WHAT PEOPLE WORE WHEN

WHAT PEOPLE
WORE WHEN

A Complete Illustrated History of Costume
*from Ancient Times to the Nineteenth Century
for Every Level of Society*

Consultant Editor Melissa Leventon

St. Martin's Griffin
New York

www.stmartins.com

Library of Congress Cataloging-in-Publication Data Available Upon Request

ISBN-13: 978-0-312-38321-3
ISBN-10: 0-312-38321-5

First U.S. Edition: July 2008

10 9 8 7 6 5 4 3

Printed and bound in China

This book was conceived, designed and produced by

Ivy Press
210 High Street
Lewes
East Sussex BN7 2NS

Creative Director: PETER BRIDGEWATER
Publisher: JASON HOOK
Editorial Director: CAROLINE EARLE
Senior Project Editor: DOMINIQUE PAGE
Art Director: SARAH HOWERD
Design: J C LANAWAY
Concept: ALAN OSBAHR
Image Reproduction: LYNDSEY HARWOOD, JOANNA CLINCH, ADAM ELLIOT

Contents

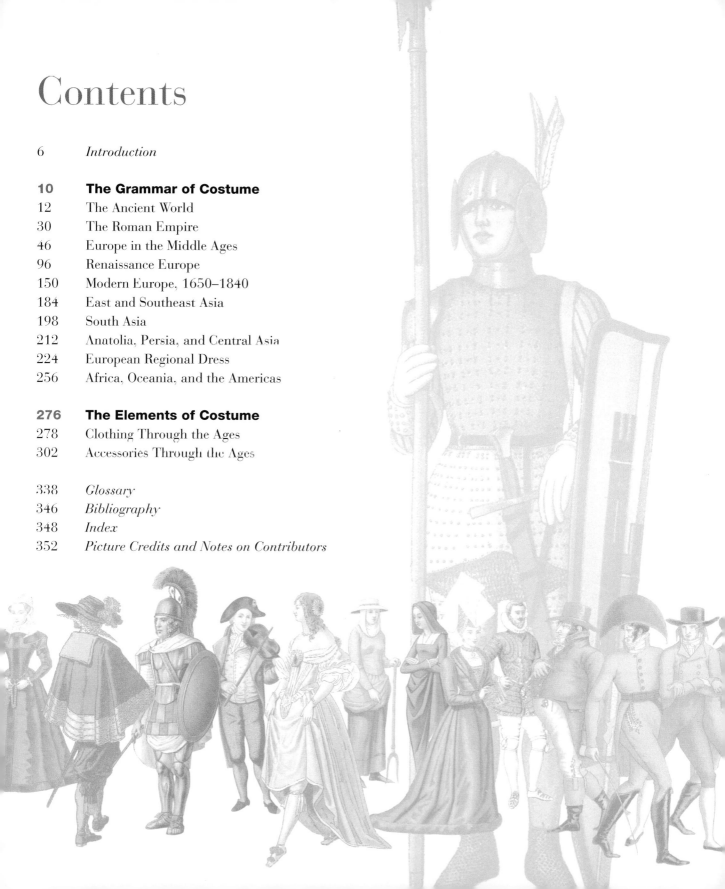

Introduction

The images in *What People Wore When* are drawn from two monumental 19th-century costume history books: Auguste Racinet's *Le Costume historique* and Friedrich Hottenroth's *Trachten Haus- Feld- und Kriegsgeräthschaften der Völker alter und neuer Zeit*. Racinet's book was originally published to subscribers in twenty installments between 1876 and 1886, and then reissued in 1888 as a six-volume work containing 500 illustrated plates and extensive commentary. In addition to costume and armor, it profiled jewelry, interiors, furniture, and, occasionally, modes of transport, spanning ancient Egypt to the turn of the 19th century and ranging from Europe to all parts of Asia, Africa, Oceania, and the New World. Racinet's images were drawn by a bevy of illustrators and were based largely, though not exclusively, on a wide variety of primary sources. *Le Costume historique* stood out not only because of its impressive scope, but also because it was the first mass-marketed costume book to use chromolithography, which came into wide commercial use in the 1860s and made publishing color images both feasible and affordable.

Hottenroth's book, which also roamed the globe across the centuries, covered similar subjects in its 200 image-crammed plates and carried

the history of European fashion forward to 1840. It was published serially between 1884 and 1891, and was also issued in a two-volume edition. Hottenroth drew his images himself and, although he did use primary sources, he relied heavily on secondary sources—including Racinet—for his images.

Hottenroth's work has since largely fallen from sight in the English-speaking world, while Racinet's has been rediscovered by new generations of readers through at least three full or partial facsimile editions published in the last thirty years. Most of these have either reproduced only the images with little or none of the original text, or provided faithfully translated but heavily abridged text. Valuable as they are, they can pose problems for the modern reader who may expect them to be literal guides to historic costume. Racinet's and Hottenroth's images are delightful but they are not always accurate. Colors

Introduction

are especially problematic and are often not to be trusted. Racinet was not above adding color to an uncolored original, and the degree of accuracy he demanded of his illustrators is unknown. As an illustrator, Hottenroth seems less concerned with accuracy and more with esthetics, and appears to have had a rather arbitrary color sense; he often seems to have chosen to color his drawings in ways that convey a different sense of the layers being worn, or of a garment's structure, than is likely to have been present in the original. Other aspects of the illustrations can also be problematic. Seemingly arbitrary changes were sometimes made, either for stylistic reasons

or, one suspects, because the illustrator did not entirely understand the garment. And indeed, illustrations from one era that copy images from earlier ones need always to be approached with a certain amount of caution. No artist can entirely divorce himself from the esthetics of his own time and, inevitably, anomalies creep in, no matter how faithful the copy. Nonetheless, despite these caveats, both books stand as valuable reminders of an earlier way of looking at the dress of other times and other peoples, and of an era when the diversity of costume worldwide seemed far more surprising than it does now.

We have relied on the published work of a great many historians, without whom this book would have been impossible to write. The book's format has not allowed for footnotes, but works consulted are listed in the bibliography. The vast trove of images on the Internet, which allowed us to track down and view in minutes works of art that might otherwise have taken weeks or months to locate, also facilitated our research. Our goal was to compare Racinet's and Hottenroth's images with their original sources wherever possible and, using information on the history of dress amassed during the last century, offer in the picture captions themselves an analysis of what the images really represent in modern terms. In this way, we hope this book can make a real contribution to the understanding of the history of costume worldwide.

THE GRAMMAR
OF COSTUME

The Ancient World

Historians popularly trace the origins of modern Western dress back to the clothing worn by ancient Mediterranean peoples, particularly the Greeks and Romans, during the eight centuries prior to the dawn of the Common Era. Dwellers in temperate climates, they wore cloth rather than animal skins: their garments were based on wide lengths of cloth woven on ground or upright warp-weighted looms that were then sewn, pinned, or tied together and often draped. Their clothes were, in turn, heavily influenced by their interactions with the peoples of the Near East and Central Asia, who contributed textiles such as fine linen, cotton, and silk to the wool and flax that the Greeks and Romans produced themselves—plus specific garments that included hoods, hats, shoes, tunics, and pants, to name just a few—all of which added to the mix of styles that over the centuries developed into Western fashion.

Classical art has influenced the depiction of the clothed and draped body in Western painting and sculpture for centuries, but we owe much of our present interest in and knowledge of the actual dress worn in ancient times to the burning interest in Classical civilizations that developed during the 18th century, fueled equally by Enlightenment philosophy and the archeological discoveries that filled public and private collections in Europe with vases, sculptures and ornaments. Both originals and published redrawings of newly discovered ancient sculptures and paintings aided the development of the first major Classical revival in dress that occurred late in the 18th century, and the subsequent revivals that have continued to appear periodically up to the present day.

Racinet's and Hottenroth's depictions of ancient dress include early Egyptian and Assyrian examples, although these had little direct influence on the much later styles of Greece and Rome, and those images appear here. As was common in 19th-century costume histories, Racinet relied on both primary and secondary sources, Hottenroth on secondary and some tertiary sources, and so there are inevitably errors and misunderstandings in their drawings and descriptions. The images in this chapter can thus really provide only glimpses of what dress as worn in the ages of Hatshepsut, Pericles, or Nero was really like.

Egypt

Military and Civilian Dress

Egyptian costume appears to have remained relatively static from about 3000 to 1550 BC. Typically, Egyptians wore a draped costume with many styles shared by men and women. One of these was the kilt-like *schenti* (originally worn only by the pharaoh) that continued to be worn by the upper classes over the years. In the earliest period, cloth was woven from vegetable fibers, especially flax. Linen was the preferred cloth as its cool, light weight was appropriate to Egypt's climate. White was a sacred color for the Egyptians, and for centuries undyed linen was used. Colored cloth began to be worn some time between 1550 and 1070 BC.

Priest: Relief from Medinet Habu, Thebes

A triangular or pyramid-shaped apron was often worn over both long and short schenti. The apron was depicted as projecting out from the schenti and so was probably heavily starched. Priests also wore a tunic with gathered sleeves and a leopard pelt.

Ptolemy II Philadelphus (r. 285–246 BC): from The Great Temple of Isis at Philae

Behind Ptolemy's short schenti is a lion's tail, an ancient Egyptian tradition symbolizing his role as chief. He wears the *pschent*, a crown representing dominion over Upper and Lower Egypt. The cylindrical base with projecting back comprised the Red Crown of Lower Egypt (*deshret*), and the egg-shaped upper portion, the White Crown of Upper Egypt (*hedjet*).

Husband and Wife: Relief from the Grottoes of el-Kab

This couple wear conical mounds on their heads. Made of scented unguents, they would fragrantly melt over their coiffures. The husband wears a shawl or cape draped around his shoulders and upper arms. First worn during the Middle Kingdom, this garment was also shown tied in a knot on the chest.

Cleopatra as the Hathor, Goddess of Fertility

A deified Cleopatra wears a Hathor headdress, high feather plumes and the *uraeus*, a symbol of kingship in the form of a fillet adorned by a central, rearing cobra. Her robe, or *kalasiris*, is held up by two straps (a single strapped version was also worn), leaving the breasts exposed. The kalasiris was eventually modified by raising the top so that it covered the breasts.

See also
Assyria, *pages 16–17*

The Goddess Mut from a Nubian Temple

Mut wears the pschent, identifying her as the counterpart of Amun Re, king of the gods. Mut's vulture cap (adopted by Nefertiti and other queens) is echoed in a figure-hugging garment comprising a bird's body and wings.

Ramses II (r. 1290–1224 BC) Battles the Hittite King: from a Painted Theban Relief

Ramses II is shown wearing the military Blue Crown, or *khepresh*. Perhaps made of rigid linen or leather, it was embellished with a raised circular surface patterning. In battle, pharaohs wore a close-fitting cloth or leather costume with scale-shaped bone or metal elements, or a short-sleeved jacket.

Assyria

Assyrian and Phoenician Dress

Austen Henry Layard and Hormuz Rassam were
the first to excavate the Assyrian site at Nimrud
(in modern Iraq). Racinet's primary sources were
Layard's publications, including the 1849 *Nineveh
and its Remains*. Many of these carved reliefs and
stelae are now held in the British Museum's
collection in London, England. Earlier Sumerian
costume consisted of lambswool garments that were
wrapped around the waist or the torso and often
topped with a cape. Under the Assyrians (*c.* 1132–
609 BC), a woven cloth replaced felt and borders
were embellished with embroidery, appliqué,
precious metals, tassels, and fringe.

Phoenician Tribute ◀
**Bearer to King
Ashurnasirpal II
(r. 883–859** BC**)**
This Phoenician
wears a cylindrical
cap. Traders of
purple dye and
clothing, Phoenicians
transmitted clothing
styles around the
ancient Near East.

See also
Egypt, *pages 14–15*

▶ **King Ashurbanipal
(r. 668–***c.* **627** BC**) and
Queen Ashur-sharrat**
Queen Ashur-sharrat
wears a crown with
crenellated elements
similar to the fortified
parapets of an
Assyrian city. The
central field of her
tasselled shawl-wrap
and lower garment
bear circular motifs,
perhaps suggesting
applied gold
ornaments. She wears
a sleeved tunic with
woven or embroidered
geometric designs.
Her flat, soft cloth or
leather shoes include
an embellished toe
compartment and
are fastened by laces
across the instep.

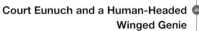

Stele of King Shamshi Adad V (r. 823–811 BC)

The royal Assyrian mitre was composed of a tapering flat-topped cylinder, a projecting conical point, and a fillet with pendant lappets. The fillet was worn only by the king or crown prince. The hem of Shamshi Adad's court robes is trimmed with elaborate, long tassels. A long, narrow belt encircles the wide waist sash and crosses over the king's chest.

Court Eunuch and a Human-Headed Winged Genie

Juxtaposed here are the images of the king's weapons' bearer and a winged protective spirit. Both wear sandals with a toe ring and heel covering, connected by thin straps. The genie's horned crown signified divinity. His semidivine status is also indicated by the long-tasseled kilt and fringed robe. Two knives and a whetstone (with an animal-headed handle) are tucked into the genie's belt.

Apes are Brought as a Tribute to King Ashurnasirpal II (r. 883–859 BC)

A Phoenician tribute bearer is depicted here wearing a fringed shawl, a garment related to Sumerian costume and also worn by Israelites and other peoples. Short boots with upturned toes were worn by Phoenicians, Syrians, and Anatolians.

Headwear
- Phoenician cap
- royal crown or miter

Hairstyles

Dress
- felted or woven wool

Upper Garments
- cape or shawl
- fringed robe
- sleeved tunic

Lower Garments
- chain mail
- kilt

Accessories
- belt
- waist sash
- bracelets

Footwear
- flat, laced shoes
- short boots
- toe-ring sandals

Anatolia

Amazons, Lydians, and Phrygians

Between approximately 1700 and 1300 BC, Anatolian dress combined styles adopted from the Greeks, Mesopotamians, and northern pastoral peoples. From around 1400 to 1200 BC, the Hittites dominated the region, until supplanted by the Phrygians. In the early 7th century BC, the Lydians became the dominant power. Famed for their luxurious way of life, they adopted many aspects of Greek culture and dress. In the mid-6th century BC, King Croesus was defeated by Cyrus the Great and Lydian territories were absorbed into the Persian Empire.

Lydians

Lydian tribute bearers were represented on the Persepolis reliefs wearing mid-calf-length tunics with elbow-length sleeves made of a pleated or striated fabric. Draped over one shoulder, as suggested here, was a long shawl. Two types of headwear were depicted: a round, brimless cap and a conical, wrapped turban.

Amazons

Amazons were typically shown in garments that the Greeks associated with "barbarian" easterners, i.e., West Asians. As illustrated here, this ensemble included tight pants and a long-sleeved upper garment topped with an animal-skin mantle (*perizoma*).

Phrygians

Phrygians wore a sleeveless, belted *chiton* over a blouse with long, narrow sleeves that was later adopted by the Greeks. A significant contribution to costume history was their tall, brimless cap of leather or felt, with a pointed top that fell to the front. The Phrygian cap often had protective flaps hanging down the back of the neck and over the ears.

Phrygian Woman

This woman wears attire similar to that of the Greek women of Ionia. A large cloak or shawl, draped and pinned over one shoulder, was worn over a long tunic. The bold patterns may represent the influence of Syrian and Phoenician varicolored costumes that were embellished with stripes, flowers and motifs.

See also
Assyria, *pages 16–17*
Greece, 500–300 BC, *pages 24–29*

Phrygians

One of the warriors is depicted wearing a crested helmet with cheek pieces (here they are folded up) and a pendant horsetail-like element. For centuries, similar crested helmets were worn in Anatolia. They are represented on the carved reliefs at Hattusas, the 2nd-millennium Hittite capital, and the 8th-century BC fortress at Karatepe.

Headwear
• crested helmet
• Phrygian cap
• turban

Hairstyles

Dress
• fitted rather than draped

Upper Garments
• cloak or shawl
• mantle, animal skin (perizoma)
• tunic (chiton)

Lower Garments
• tight-fitting pants

Accessories

Footwear

West Asia

Medes, Persians, and Arabs

The Persians were vassals of the Medes and shared a common origin from Indo-Iranian tribes. Around 550 BC, Cyrus the Great conquered Media and the Persians inherited their kingdom. Herodotus, the Greek historian who traveled extensively in the Near East around 460–454 BC, is one of the best sources on the Achaemenid Persians. According to Herodotus, ancient Persians first wore animal hides and felt tiaras. Later, the long robes worn by Persians were found to be cumbersome in battle, so Cyrus adopted Median dress and gave Median robes as gifts of honor to his nobles. Herodotus mentions battle attire that included purple tunics and bronze or gold scaled corselets worn by the king and his army of the "10,000 Immortals."

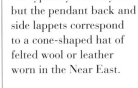

Median Soldier

Loose pants tucked into boots or, as shown here, bound with ankle straps, were introduced by steppe nomads. This figure's headgear is not typically worn by Persians or Medes, but the pendant back and side lappets correspond to a cone-shaped hat of felted wool or leather worn in the Near East.

Medes

Wearing a knee-length belted tunic over tight-fitting pants, the figure on the left may represent a Mede. This costume originated with the Medes and was also worn by Persians, Armenians, and Cappadocians. Medes are also depicted on Achaemenid reliefs wearing long-sleeved overcoats with turned-back or fur-trimmed collars. His hat may be an exaggeration of the egg-shaped soft Median cap.

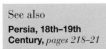

See also
Persia, 18th–19th Century, *pages 218–21*

Headwear
- fluted headdress
- Median cap
- tiara
- turbanlike cap
- veil

Hairstyles
- shoulder-length hair and full beards (Persians)

Dress
- long-sleeved robe (thob)

Upper Garments
- circular shawl
- knee-length tunic
- long tunic with pleated sleeves and skirt

Lower Garments
- pants

Accessories
- leather belt
- torque

Footwear
- shoes with straps and buttons (Persians)

Arab Woman with Children

Arabs paid tribute to the Achaemenids with textiles and other goods. An Arab woman wears a veil for modesty over a long-sleeved garment with a front neck opening similar to the robe (*thob*) still worn by Bedouin women.

Persian Noble

One of the traditional costumes of Persian nobility worn in the Achaemenid period included a long garment with pleated sleeves and skirt, and a wide leather waist belt that was knotted in the front. Covering the upper body was a long circular shawl as depicted here. The distinctive fluted headdress was a shorter version of the king's tiara. Persian shoes were depicted with three straps and buttons on the instep.

Achaemenid Persian King in War Costume

Probably derived from a Pompeian mosaic depicting the 333 BC battle between Darius III and Alexander the Great, Darius wears a turban-like cap that draped over the ears and covered the chin. Circling his neck is a gold Persian torque with lion-head terminals. According to the 1st-century AD author Curtius Rufus, the king dressed for battle in a belted purple tunic, a gold-embroidered cloak, and a headdress (*cidaris*) decorated with violet-colored lace.

Etruscans

The Greco-Roman Era

The ancient peoples of the Mediterranean all wore variations on the same garments: a tunic called a chiton by the Greeks, and several types of mantle that went by various names at different times and places. The Etruscans, whose distinct culture seems to have developed after about 800 BC, probably adopted the chiton from the Myceneans and Near Eastern peoples, and Etruscan dress subsequently both influenced, and was influenced by, Greek and Roman styles. In fact, there was an active exchange of garments and clothing styles among the three cultures between the 7th and 1st centuries BC, and it can be difficult to discern the origin of a particular garment or style. On these pages are examples of garments that are clearly Etruscan as well as those that may be Greek or Roman.

Goddess ◁

The sculpture of a goddess shows her in a loose pleated linen chiton with a mantle wrapped around her shoulders and covering her head. Etruscans adopted the linen chiton from Ionia in about 550–540 BC; it then made its way into Greek fashion between about 540 and 530 BC.

See also
Greece, 500–300 BC, *pages 24–27*
Greek Armor, *pages 28–29*
Rome, *pages 34–37*

▶ **Muse**
Taken from a bas-relief in a private collection, this figure of a Muse is dressed in a soft Ionic chiton of pleated linen with an unusual V-shaped neckline and a necklace. That, and the raised waistline, may indicate that this is a Roman figure; however, the mantle draped around her hips is typically Etruscan.

Headwear

Hairstyles

Dress
• draped rather
than fitted

Upper Garments
• cuirass
• mantle (Etruscan
mantle, tebenna)

Lower Garments
• greaves

Accessories
• necklace

Footwear

Diana

The goddess of hunting, Diana, wears a mantle with rounded edges that is probably linen, given the softness of the folds that she holds in her right hand. Unlike the Greeks, whose mantles were primarily rectangular, the Etruscans wore different-shaped mantles that were created as they were woven; their clothing was not shaped through cutting.

Mars

The god of war is dressed in Roman armor, which was influenced by its Etruscan and Greek counterparts. His cuirass, probably of leather, is molded to the muscular contours of his chest, and below it he wears a short tabbed skirt showing a short chiton beneath. His legs are protected by greaves.

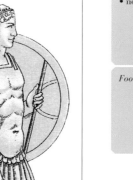

Vulcan

The Roman god Vulcan wears the *tebenna*, a characteristically Etruscan mantle with rounded edges that later developed into the Roman toga. The tebenna is wrapped diagonally around his body, and despite the stylization of the folds, it is clear that the zigzag drapery is curved along its bottom edge.

Venus

Venus, goddess of love, also wears an Ionic chiton under her mantle. The chiton sleeves are not woven to shape; rather, they are formed by pinning together the wide edges of the linen along the shoulder, leaving an opening in that seam for the arm, and allowing the rest of its length to drape beneath.

Greece, *500–300 BC*

Men in the Golden Age

During this period the Greeks used wool and linen for
their clothes, based on uncut, relatively lightweight
woven cloth that draped fluidly. There is a
misconception that ancient Greek clothing was mainly
white, fostered by depictions in surviving sculpture and
paintings. Although color references in contemporary
sources can be vague, primary colors were certainly
worn. The basic garment for males was the chiton,
worn short or long, depending on the wearer's
occupation and age. It was based on one or two
uncut rectangles of cloth, sewn or pinned, and girdled
at the waist. Over the chiton men wore primarily the
himation, a long, draped cloak, and the *chlamys*,
a shorter cloak worn pinned closed.

Draped Himation

This strolling musician is naked
except for a himation draped
casually around his body.
Heroic nudity as the celebration
of the beauty of the body is
common in Greek depictions of
young gods and young men, but
it was more an artistic convention
than an aspect of everyday life.
In the late 8th century BC,
however, Greek athletes did
abandon their loincloths and
begin to compete nude.

Doric Chiton

This man wears the
Doric style of chiton,
a loosely fitted wool
version that lacks
the width and fine
pleats of the linen
Ionic chiton. His
himation drapes
fluidly around his
body. It is patterned
simply with a border
stripe, but himatia
were often more
elaborately decorated.

Short Cloak

This man is dressed for walking in a chlamys, the short cloak that was a favorite among Greeks. It is pinned on his right shoulder, leaving his right arm free, perhaps the way the cloak was most commonly worn. Hanging at the back of his neck he wears a *petasos*, a felt hat with a round crown and flat brim.

Ionic Chiton

The long Ionic chiton is almost completely obscured by the large wool himation that swathes the wearer's body. Himatia did not allow for unfettered movement; it is clear that this garment would have required the wearer to manage it carefully in order to keep it properly arranged as he walked.

Chlamys Variation

Here the chlamys is pinned at the base of the throat and worn thrown back over both shoulders. The contrasting border stripe would have been woven in. Beneath the chlamys the man wears a short, pleated linen chiton. What looks to be a broad sash at the waist may, in fact, be the chiton draped to form a small overlap.

See also
Etruscans, *pages 22–23*
Greece, 500–300 BC, *pages 26–27*
Greek Armor, *pages 28–29*

Greece, 500–300 BC

Women in the Golden Age

The primary sources for Greek dress are often oblique references to clothing in ancient texts and the stylized, idealized depictions on sculptures and black- and red-figure vases. Recent studies suggest that garments may have been more varied in style, color, and pattern. Tunics and mantles were essential items. The sleeveless or short-sleeved chiton, and the *peplos*, a tubular, open-sided garment with an overfold, could be worn individually or one over the other. Goddesses, huntresses, athletes, and entertainers may be depicted in short ones; Greek matrons would have worn them long. The himation (*see page 24*) was worn in different sizes and variously draped.

See also
Greece, 500–300 BC, *pages 24–25*
Etruscans, *pages 22–23*

Bloused Chiton
This sleeveless (Doric) wool chiton blouses over a belt at the waist; this was one way to adjust the tunic's length. The bulge created at the midriff is called a *kolpos*. The decorative borders were woven in or embroidered on.

Sleeveless Tunics
Around AD 180 the Roman author Aelian wrote of luxurious tunics worn by women in ancient Greece, their shoulders "fastened with gold pins and silver brooches," as shown here. The fabric is pinned on each shoulder, creating a draped neckline and a waist-length overfold. The smaller images show how the shoulders were pinned; the overfold hides a belt. In the main image, the belt passes just under the breasts, to give an "Empire" waistline.

Foreign Dress
Racinet intended this to represent an Ionian (linen) chiton but its long, tight sleeves suggest Asiatic or other foreign dress. The close fit is more artistic license than real, for Greek clothing was untailored. The hint at transparency may mean that this is a courtesan's semisheer tunic of wild silk.

Side View
This side view of a peplos suggests that its fabric was striped on three sides. Peploi were open-sided, but the depiction of the woman's drapery suggests that this one has been sewn or pinned up the side, parallel to the inner edge of the stripe.

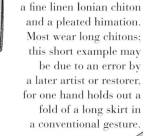

Kore, c. 500 BC
Korai were made as votive or commemorative sculptures. This one has a fine linen Ionian chiton and a pleated himation. Most wear long chitons; this short example may be due to an error by a later artist or restorer, for one hand holds out a fold of a long skirt in a conventional gesture.

Ionian Linen Chiton
Art does not always reflect real dress, and the reasons why women are depicted as they have often been lost over time. This dancing figure, probably from a vase painting, wears a loose, Ionian linen chiton under an abbreviated mantle. Her calf-length chiton is unusual; whether because she is a reveler or for another reason is not known.

Headwear

Hairstyles

Dress
• draped rather than fitted

Upper Garments
• long mantle or cloak (himation)
• robe, open-sided (peplos)
• tunic (chiton)

Lower Garments

Accessories
• belt
• brooch or pin

Footwear

Greek Armor

Warriors

Greeks first made bronze armor and helmets between 1450 and 1350 BC. Evidence for their continued use in the Greek Dark Ages (*c.* 1100–800 BC) is scant, but by the early 8th century BC bronze was again used in Greece for plate armor, for helmets, and for reinforcing wooden shields. The backbone of Greek armies in the Classical period were the *hoplites*, infantrymen who fought massed in phalanxes. They were usually equipped with a bronze cuirass or corselet, greaves, helmet, spear, and shield.

Officer

This officer's cuirass is either a laced composite or scale armor. According to a scene on a 5th-century BC vase painting, the garment would fasten down the center front, with the broad shoulder flaps then laced to the corselet's body. The officer's legs are protected from knee to ankle by shining bronze greaves.

The Legendary Aegis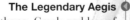

Athena, Greek goddess of war, wears the *aegis* over her shoulders. The *Iliad* describes the aegis as Zeus's shield, adorned with gold tassels and the image of Medusa's head. Attic vase painters often represented the tassels as a fringe of snakes, which confirms that the aegis is not a real piece of armor.

Hoplite

Herodotus, in *c.* 450–440 BC, wrote of Persian soldiers wearing "a coat of mail looking like the scales of a fish." Greeks wore a similar version, with bronze scales probably fixed to a linen or leather base. The protective skirt was a mid-5th-century BC innovation. The Corinthian helmet shown here was worn in Greece from the early 7th century BC until at least the early 5th century BC.

Soldier, 5th–4th Century BC

This soldier wears a Thracian helmet and a "muscle" or "classical" cuirass, first seen early in the 5th century BC. Commonly made of bronze, with a breastplate and backplate joined at the sides, the cuirass had to be fitted to the wearer quite precisely. It usually extended over the stomach to protect it; however, this man's leather apron hides the lower part of the cuirass.

Archer

This archer is equipped with a battle-ax as well as his bow, a quiver of arrows, and a short sword in a scabbard slung under his left arm. He wears a skirted cuirass of either leather or quilted linen that faintly resembles the later Roman *lorica segmentata* (*see page 33*), as well as leather greaves and a long-tailed leather hat.

Hairstyles

Dress
• plate armor

Upper Garments
• cuirass, comprising breastplate and backplate
• short cloak (chlamys)

Lower Garments
• greaves
• leather apron

See also
Roman Armor,
pages 32–33

Accessories
• circular shield
• Zeus's shield (aegis)

Footwear

Infantryman, 5th–4th Century BC

Hoplites first appeared in Greece in the late 8th century BC. This heavily armed hoplite wears a bronze helmet with earpieces and an eye-catching multicolored crest. His molded "muscle" breastplate, shield, and greaves are also bronze, and he wears a protective skirt of multicolored strips. On top of it all is a chlamys, which began as a military cloak before crossing over into civilian wear.

The Roman Empire

Roman society was extremely stratified, and dress was an important way of establishing and maintaining the social hierarchy. Rank could be denoted by a wide variety of factors, such as the quality or nature of a garment's material, its type, size, or color, or the way it was worn. Roman soldiers, for instance, commonly distinguished themselves by wearing their tunics shorter than civilian men. Slaves, on the other hand, could be identified by their footwear, or lack of it, as they were forbidden to wear the characteristic Roman ankle-high shoes called *calcei*. Society's civic and moral values, such as dignity (for men) and chastity (for women), were also embedded in the style of dress chosen and the way articles such as the *toga* and the *palla* were managed. Depending on the context, those same garments might also serve as punishments: a woman divorced for adultery was condemned to wear a plain toga (a garment otherwise not worn by adult females save for prostitutes) as a constant and visible sign of her sin. How successfully these sumptuary regulations were enforced is difficult to know, but the fact of their existence underscores the importance of clothing in reinforcing Roman distinctions of rank, age, and sex.

The Romans borrowed a number of garments from their Mediterranean neighbors, particularly the Greeks and Etruscans. Indeed, the single most characteristic Roman garment, the toga, was Etruscan in origin. Romans also shared the Etruscan taste for a more fully covered body and for clothes made from heavier cloth with more complex patterns; although in Etruria, as in Greece, pattern was primarily decorative, whereas in Rome it was symbolic. Despite their relative conservatism, Romans were also surprisingly open to outside sartorial influences from non-Mediterranean peoples, garnered through both conquest and trade. As a result, new garments such as pants (*braccae*) and distinctive round, hooded cloaks like the *paenula* and *cucullus* crept into the Roman wardrobe. Conversely, the spread of the Roman Empire, which at its height in the 1st century AD stretched from Britain and Spain east to Armenia, and from the Danube in the north to Egypt in the south, brought Roman clothing to subject peoples, although Roman-style dress never fully supplanted local styles.

Roman Armor

Battle and Gladiator Dress

The Roman army would adopt any superior technology and equipment it found among its erstwhile enemies, but these borrowings can be hard to tease out from the visual and archeological records. Greek styles—in particular the "muscle" cuirass and scale armor of the 4th century BC— appear often in depictions of Roman soldiers, but whether this portrays combat armor accurately is uncertain. Stylistic conventions of Roman art were heavily influenced by Greece, and artists would use a sartorial shorthand to show a figure's rank. One of the first pieces of Roman art that verifiably depicts men in contemporary armor is Trajan's Column, completed in AD 113, from which several figures shown here derive. Nonetheless, the elaborate details and rich colors here (*see also pages 28–29*) go beyond the information that can be gleaned from original sources. Such touches can only suggest what armor might have looked like.

Infantryman, 1st Century AD

His torso is protected by a segmental cuirass (lorica segmentata); the small "apron" of straps below it probably developed as an elaboration of the belt terminals. Some comprised as many as eight studded straps (*see opposite*). In reality he would probably have worn an apron and carried a sword, details likely omitted by the original sculptor. A new feature of his Imperial-style helmet is the cutout over the ear, which helped a soldier to hear while he was wearing it.

Gladiator

Gladiators were entertainers. Their armor combined strength and vulnerability: an elaborate enclosed helmet and a heavy, articulated armor sleeve, leaving the left shoulder bare. The leg greave and long shield protected his left side when he lunged with his sword.

Cavalry Officer, Early 2nd Century AD

This cavalry officer from Trajan's Column wears a mail shirt over a blue wool tunic and carries an elaborately blazoned oval shield. Mail was adopted from the Celts and worn by both legionaries and cavalry during the Republic and early Empire. Both ranks wore leggings that extended just below the knee, although what they were made of is unknown.

Standard-Bearer, 3rd–4th Century AD

His helmet corresponds most closely with a type seen in the 3rd and 4th centuries AD that featured a horizontal brow plate, wide cheek pieces, and a long crest. Earlier in the Empire, standard-bearers were usually depicted with small, round shields that could be tucked under the arm; but this large, painted shield, with its protruding boss, cannot be carried in this way.

See also
Greek Armor,
pages 28–29

Citizen Soldier, c. 2nd Century AD

He wears a lorica segmentata above two tiers of protective lappets. This type of cuirass, first depicted on Trajan's Column, is the armor worn by Roman citizen troops. Its iron girth hoops, shoulder straps, and hinges were long thought to have been laced to a supporting leather tunic, but 20th-century reconstructions demonstrated that the elements of the cuirass must have been articulated on leather straps.

Emperor, c. AD 140–160

Each of his two narrow crossed belts holds a sidearm, although this was shortly to give way to a single, wider belt supporting both sword and dagger. His helmet, decorated in relief, has a bright feather crest and long earpieces that overlap under his chin. Racinet intended the bright color to denote imperial purple.

Headwear
• helmet

Hairstyles

Dress

Upper Garments
• mail shirt
• segmented cuirass (lorica segmentata)

Lower Garments
• greaves
• leather skirt
• leggings or breeches

Accessories
• shield
• wide belt

Footwear

Rome

Togas and Other Mantles

The toga is the garment most closely associated in modern minds with ancient Rome. To the Romans it symbolized both the power of the Empire, and Roman humanity and culture. It was worn by men and women in early Rome, but by the 2nd century BC its use was largely reserved for male citizens, and within that group a strict hierarchy of color, decoration, and drape evolved that instantly conveyed to the initiated the rank and status of its wearer. As the Republic gave way to the Empire in the 1st century BC, the toga became considerably larger and harder to manage, and its popularity as everyday wear declined, although it continued as a ceremonial and festive garment until the 4th century AD. It was never the only mantle Roman men wore: depictions of rectangular and rounded garments often appear in surviving Roman art.

◉ Early Empire Togas

Togas conveyed rank and status through color and striping. The *toga pura*, the everyday garb of the average citizen, was probably off-white or grayish. The *toga pulla*, a dark toga, was worn for mourning. The *toga praetexta* had a 3 in. (7.5 cm) purple stripe along the border and was reserved for magistrates, priests, and boys. The purple toga, or *toga purpurea*, which is probably what the figure on the right is wearing, was reserved for the emperor.

See also
Rome, *pages 36–37*

Headwear

Hairstyles

Dress
• draped rather than tailored

Upper Garments
• cloak (paludamentum)
• toga
• tunic

Lower Garments

Accessories

Footwear

Purple Mantle

This tribune wears a purple mantle, one of the most high-status and expensive colors during the Republic and Empire. Romans wore many shades of purple, and a number of different dyes were used to make them. The most expensive was "murex," made from a mollusk that produced an imperial purple.

Wool Tunic

Unlike Greek chitons based on rectangles, Roman tunics like this one often had their sleeves woven in, which gave them a less draperylike quality. Such tunics, and the mantles worn over them, were most often made of wool, which was available dyed in a surprisingly wide variety of colors.

Statesman, *c.* 5th Century AD

This man, a high-ranking state functionary, wears a large *paludamentum* (cloak), the Romanized version of the Greek chlamys. His is long, as was typical for an official, and is decorated with a rectangular panel known as a *tablion*. The paludamentum replaced the toga as a Roman symbol of power and authority in the 5th century AD.

Senator

The senator may be wearing a *toga candida*, the white toga worn by those seeking office (candidates). He dates from the period between the late 1st century BC and the 2nd century AD when the toga became a stately garment 15–18 ft (4.5–5.5 m) wide that could not be put on without assistance.

Rome

Women's Dress

Dress for Roman women, as for men, was concerned with denoting rank and status. Any viewer could place a Roman female by her clothes. Girls, like boys, wore the toga praetexta with a narrow purple stripe until they were of marriageable age; once married, they gave up the toga in favor of the *tunica, stola*, and palla. The tunica, a sliplike dress worn next to the skin, was reserved for chaste married women. Above the stola, a carefully draped, toga-like enveloping robe, was the palla, a large mantle that also served as a veil. Once married, a Roman woman always veiled her head in public; the veil acted as an indicator of her marital rank, a symbol of her husband's authority over her and a protector of her purity.

Woman, Late 1st Century BC
Wealthy Romans favored startling colors in the late Republic and early Empire periods. *Galbinus*, which Pliny described as a greenish yellow, was perhaps what was intended by the color given to this woman's palla. It seems to have been favored because it was expensive.

See also
Rome, *pages 34–35*

Modest Matron
This seated matron of unknown identity is in a conventional Roman attitude of *pudicitia*, or modesty, holding her palla up to cover part of her face. This is a pose frequently seen on tombstones.

Pudicitia

Pudicitia was the personification of chastity and modesty, and here she is dressed like a proper Roman matron, in tunica, stola, and a palla that discreetly veils her head. Beneath the veil she wears a diadem that resembles those found in Greek sculpture.

Young Girl

This is a statue of a young girl, possibly one dressed for her wedding in the *tunica recta* (straight tunic), traditionally woven by the bride herself on an old-fashioned warp-weighted loom, and a bridal veil, the *flammeum*. The veil as shown here is a dull mustard yellow but according to Festus, writing probably in the 2nd century AD, the flammeum was the color of lightning, while Pliny the Elder likens its hue to that of an egg yolk.

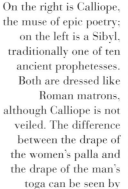

Palla vs. Toga

On the right is Calliope, the muse of epic poetry; on the left is a Sibyl, traditionally one of ten ancient prophetesses. Both are dressed like Roman matrons, although Calliope is not veiled. The difference between the drape of the women's palla and the drape of the man's toga can be seen by comparing these two figures with the orator pictured in the center.

Headwear
• bridal veil (flammeum)

Hairstyles

Dress
• heavily draped

Upper Garments
• draped robe (stola)
• dress (tunica)
• long, full mantle (palla)

Lower Garments

Accessories
• diadem

Footwear

Gauls, Celts, and Britons

Tunics, Pants, and Tattoos

There are few sources of information on dress in Celtic Europe in the era prior to AD 500: a handful of bas-reliefs, sculptures, and written accounts, mostly left by the Romans who conquered Celtic tribes during the 1st century BC. As a result, some historians have extrapolated back from later examples. Celtic men wore pants, unlike the Romans, and the shape and length of men's tunics appear to have been different in Gaul. Roman commentators were struck by the body paint or tattoos Britons wore, without necessarily understanding them. William Camden's *Britain* of 1610 repeats Roman geographer Pomponius Mela's comment: "Whether the Britons died their bodies with woad for a beautifull shew, or in some other respect, it is uncertaine." Whether woad was actually used is questionable; although Latin accounts were popularly translated that way for centuries.

Warrior and Peasant

Based on a figure from Trajan's Column (early 2nd century AD), the warrior (*left*) wears a sleeveless, belted tunic with bracelets and anklets adorning his arms and legs, copied by Racinet from surviving ornaments. The peasant's dress (*right*) is a composite of several sculptures; he wears a tunic with long, tight sleeves, a type thought to have been introduced to Rome from Gaul, and a red Phrygian cap, probably here a symbol of his non-Greek and non-Roman identity.

Gallic Woman

She wears a simply cut ankle-length tunic beneath a hip-length one with very wide sleeves; both garments appear to be unbelted, and she is barefoot. There is little difference between her hairstyle and that worn by the peasant in the image below.

Hood and Pants

This peasant figure wears several characteristically Gallic garments, particularly his loose pants and his hood, known as a cucullus. His wide-sleeved tunic is decorated with parallel bands and seems nearly identical to the one worn by the woman to his left. The muted colors he wears do not reflect the bright colors mentioned by many contemporary chroniclers as having been favored by the Gauls.

Irish Couple

Racinet also took this couple from Meyrick and
Smith's work (*see below, left*); they in turn relied
on the description of "a wild Irishman and wild
Irishwoman, in the time of James" (early 17th
century) in John Speed's *The Theatre of the
Empire of Great Britaine* (1627), for their
imaginative re-creation of the dress of a much
earlier time. The man wears a jacket and
pants (the latter looking much like the men's
snug pantaloons fashionable in around 1815)
beneath a patterned cloak; the woman wears a
poncholike garment trimmed with a fringe.

Roman and Non-Roman

A Romanized Briton is contrasted with a
fully tattooed man. The former wears a full,
short belted tunic with long sleeves and
a mantle (*pallium*), rather improbably
rendered in pink and white plaid. The
imaginative treatment extends to his
companion, who is drawn as if wearing
a leotard printed with crude animal and
geometric figures. Both images were taken
directly from Meyrick and Smith's *Costume
of the Original Inhabitants of the British
Islands*, published in 1815; Racinet,
however, chose different colors.

See also
Post Roman Empire,
pages 42–45

Hairstyles
• long and loose
(Gauls); short
(Celts and Britons)

Dress
• draped
• fitted

Upper Garments
• jacket
• mantle (pallium)
• tunic, usually
sleeved

Lower Garments
• pants

Accessories
• anklets
• bracelets

Footwear

Byzantium

Royal, Noble, and Clerical Dress

In AD 330 Byzantium (Constantinople), the medieval world's most important commercial center, became capital of the Roman Empire. Its commercial success was due to its strategic location on the trade route between Europe and Asia, and to its silk industry. Byzantine silks were high quality, highly prized, and very costly. The favored style—richly colored, with dense, repeating patterns and heavy use of gold thread —became widespread throughout the Empire, and, through the voluntary or forced migration of its silk workers, Byzantium influenced the development of silk industries in places such as Italy. The clothes worn in Byzantium retained the influence of Rome for centuries. Both men and women wore T-shaped tunics under a variety of rectangular mantles. The tunics had long, tight sleeves and were usually trimmed with decorative bands along the hem and at the wrists.

See also
Rome, *pages 34–37*

Byzantine Ascetics

These three figures represent Byzantine ascetics from the 9th century. All wear loose, knee-length tunics with long, tight sleeves, girdled at the waist, and trimmed with decorative bands around the wrists and hem; each wears a knee-length pallium knotted around his neck, figured cloth hose on his legs, and gilt leather buskins on his feet. The bright, solid colors of the garments are characteristic of the period.

Headwear
• imperial crowns

Hairstyles
• mostly long

Dress
• Roman-influenced

Upper Garments
• mantle (pallium)
• military cloak (paludamentum)
• tunic (dalmatic)

Lower Garments
• hose

Accessories
• girdle

Footwear
• buskins

Men's Imperial Dress

This depiction of the Emperor Nicephorus III Botaniates (r. 1078–81) comes from a contemporary illuminated manuscript now in the Bibliothèque Nationale in Paris, France. The original painting shows the demarcation between his richly colored, gold-figured silk tunic and embroidered pallium (depicted in its later, more stylized version) far more clearly than the version shown here, but both effectively convey the luxuriousness of Byzantine imperial dress.

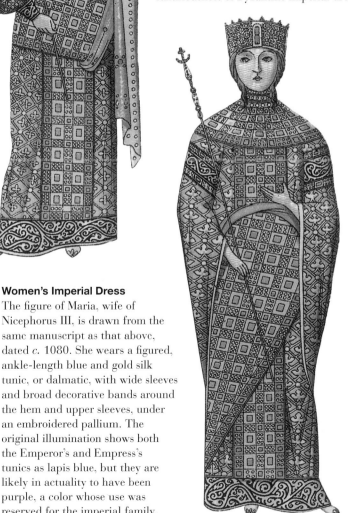

Early Royal Dress

This figure of an unidentified Byzantine emperor most likely dates to the earlier period of Byzantine history, since he wears an earlier style of royal dress: a loose, ankle-length outer tunic under a splendid, Roman-style paludamentum (a military cloak) pinned closed on one shoulder. His paludamentum is purple; the arrangement of its motifs within roundels is characteristic of Byzantine silks.

Women's Imperial Dress

The figure of Maria, wife of Nicephorus III, is drawn from the same manuscript as that above, dated *c.* 1080. She wears a figured, ankle-length blue and gold silk tunic, or dalmatic, with wide sleeves and broad decorative bands around the hem and upper sleeves, under an embroidered pallium. The original illumination shows both the Emperor's and Empress's tunics as lapis blue, but they are likely in actuality to have been purple, a color whose use was reserved for the imperial family.

Post Roman Empire

Scandinavians, Celts, and Anglo-Saxons

Scandinavians, Celts, and Anglo-Saxons were separate tribes, probably of Germanic origin, who engaged with the Roman Empire. So little information survives from early periods that the garments pictured here are more imaginative re-creations than accurate representations. The use of pants by non-Romans can, however, be documented. The Celts wore pants, items they probably adopted through contact with Scythians and Persians in the 3rd century BC. Subsequent Celtic migrations helped to spread pant-wearing elsewhere through western Europe. Even the Romans used pants of a kind in military dress, possibly after the conquest of Gaul (1st century AD), or through earlier contact.

Anglo-Saxons

The man's short pants recall the below-the-knee-length leggings worn by some Roman soldiers in the late Republic and early Empire, while the neckline detail of his tunic looks forward to those in the Bayeux Tapestry. His Phrygian cap is associated with freedom and non-Roman (eastern) identity, but it was also worn in the Roman Empire on festive occasions and by freed slaves.

Scottish Dress

The earliest-surviving written references to Scottish dress (11th and 12th centuries) mention only that Scots usually had bare legs and feet and wore shaggy wool cloaks; one also mentions dark colors. The plaid, kiltlike costumes worn by these two Highlanders are imaginary, probably based on the formalized 19th-century Scottish kilt, improbably extended upward to cover part of the torso.

Scandinavian Woman, Iron Age

Hottenroth based this drawing on finds from an Iron Age grave near Aarhus in Jutland, Denmark—possibly on Huldremose Woman, found in 1879; or possibly on another burial now unknown. The clothing discovered included a short-sleeved blouse with a slit neck opening, a gathered skirt, and a long braid girdle that wrapped around the waist several times.

Scandinavian Warrior

It is possible, although not certain, that he is intended to represent a Viking. Vikings were Norsemen who raided a vast territory that stretched from Britain to Baghdad between the 8th and 11th centuries. He wears a short mail shirt, a length favored by foot soldiers, over a knee-length, full-skirted tunic and ankle-length *braies*, or pants.

See also
Gauls, Celts, and Britons, *pages 38–39*
Scotland, *pages 232–33*

Irish Couple

This pair highlight the problems with interpretive redrawings of earlier images. They originated in John Speed's 1627 *The Theatre of the Empire of Great Britaine.* This is Hottenroth's version; Racinet's can be seen on page 39. There are notable differences in pose, hairstyles, and colors. The direct source for both of these versions was Meyrick and Smith's *Costume of the Original Inhabitants of the British Islands,* and a comparison shows that Racinet faithfully reproduced Meyrick's hairstyles and poses, while Hottenroth more accurately reproduced the colors and textiles.

Headwear
• Phrygian cap

Hairstyles

Dress
• draped
• loosely fitted

Upper Garments
• cloak
• mail shirt
• short-sleeved blouse
• sleeved tunic

Lower Garments
• skirt
• pants (braies)

Accessories
• girdle

Footwear

Post Roman Empire

Gallo-Roman, Merovingian, and Carolingian

Celtic Gaul, which included parts of modern France and Germany, was conquered by Julius Caesar in the middle of the 1st century BC as Rome made the transition from Republic to Empire. Rome ruled Gaul for six hundred years, but late in the 5th century AD the last Roman governor was defeated by Clovis I, king of the Franks, and the Merovingian Dynasty began. This, in turn, gave way to the Frankish Carolingian Dynasty in 751. The most famous Carolingian king was Charlemagne, who ruled from 768 to 814 and who, in a neat reversal of history, conquered Italy and had himself crowned emperor by Pope Leo III in 800. Primary sources concerning the dress of this period are scarce. What does survive suggests that the Romans were as ready to adopt Gaulish garments, like braies or breeches, as they were to bring their own garments to Gaul.

● Gallo-Romans and Franks

All these men are Gallo-Roman, except for one Frank on the far right. Their costume consists generally of tunics in different lengths, with several men also wearing braies. The plaids many wear are also striking, although their colors or deployment may not be entirely accurate.

See also
Gauls, Celts, and Britons, *pages 38–39*
Post Roman Empire, *pages 42–43*

● Charlemagne, 9th–10th Century

This image of Charlemagne probably came from a 10th-century copy of a 9th-century manuscript. Hottenroth did alter some clothing details but he faithfully reproduced its color, which is indeed this unlikely combination of orange and green. In the manuscript his mantle seems longer, the border trimming his tunic hem is broader, and his conical hat is stepped, taller, and narrower.

Gallo-Roman Man

His dress shows a blend of Roman and Celtic elements. His short tunic has the long, tight sleeves typically worn in Gaul by both sexes and it is decorated with woven stripes down the front. His short, calf-length pants appear to be of the snug-fitting style adopted from the Celts by the Romans. His tall sandals and the rectangular cloak fastened on his right shoulder may be Roman in origin.

Romanized Garments

This woman appears to be dressed in full, draped Romanized garments, but a closer look at her mantle reveals that it seems, oddly, to be half mantle and half cloak, with a sawtooth slit cut into its right side for her arm to pass through. Hottenroth failed to identify his source, so it is difficult to know how to interpret it.

Druid Priest

Druids were the priests of Europe's Celtic tribes; their nature-loving, polytheistic faith was ultimately supplanted by the Roman government and Christianity. This drawing appears to be based on an 1845 engraving from a Roman-era bas-relief discovered at Autun, France. His long white cloak fastens on his left shoulder with a ring, and he is crowned with a wreath of fresh oak leaves—oaks being an object of Druidic veneration.

Bardocucullus

This man is dressed in a short plain tunic and hooded cloak, known as a *bardocucullus*, originally a Roman import. This Gaulish form of bardocucullus, with an upturned peak on its hood, was very popular among Romans.

Headwear
- conical hat
- hood

Hairstyles

Dress
- mixture of Roman and local styles

Upper Garments
- cloak
- hooded cloak (bardocucullus)
- mantle
- sleeved tunic

Lower Garments
- pants/breeches (braies)

Accessories
- headband
- ring brooch
- wreath

Footwear
- leather shoes or boots
- sandals

Europe in the Middle Ages

Compared to today's lightning-fast changes in fashion, men's and women's clothes evolved relatively slowly before the Renaissance dawned in Italy during the 14th century. Dress at the beginning of this period was similar for both sexes, as it had been during earlier times, and consisted of two or three tunics or gowns, one worn on top of another, with a washable linen one usually closest to the skin. These garments were known by a variety of different names in different places and times, and could be either knee-length or long for men, but were invariably long for women.

As the era progressed, the appearance of men's and women's dress reflected an increasing divergence. By the 11th century it was clear that European dress was becoming more elaborate and extravagant, using richer materials and more surface decoration than heretofore. In both the 12th and 14th centuries styles became much more fitted. These changes resulted in part from the influences and goods that came to Europe from the Middle East in the wake of the Crusades, coupled with the development of an urban middle class and growing sophistication in cutting and tailoring. Also important in increasing the luxuriousness of European dress was the establishment of sericulture and silk weaving in Spain and Italy in the 7th and 8th centuries respectively. By the mid-13th century Italy was both a key importer of Chinese silks and Europe's most important center for manufacturing silk cloth.

Yet perhaps the most significant development during this period was the evolution of the complex system of constantly changing modes, divorced from fixed hierarchies of rank and locale, that comprises modern fashion. Scholars believe that this system arose during the 14th or early 15th centuries, originating either at the luxurious Burgundian court or in Italy before shifting to Burgundy just as the Renaissance began to take hold. Burgundy, which at this time controlled Flanders and much of what is now France, was enormously wealthy, with a sophisticated, elegant, and powerful court whose elaborate ceremonies provided the perfect fashion arena, a rising middle class, and access to high-quality materials—all the ingredients that fashion needed.

Armor, *9th–12th Century*

Mail and Plate Armor

Mail, which is armor made from interlocking metal rings, probably originated with the Celts in the 6th or 5th century BC. It became the most common form of armor among European mounted and foot soldiers until the 13th century. It was commonly worn over a padded undertunic, called an *aketon* in medieval Europe, that would cushion the body from abrasion and cuts from the mail. The development of European plate armor, which was stiffer than mail and better able to withstand direct blows to the body, began with the appearance of *hauberks* covered with overlapping iron scales, or plates, in the 11th century, similar in appearance to the scale armor worn in ancient Greece and Rome.

▶ Knight, 12th Century

He wears an unusually long mail shirt slit for riding—although his long gown seems unsuitable for this— that is fitted to his body in keeping with the 12th-century fashion for tighter clothes. His conical helmet is probably of eastern origin and the face shield worn below it is punched with breathing holes.

See also
Greek Armor,
pages 28–29
Roman Armor,
pages 32–33

Full Mail, 12th Century ◀

These three soldiers wear mail from head to foot, from the full mail hose covering their legs to the knee-length hauberks with full mail sleeves that extend to form mail gloves, to the *coifs* beneath their conical and flat-topped helms. Typically, each of the helms has a nose guard, or *nasal*, to protect the face.

Mounted Knight, 11th–12th Century

This knight was plainly mounted in the source image, although Hottenroth omitted the horse here. What appears to be a mail jumpsuit in this picture is most likely a misrepresentation of the slit knee-length hauberks favored by cavalry, which allowed them to sit astride a horse more easily.

Mail, 11th Century

This is a front view of armor similar to the hauberk pictured above. Here Racinet has better interpreted its structure as a mail shirt slit for riding at the bottom center, front and back. His conical banded helm is of a type widely adopted in Europe and used for centuries, and his kite-shaped shield is the type commonly carried by cavalrymen. This is the style of armor depicted in the Bayeux Tapestry (*c.* 1066–77).

Knight, Early 9th Century

This French knight from Charlemagne's time wears a cuirass of iron plates, more likely a variation of classical scale armor than an ancestor of European plate armor. His helm and face plate are in a style used by Roman soldiers at least six hundred years earlier.

Headwear
- conical helmet
- face shield
- flat-topped helmet
- nose guard (nasal)

Hairstyles

Dress
- mail
- scale, or plate, armor

Upper Garments
- cuirass
- hauberks
- padded undertunic (aketon)

Lower Garments
- mail hose

Accessories
- kite-shaped shield

Footwear
- mail hose

England, *11th–13th Century*

Anglo-Saxons and Anglo-Normans

The Roman Empire was in serious decline by the mid-11th to the early 13th centuries, a period when Norman-French and Anglo-Saxon cultures intertwined in England. The Bayeux Tapestry, an important source for 11th-century dress, chronicles the beginning of their cultural melding in the successful Norman invasion and conquest of England. It makes little distinction between the dress of the Normans and that of the English, although there is a clear difference in the way the two groups wear their hair. The Normans' hair is cut very short, high above the nape of the neck, while the English wear theirs long, a style that the Normans soon adopted.

King, 13th Century

The crown on his mail coif confirms his rank; the small amounts of protective plate armor on elbows (*couters*) and knees (*poleyns*) suggest the 13th century. Heraldic devices are thought to have been introduced to England by the Normans; the lions or leopards on his surcoat are associated with both the Normans and the English monarchy from *c.* 1133–*c.* 1340.

Norman Knight, *c.* 11th Century

Hottenroth identified this knight as Norman, and indeed he closely resembles the Norman knights depicted in the Bayeux Tapestry. The slit in the skirt of his *haubergeon* (knee-length hauberk) allowed for riding, and some are thought to have had extra thigh protection via a flaplike extension in the back that could be pulled between the legs and laced to the skirts in front.

Full Suit of Mail, Late 12th Century

The suit has armored hose (*chausses*) laced around the leg and a hauberk whose sleeves completely cover the wearer's hands. The drawing suggests that a plate *gorget* protects his neck, but since those did not come into use until the late 13th century it is likely that his coif is made of mail only.

Civilians, 13th Century

The tunic sleeves of the man on the right suggest the tapering shape characteristic of the 13th century. The man on the left appears to be wearing the hooded garment called a *gardecorps*, which appeared mid-century. It had full sleeves that were slit to allow the wearer's arms to move freely.

See also

Armor, 9th–12th Century, *pages 48–49*

Knights, 11th Century

The soldier in the background is probably Norman, as his very short hair suggests the way the invading Normans in the Bayeux Tapestry wore theirs. The knight in front wears typical 11th-century mail: a coif and haubergeon with elbow-length sleeves, and what may be quilted leggings reinforced with mail strips. He could be either Saxon or Norman.

Headwear
• crown
• hood
• mail coif
• plate gorget

Hairstyles
• shoulder-length (Anglo-Saxon)
• very short, shaved at back of neck (Norman)

Dress

Upper Garments
• elbow armor (couters)
• hauberk (haubergeon)
• hooded robe (gardecorps)
• sleeved tunic

Lower Garments
• armored hose (chausses)
• knee armor (poleyns)
• leggings
• mail leggings

Accessories

Footwear

England, *14th Century*

Men's and Women's Dress

There is far more information about dress in the 14th century than in the 13th. Much of it comes from inventories, such as the great wardrobe accounts of the English royal court, some of which survive. The great wardrobe supplied the royal household with its clothing and its furnishing textiles. The clothing encompassed not only what the royal family wore, but gifts to knights and ladies and others of lower rank, both inside and outside the royal household, which were a regular and important aspect of medieval economic and social exchange. An analysis, therefore, of the descriptions of the garments made, stuffs used, and expenditure on materials and labor for such a wide range of people can reveal much.

Minstrel
14th-century musicians are often depicted in clothing made from fabrics decorated with brightly colored narrow and broad stripes, which served as a form of uniform or livery. Striped fabric, much of it woven in Ghent, Flanders, was cheap and ordinary, and would have been affordable even for a musician.

> **See also**
> **France, 14th–15th Century,** *pages 64–65*
> **Germany, 14th Century,** *pages 74–75*

Historic Anomalies
The squarer shape of the neckline seen on the right, while perhaps not as pronounced in life as Hottenroth has made it, seems to have been an English phenomenon. So, too, are the pocketlike slits in the skirt of the *surcoat*, or overdress, which allowed the wearer to slip her hands inside to warm them. Both features appear on a *c.* 1364 brass of Lady Stapleton.

Headwear

Hairstyles

Dress
• increasingly close-fitting

Upper Garments
• gown (houppelande)
• overdress (surcoat)
• tunic

Lower Garments

Accessories

Footwear

Open-Sided Surcoat

This surcoat is lined with ermine. The undersleeves are fastened with myriad small buttons. It is hard to judge the length of the train, but a similar surcoat on Margaret, Lady Despencer's mid-century effigy has a train about 10 in. (25 cm) long.

Fitted Tunics, 1360–80

The shorter, tighter tunic worn by both men is a style that can be traced in England through manuscript illuminations and effigies made after 1340. It caused some consternation among English chroniclers, who condemned it as both foreign and outlandish, and looked longingly back to the "good old days" when longer, larger tunics offered what they considered to be proper coverage of the body.

Houppelande, c. 1390–1400

This style of gown appeared at the end of the 1300s. The early houppelande was distinguished by its very high collar—so high that the hair on the nape of the neck was often shaved to accommodate it and its enveloping quality. This one has wide bombarde sleeves with dagged edges and is sewn with gold bezants—thin disks of metal that jingled softly as the wearer walked.

England, *15th Century*

Men's Dress

The relative wealth of documentary evidence for dress in England in the 14th century notwithstanding, English fashion in the 15th century is difficult to determine from the sources, which are both scarcer and inferior to those produced elsewhere in northern Europe. Surviving garments from the period are even rarer, so there is little to add to the documentary evidence to establish what the English wore. Accounts by foreign visitors report that English clothes were strange and old-fashioned, so it seems clear that fashion leadership in the 15th century was elsewhere. Nonetheless, images that do exist indicate that the English generally followed northern European fashion trends, a habit doubtless reinforced by their occupation of northern France during the first half of the century.

Bag Sleeves, First Quarter, 15th Century

Early houppelandes are usually shown as having wide sleeves, called *bombarde* or *ducale* sleeves, but a popular variation during the first quarter of the century gathered those sleeves tightly around the wrist, leaving the fullness to fall like a bag from the forearm. The man on the right wears a long chain fitted with small bells across his chest.

Geoffrey Chaucer, Early 15th Century

The gray-clad figure is based on a portrait of Chaucer in a surviving manuscript of *The Canterbury Tales*, which itself was probably based on a portrait painted shortly after his death in 1400 by Charles Hoccleve, who knew the poet personally. Chaucer's calf-length gown with closed, baglike sleeves and a small hood is far less extravagant than those worn by his three, later, companions.

Short Gown, Third Quarter, 15th Century

This style of very short gown, with ordered pleats narrowing into the waist and fanning out below it, had appeared by 1460 and remained in fashion for at least a decade. The two-piece sleeve suggests the slightly later date. The bagginess of his hose at the knees and buttocks indicates that they are cloth rather than knitted.

See also
France, 1364–1461,
pages 62–63
Germany, 15th Century,
pages 76–77

Sober Styles, Late 15th Century

The men facing forward are soberly dressed, showing none of the extremes of end-of-the-century fashion (low-cut doublet necklines and short sleeves to reveal a billowing shirt). The man on the far right resembles Henry VII, known for his lack of interest in fine clothes.

Particolored hood

The fashion for two-tone hoods is supported by documentary evidence. The 1459 wardrobe inventory of Sir John Fastolf, compiled by John Paston, lists four particolored hoods and others made of two different fabrics of the same color. The Paston Letters also list a 1467 purchase of three-quarters of a yard (80 cm) each of damask and sarsenet for a hood for Anne Paston.

Headwear
• hood, in various styles

Hairstyles

Dress
• broadened shoulder line

Upper Garments
• gown (houppelande)
• short, pleated gown

Lower Garments
• hose

Accessories
• chain

Footwear

England, *15th Century*

Women's Dress

As previously noted, English fashion generally followed in France's wake during the 15th century, but a comparison of the two reveals some differences. The line of English clothes was generally a little squarer than in France, and gowns and surcoats often fitted the body more loosely. English upper-class life, then as later, was more centered around the country than the court; as a result, styles from abroad were slower to be adopted, fashions changed a bit more slowly, and the materials used for clothing were less luxurious. Indeed, it could be challenging for anyone stuck in the country to obtain the necessary fabrics for clothes for themselves and their family without sending to London for them. Margaret Paston, writing from Norfolk to her husband in London in the 1450s, repeatedly asks for fabric for hoods, gowns, and other garments for herself and her children, and laments in one letter that "there is neither good cloth nor good frieze in this town."

Northern European Styles, Early 15th Century

The open-sided surcoat is a 14th-century fashion that persisted as upper-class formal and ceremonial dress throughout the 15th century. This depiction may have been drawn from a tomb sculpture; a similar one, dating from *c.* 1470, exists in Norbury, England. The houppelandes and the wired butterfly headdress seen on the left were also styles found elsewhere in northern Europe. Similar headdresses appear in the *Très Riches heures du Duc de Berry* (1412–16) and Christine de Pisan's *Book of the City of Ladies* (1410). The square headdress (*center*) may be a misreading of an English hairstyle of the 1420s, in which netted horns of hair worn at the sides of the head were covered with a crimped veil.

See also
France, 15th Century,
pages 68–69

Headwear
- butterfly headdress
- crimped veil
- gable or pediment hood
- horned headdress
- undercap

Hairstyles
- central parting
- horned, secured with a hairnet

Dress
- high-waisted, fitted, floor-length

Upper Garments
- gown (houppelande)
- long-sleeved tunic (kirtle)

Lower Garments

Accessories

Footwear

Ungainly Headdresses, Second Quarter, 15th Century

On the left is most likely Cicely Nevill, Duchess of York, as depicted in a book of hours in the Bibliothèque Nationale, Paris, France In the original version her houppelande is brocade lined with miniver, and her bejeweled headdress has a linen veil pinned to its horns.

English Wool

This woman's gown is probably made of wool, for which the English had a fine reputation. Fleece was an important English export in the 13th and 14th centuries, but domestic demand grew so much during the 15th century that export was discouraged.

Gable Hood, *c.* 1500

The distinctively English gable or pediment hood appeared during the 1490s. It was worn over an undercap and its shape was achieved with wire. In its earlier form, shown here, it reveals a bit of center-parted hair, a feature that disappeared after 1525. The lappets that frame the face often bore rich embroidery or jewels; here, these appear to be made of gold net, a fitting match for her silk velvet or brocade ermine-trimmed *kirtle* (long-sleeved tunic).

France, *12th–13th Century*

Kings and Queens

Illuminated manuscripts and sculpture are important primary sources that antiquarians rely on for information about medieval clothing. These church sculptures of early French kings and queens were identified by Racinet as King Clovis I (*c.* 466–511), his wife Clotilda, their son Childebert I, king of Paris (*c.* 495–558) and his wife Ultrogothe. He notes that no attempt was made to replicate the dress of the monarchs' own day; instead, they appear in styles from the 12th and 13th centuries when the sculptures were carved. Contemporary sources are vague about the influence of the Crusades (1075–1270) on western fashions, but many historians feel that contact with the East contributed much to the growing sophistication of dress at this time.

King of Paris

Childebert I is shown with shoulder-length hair beneath his jeweled crown and with a full beard and mustache. Both the long hair and beard are thought to be signs of eastern influence; they begin to appear regularly in depictions of western men in the 11th century and are widespread by the 12th. The mantle he wears over his long-sleeved, belted tunic is fastened with a ribbon across his chest that he pulls down with his left hand in a gesture that appears frequently in sculpture of the period.

Queen of Paris

This statue of Queen Ultrogothe comes from the church of Sainte-Geneviève de Paris. Her looser tunic and long, buckled belt are in the style of similar sculptures from the early to mid-13th century. Ironically, this same sculpture was the source for a similar costume plate published in the 1830s as an example of 6th-century costume.

Enveloping Mantle

There are few details of the dress to be seen on this statue of St. Geneviève from the portal of St. Germain-l'Auxerrois. The mantle, drawn veil-like over her head, is reminiscent of the Roman palla, but it also has the ribbon closure that was often found on fashionable mantles during the 12th and 13th centuries.

See also
Rome, *pages 34–35*
Byzantium, *pages 40–41*

Headwear
• royal crown

Hairstyles
• long hair, mustache, and beard for men

Dress
• showing oriental influence

Upper Garments
• cloak/mantle (pallium or paludamentum)
• gown
• tunic
• undertunic (cotte)

Lower Garments

Accessories
• buckled or knotted belt
• ribbon closure

Footwear

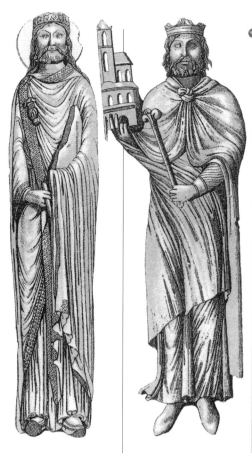

Tight-Fitting Gown

Queen Clotilda wears a tight-fitting style of gown often depicted in the 12th century. The pleated or crimped bodice, slit at the neck to show the undertunic, was fitted to the torso with buttons or lacing down the side. She has huge sleeves and a long belt knotted low on her hips.

Clovis I

This 12th-century sculpture from Notre Dame de Corbeil is thought to depict Clovis I. He seems to be dressed in a long fitted tunic with a fuller skirt that falls in folds at his feet. This is largely concealed under his embroidered cloak, which looks similar to a paludamentum, the one-shouldered cloak used since ancient Greek times.

Fitted Tunic

Here the king is wearing a tunic in the more fitted 12th-century style. This is accompanied by what appear to be long, pleated, or goffered sleeves fitted at the wrists with a band of embroidery. His cloak is in the style of the Roman and Byzantine pallium, an item that was worn knotted around the neck.

Cotte and Overtunic

This 13th-century sculpture clearly shows the king is wearing two layers: the undertunic, or *cotte*, which both sexes commonly wore next to the skin, and a calf-length overtunic with full sleeves cut in one with the tunic's body and tapering to the wrist. He wears a long-tongued buckled belt at the waist.

France, *13th–14th Century*

The Middle and Working Classes

Depictions of the dress of ordinary people are less common in the Middle Ages than those of the upper classes, but a number of examples like these have come down to us by way of illuminated manuscripts. Judging from their clothing, these drawings may present an idealized view of 14th-century laborers' dress, as the peasants appear rather prosperous and well-kempt. Working men generally wore upper garments that extended no farther than knee-length and were often shorter, which enabled them to move more easily as they worked. Women's clothing, usually consisting of a long-sleeved tunic (kirtle) worn over a chemise and occasionally topped by an overgown, was invariably long—ankle-length at least—but working women were often portrayed with at least their outermost skirt looped up or caught back to make movement easier. Aprons, which later were a staple of working dress for both sexes, were only just beginning to be worn in the 14th century.

Doublets, Tunics, and Hoods

These three laborers all wear variations on the same garments—a doublet (short, close-fitting jacket worn on top of the shirt) and a short, round-necked tunic belted at the waist, which was a standard garment for laborers for centuries. The hoods worn by two of these men were also worn by country people over a long period of time; in addition to their hoods, each man has a straw or felt hat.

Headwear
- hat (broad-brimmed or acorn-shaped, straw or felt)
- veil

Hairstyles
- shoulder-length

Dress
- shorter, more practical than aristocratic dress

Upper Garments
- chemise
- doublet
- long-sleeved tunic (kirtle)
- overgown
- short tunic

Lower Garments
- cloth hose

Accessories
- apron
- linen bag (panetière)

Footwear
- boots with pointed toes (poulaines)

Broad-Brimmed Hat

This gardener wears a blue overgown fitted relatively closely to her torso; its skirt is looped up to reveal a red kirtle (tunic) beneath. A linen veil is wrapped around her head and she wears a broad-brimmed straw hat, a style worn only by the working class at this period.

Middle-Class Men

These three men, taken from an edition of Jean Froissart's *Chroniques*, are intended to represent fashionable dress of the middle class in 1341, but their dress comes closer to reflecting the early to mid-15th century than the mid-14th century. The broad shoulderline and puffed sleeves of two of the three, the slightly dropped waistline, and the acorn-shaped hat are all of the later period.

See also
France, 15th Century, *pages 68–69*
Northern Europe, 14th Century, *pages 78–79*

Panetière and Poulaines

This man is a cowherd; over his doublet he wears a very short tunic that barely covers his buttocks. Although it looks as though he is barelegged, he is wearing flesh-colored cloth hose that are tied onto his doublet beneath his gown. Ankle-high black boots (*poulaines*) with long, pointed toes complete his outfit. Around his waist is a *panetière*, a white linen bag used to carry bread or other comestibles.

61

France, *1364–1461*

Noblemen and Noblewomen

Most of these figures are 14th- or 15th-century French
royals and nobles, many related by blood or marriage.
The men's dress reflects the luxurious textiles, furs, and
lavish embroidery then in vogue in both the French and
Burgundian courts. The women wear examples of 14th-
century dress that fossilized into the *robe royale*, a suit
of four or five garments worn on state occasions by royal
and aristocratic Frenchwomen until the end of the 15th
century. The most distinctive of these is the open-sided
surcoat, which is an overdress with a bodice that is
stiffened in front and cut out at the sides from shoulder
to hip, revealing a fitted gown beneath.

Figures from Illuminated Manuscripts

The man is reproduced fairly
accurately from *King René's
Tournament Book* (*c.* 1460), but
in the original his sleeves, cap,
and shoes are more exaggerated.
Isabella Stuart, Duchess of
Brittany, from a book of hours
c. 1417–18, wears an open-sided
armorial surcoat with an ermine-
clad bodice. In the original her
bodice is narrower and curvier
with a wider neckline, a red
gown beneath, and clearer
armorial embroidery.

See also
**France, 14th–15th
Century,** *pages 64–65*
France, 15th Century,
pages 68–71

Marie d'Anjou,

This image of Charles
VII's queen was
copied from a 19th-
century engraving
that rendered many
details of her steeple
headdress incorrectly.
Originally, her mid-
15th century
headdress would have
sat a bit farther back
on her head and
been less lumpish in
shape. The veil would
have been more
transparent, and
would most likely
have been draped over
the headdress rather
than beneath it, and
folded back just to the
edge of the forehead.

Headwear
• hood
• steeple headdress
• veil

Hairstyles

Dress
• much use of fur, especially ermine

Upper Garments
• bodice
• court ensemble (robe royale)
• gown (houppelande)
• mantle
• surcoat

Lower Garments

Accessories
• decorative streamers (tippets)

Footwear

Louis, King of Naples and Sicily

Louis, the titular king of Naples and Sicily, is shown here in a drawing after a shoulder-length portrait by an unknown artist dated *c.* 1412–15. The dagged red hood twisted like a turban and the high collar of his red-and-gold brocade houppelande are fairly well represented from the original, but all the other details of his clothing below his shoulders were added by Racinet.

Marie de Berri

Marie married Jean I, Duc de Bourbon, in 1401; this portrait may date from around that time. She is one of a handful of royal and noble English and French women from 14th- and 15th-century manuscripts and brasses who wear heraldic surcoats. Hers is a closed surcoat with an ermine bodice whose short sleeves are garnished with long streamers called *tippets*.

Jean, Duc de Bourbon

His enveloping mantle, of small embroidered gold fleurs-de-lis on a blue ground, reproduces the coat of arms used by the Dukes of Bourbon from 1327 to 1410. Ermine, which lines his mantle, was popular with the upper echelon of society in this period, but fur of all kinds, from squirrel to lamb to fox, was very popular with people of all classes.

France, *14th–15th Century*

Men and Women Depicted in Illuminated Manuscripts

Racinet relied heavily on illuminated manuscripts for medieval clothing. Many of the images in this book are taken from manuscript illuminations, and they are perhaps the most important surviving visual sources we have for pre-Renaissance dress, offering brilliantly colored images of clothing and how people actually wore their attire. In addition, they sometimes depict middle- and working-class dress. However, the majority of illuminated manuscripts were devotional books, peopled with characters who may not always wear straightforward dress of the time, so we cannot take the representations too literally.

See also
France, 15th Century, *pages 68–71*

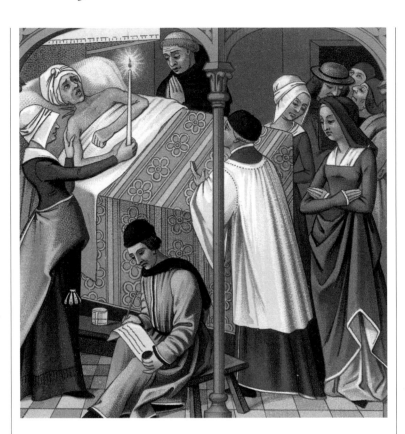

▶ **Jailer and Messenger**
Both men wear knee-length gowns with belts that mark a slightly dropped waistline. The wide, dagged sleeves of the jailer's gown and his companion's short hair and tall collar were fashionable early in the 15th century. The jailer's headgear is more often depicted in contemporary manuscripts with its long crown worn folded back over the crown of the head.

◀ **Nightclothes, Late 15th Century**
This deathbed scene, from the *Stile du droit français,* indicates that many people at the end of the Middle Ages were still sleeping naked save for a nightcap of some sort, here a linen towel wrapped like a turban. The stubby headdress with the folded-back front worn by the woman at the foot of the bed is a type favored by lower-class women.

Headwear
• headdress made from padded rolls of fabric (bourrelet)
• nightcap
• steeple headdress
• turban

Hairstyles
• short hair for men

Dress
• fitted to the body with padded, ordered pleats

Upper Garments
• doublet
• gown
• surcoat

Lower Garments

Accessories
• belt

Footwear

Foreigners, Early 15th Century

The source for this image was a French manuscript, but it is intended to represent clothing from Spain. Foreignness is suggested by the headgear, especially of the two men in the middle, and the shape of the hem of the dagged white gown.

Gown and Doublet, *c.* 1460

The doublet on the right, so short that it barely covers the buttocks, has the characteristic rounded folds of the period in its skirt and would probably originally have had them in the torso as well. A similar doublet is probably beneath the long brocade gown worn by his companion, as its stand collar is visible above the gown's fur-trimmed neckline. His unusual tall cap resembles the steeple headdresses worn by women at this time.

The Suicide of Lucretia, *c.* 1415

Lucretia, a legendary noblewoman of ancient Rome, is dressed as an upper-class Frenchwoman in a wide-necked surcoat with trailing, ribbonlike sleeves. She wears a padded *bourrelet* on her head.

France, *1364–1461*

Battle, Joust, and Tournament Dress

During the 15th century armor reached its highest level of sophistication, with the finest examples being made by German and Italian craftsmen, who produced suits that were both beautiful to look at and protected the wearer in battle. Jousts and tournaments were the war games of the Middle Ages and early Renaissance, and they served both as popular forms of entertainment for royalty and the nobility and as useful practice for war. Although generally fought with blunted weapons, these were still dangerous pastimes, and deaths sometimes occurred.

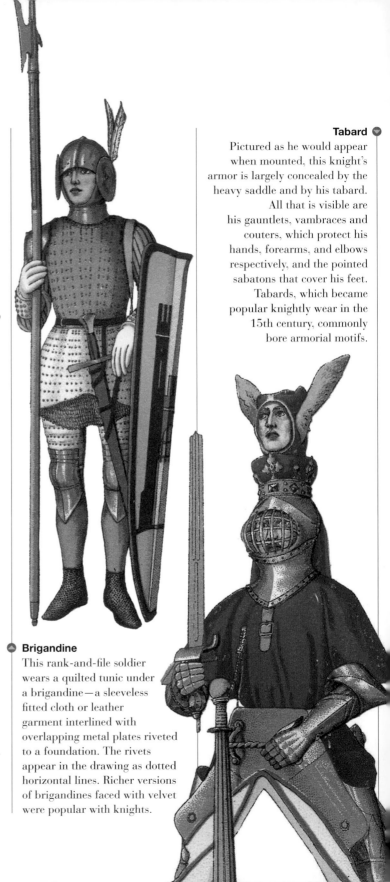

Tabard
Pictured as he would appear when mounted, this knight's armor is largely concealed by the heavy saddle and by his tabard. All that is visible are his gauntlets, vambraces and couters, which protect his hands, forearms, and elbows respectively, and the pointed sabatons that cover his feet. Tabards, which became popular knightly wear in the 15th century, commonly bore armorial motifs.

Memento Mori
Crested helms like this foreboding memento mori were worn in battle until about 1380; after that, they became tournament wear only.

Fanciful Crest
The buckled strap probably shows how this crest fastened to the helm. Some surviving helms have holes for crest ties; others have metal loops at the top of the crown.

Brigandine
This rank-and-file soldier wears a quilted tunic under a brigandine—a sleeveless fitted cloth or leather garment interlined with overlapping metal plates riveted to a foundation. The rivets appear in the drawing as dotted horizontal lines. Richer versions of brigandines faced with velvet were popular with knights.

See also
France, 15th Century
pages 70–71

Frog-Mouth Helm

A jousting knight's goal was to unhorse his adversary with his lance, so jousting armor was designed to offer maximum protection from the oncoming weapon. Hence the popularity of the so-called frog-mouth helm worn by this knight, which provided only the narrowest of slits for seeing but effectively protected the face. The shield, which is fastened to the armor, has a bricklike pattern raised on its surface, that would help deflect an opponent's lance.

Swan's-Neck Crest

Elaborate crests like this swan's neck were often made of leather cut to shape, wetted, and molded into a three-dimensional form. Once dry, it could be further sculpted with a plasterlike material or simply painted. This crest has a mantle cut into long, dagged streamers that would have fluttered in the wind.

Crossbowman

This crossbowman wears mainly upper-body armor, consisting of a short-sleeved mail coat (known as a haubergeon) underneath a cuirass marked with a cross, a standard, or mail neck guard, and a visorless helm.

Headwear
- frog-mouth helm
- helm (often crested)

Hairstyles

Dress
- quilted armor
- plate armor

Upper Garments
- cuirass
- gauntlets
- overtunic (brigandine)
- short-sleeved mail coat (haubergeon)
- vambrace

Lower Garments

Accessories
- shield

Footwear
- pointed sabatons

France, *15th Century*

Men's and Women's Dress

All four of these scenes were taken from the *Stile du droit français*, a manuscript about French law from the second half of the 15th century that shows people of different classes. Racinet boasted that his reproductions were just as grand as the originals, but they can be difficult to interpret out of context. The manuscript is dated to the second half of the century but some of the clothing is of an earlier style, for what reason it is hard to say. There are also several figures that seem to be allegorical rather than fashionable. Racinet was aware that not all the images were straightforward: in his introduction to the plate he mentions that the veil worn by the woman in the upper plate on this page and the entire ensemble worn by the priest in the lower plate are "apocryphal."

Allegorical Figure

Beneath her veil, this woman seems to wear the basic cotte worn by most working-class Frenchwomen. Hers is decorated at the hem and wrists, though, which peasants would have unlikely afforded. Surviving inventories indicate that most peasants had only a few clothes. They were often made from dyed blue woad, as it was both a plentiful and inexpensive fabric.

Old-Fashioned Dress

The man's fur-lined short houppelande, with its natural shoulders, dropped waistline, and fullness at front and back, is in the style of the 1430s. It is not known whether the original was intended to depict the past or whether it is simply meant to convey that its wearer's clothes are out of fashion. He has slung a long black hood over his shoulder by its pate, the part that would cover his shoulders if it were worn.

See also
France, 14th–15th Century, *pages 64–65*
France, 15th Century, *pages 70–71*

Courtroom Scene

In this medieval courtroom several classes are represented: the working people, such as the two men in black hats, more old-fashioned and countrified, and the middle- and upper-class people, more chic. In describing this scene, Racinet credited the relative simplicity of the dress to reforms instituted by Louis XI (r. 1461–83) and explained that only lawyers, clergymen, and men of letters wore long gowns at this time.

Headwear
• hood
• veil
• wimple

Hairstyles

Dress
• variable waistlines and degrees of fit

Upper Garments
• gown (houppelande)
• riding gown
• undertunic (cotte)

Lower Garments

Accessories

Footwear

Miniver Lining

The man in his miniver-lined gown slit for riding is plainly far wealthier than the woman in cotte, wimple and regional veil. Miniver—gray squirrel belly—was one of the most popular furs in the Middle Ages. The pelt had a distinctive white shield shape in the center and a narrow border of gray fur, making it easy to identify in paintings.

France, *15th Century*

Tournament Dress

The crowd scenes here derive from *King René's Tournament Book*, written around 1460 by René of Anjou and illuminated by an anonymous painter known as the Master of René of Anjou. The king was famous for the tournaments he mounted in the 1440s, and he claims to have written the book to record how he thinks tournaments in France should be organized, based on his own experience and on his study of practices elsewhere in Europe. Using as examples the Duke of Brittany as challenger and the Duke of Bourbon as defendant, he sets forth in minute detail the proper ways of conducting all aspects of the contest, and he also describes the fashion and style of the weapons and armor, and the prizes to be awarded.

Before the Tourney ◀
Here the Duke of Bourbon is arriving to take his tournament oath. Drawn from a copy (*c.* 1488) of the *c.* 1460 original, this version reproduces the original carefully, but some details reflect the later period—for example, the broader-shouldered silhouette, and the rounder, shallower hat worn by the duke.

Courtiers, *c.* 1490 ◀
These men and the courtier opposite are fashionably attired, hatted, and coiffed. Their most prominent garment is the fur-lined, broad-lapeled gown. The long sleeves are worn pushed up but are also slit so they can be worn hanging. All wear belts that dip slightly lower at the front.

Headwear
• brimmed hat

Hairstyles

Dress

Upper Garments
• long

Lower Garments

Accessories
• belt

Footwear

Courtier, *c.* 1490

This courtier and the two on the opposite page come from a third manuscript of *King René's Tournament Book* (*c.* 1490). Interestingly, although the colors Racinet used are often incorrect, these follow the shades in the original painting quite closely.

Back View Before the Tourney, *c.* 1460–88

This scene and the scene on the opposite page were originally part of the same large picture. These people are watching the Duke of Bourbon's arrival, and they offer a rare rear view of men's headgear and gowns. Although they, too, come from the later manuscript, their wide-shouldered, firmly pleated gowns seem more accurate renditions of the original source.

Herald of Arms

This herald is in tournament dress. According to King René's rules, three or four heralds should accompany the king of arms (essentially the chief herald) when he visited the courts of the challenger and defendant. The heralds also played an active role during the tourney itself.

See also
France, 15th Century
pages 68–69

71

Germany, *6th–13th Century*

Medieval Development

German clothing during the Middle Ages was an amalgam of its own past plus influences from the Near East and Central Asia, France, and the Roman Empire. Germany's feudal system, which developed in the 11th century, was headed by an elected king who lacked the power of an absolute ruler. As a result, Germany in the later Middle Ages became a confederation of independent cities that were competitive with each other and, thanks to entities like the Hanseatic League, economically powerful. The Hanseatic League was an organization of German merchants in as many as a hundred cities and towns, and controlled trade on the Baltic and North Seas.

Medieval Jew

Hottenroth identified the man on the left as a Jew. He does not wear the *judenhut*, the conical hat in which medieval Jews are often pictured, but his tunic is yellow. In 1215, Pope Innocent III's Fourth Lateran Council ruled that both Muslims and Jews in Christian Europe must wear identifying dress; for Jews it was a yellow badge, which was notoriously revived by the Nazis in the 20th century.

Goffered Bodice, Mid-12th Century

Hottenroth described and drew this unusual dress as a tunic under a girdle quilted like armor lining and laced closed. But this seems to be a misunderstanding of his source, a sculpture of Queen Juda from Chartres Cathedral in France, who wears a long tunic with a goffered bodice.

See also
Germany, 14th Century, *pages 74–75*
Germany, 15th Century, *pages 76–77*

Man of Rank, 11th or 12th Century

German tunics in the 11th century were often knee-length; this one is longer, although still short enough to show a linen undertunic. Its wrists and neckline are embroidered, and it may have the diagonal neck opening used until the 13th century.

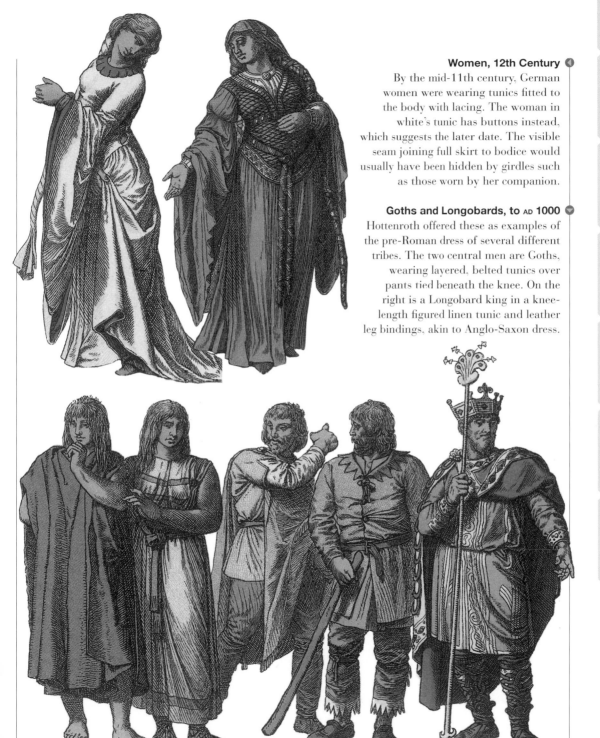

Headwear
• conical hat

Hairstyles

Dress
• layers of tunics

Upper Garments
• goffered bodice
• long tunic
• undetunic

Lower Garments
• leg bindings
• pants

Accessories
• girdle

Footwear

Women, 12th Century

By the mid-11th century, German women were wearing tunics fitted to the body with lacing. The woman in white's tunic has buttons instead, which suggests the later date. The visible seam joining full skirt to bodice would usually have been hidden by girdles such as those worn by her companion.

Goths and Longobards, to AD 1000

Hottenroth offered these as examples of the pre-Roman dress of several different tribes. The two central men are Goths, wearing layered, belted tunics over pants tied beneath the knee. On the right is a Longobard king in a knee-length figured linen tunic and leather leg bindings, akin to Anglo-Saxon dress.

Germany, *14th Century*

Men's and Women's Dress

Clothing styles were relatively consistent across western Europe in the 14th century, although there were certainly local variations. The contemporary taste for parti-colored clothing, for instance, is particularly strongly reflected in these drawings of German dress, appearing not only in hose but also in doublets and tunics as well. Some striped garments appear in German illuminated manuscripts of the 14th century but for the most part clothing is rendered in solid colors, with the combination of under- and over-garments of contrasting shades adding to the *mi-parti* effect. The dagged edges of hoods, sleeves, and tunics were a German speciality that quickly spread to the rest of Europe.

Female Costume

A comparison of these three women with the men pictured on these pages underscores the similarities between men's and women's dress in this period in terms of silhouette, position of the waist, and decorative details such as buttons. The differences are in the necklines, hemlines, and headgear—here, hoods for men, and for women barbets and layered, frilled, or crimped veils. The latter were popular in Austria, Hungary, and Bohemia.

Hoods and Sleeves, Mid-14th Century

The two men together give a front and a rear view of the 14th-century hood as it looked when worn pushed back off the head. The kneeling man's sleeve buttons are a new fashion, which allowed people to button their sleeves instead of sewing them closed each time they got dressed.

Dentate Dagging, Mid-14th Century

The German love of dagging shows in the way the shoulders of this man's hood, the edges of his trailing sleeves, and the hem of his overtunic are all finished. The low-slung belt encouraged a more serpentine stance and led in the 1350s to the introduction of padding over the belly.

See also
Germany, 15th Century, *pages 76–77*
Northern Europe, 14th Century, *pages 78–79*

Stockings, 1340s

This drawing shows how baggy cloth hose could be. Stockings were seamed up the back, probably cut on the bias to allow them to stretch, and would have been made to measure by a hosier. Knitted stockings were luxury goods and not widely available until the process of making them was mechanized during the 17th century.

Hanging Sleeves, *c.* 1340

In the 1330s the sleeves of the overtunic began both to shorten and widen, and by 1340 had developed into the sort of striplike hanging sleeve seen here. Her coiffure, with its spirals of hair over the ears, is still in vogue in around 1340 but went out of fashion shortly thereafter.

Knight, 1330s–40s

The mail coif and the richness of the ermine-lined overtunic identify this man as a knight. His waistline is beginning to drop to hip level and it is just possible to make out small buttons on the snug sleeves of his tunic.

Headwear
• cap fastened under chin (barbet)
• hood
• mail coif
• veil

Hairstyles
• women: coiled over ears

Dress
• fitted to the torso and sometimes padded

Upper Garments
• overtunic

Lower Garments
• cloth hose
• stockings

Accessories
• belt

Footwear

Germany, *15th Century*

Men's and Women's Dress

Germany as a unified nation did not exist in the 15th century. Despite substantial dominions, stretching from Brussels in the east to near Krakow, and from Hamburg in the south to Siena, it was primarily a loose confederation of localities, each more influenced by the non-German areas with which it came into regular contact through trade than by any idea of a national sartorial identity. As a result, German dress in this century shows Franco-Burgundian and Netherlandish styles and elements absorbed from eastern Europe that seem at odds with the fashions of western Europe. Still, toward the end of the century, some distinctive German elements crept into mainstream European fashion.

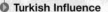

Turkish Influence

The central figure's pointed beard and headdress, and the rather odd arrangement of a short fur-trimmed gown over a long one, have a Turkish look. The Ottoman Empire was of great interest to 15th-century Europeans, and images of Turks, many copied from Nicolas de Nicolay's *Les Quatres premiers livres des navigations et peregrinations orientales*, published in 1567, abound in the costume books of that era.

Heuque

The man on the right probably wears a fur-lined *heuque*, defined as a sleeveless overgarment worn by men but generally not by women. They are described in wardrobe accounts from the first quarter of the century in ways that suggest they were often connected with livery.

See also
Germany, 15th–16th Century, *pages 120–21*
Anatolia, 16th–18th Century, *pages 214–15*

Netherlandish Influence, Mid-15th Century

This simple red kirtle (tunic) worn with tied-in contrasting oversleeves, linen veil, and kerchief recalls those in Netherlandish portraits, and suggests that the woman is from the part of Germany open to Flemish influence. This basic dress, often worn under an overgown, was common across classes.

Houppelande, Early 15th Century

This houppelande's silhouette largely follows fashionable norms for the first decades of the century, but its extreme, ribbonlike slashing and overlong striped cuffs are outside the fashion mainstream and it lacks the high collar common in this era. The gold spots are bezants— loose metal discs that would gently clink as the wearer moved.

Tight Clothes, c. 1480–1500

These dresses reveal embroidered chemises at the low-cut necklines and tight, split sleeves. The dress with overlong sleeves suggests middle-Rhenish styles of the 1480s. The center headdress hints at lingering Italian influence, recalling the bulbous Italian *balzo* of earlier in the century.

Laced Closures

The central figure and the man to his right are Hottenroth's embellished versions of drawings from Carl Köhler's 1871 *History of Costume*, and represent men's dress from the first half of the century. Both wear garments that lace closed in front, a common fastening that became more prominent and decorative in the second half of the century.

Headwear
- headdress
- veil

Hairstyles
- men: chin or shoulder-length

Dress
- tight, often revealing underlayers

Upper Garments
- chemise
- gown (houppelande)
- long-sleeved tunic (kirtle)
- sleeveless overgarment (heuque)

Lower Garments

Accessories
- gold discs (bezants) as ornament
- kerchief

Footwear

77

Northern Europe, *14th Century*

Developments in Tailoring

In around 1340, changes in tailoring in Europe triggered significant advances in clothing styles. Sleeves, previously cut in one with the body of a gown or tunic, began to be cut separately and set into a high, tight armhole, and could thus be better fitted to the arm. This meant that the garment as a whole could be more tightly fitted to the torso—so much so that it could no longer be pulled on over the head. Front openings appeared, and the buttons that fastened them became, for the first time in the West, important decorative features. By 1360, the latest fashions for men show a burly, rounded chest created with padding that contrasted with a tight waist and slender hips emphasized by a low-slung belt.

See also
France, 13th–14th Century, *pages 60–61*
France, 14th–15th Century, *pages 64–65*

Knightly Mantle, *c.* 1360s
This unknown king is probably in the fashionable dress of the 1360s, although few details of his doublet or jacket are visible beyond the low belt sitting just above its dagged hem. His mantle is the side-fastening cloak descended from ancient Greece and Rome, and traditionally worn by knights, who needed their right arms free to draw their swords.

Hairstyles
In Western art long, loose hair symbolized virginity or purity. In 14th-century upper-class life it was worn only by young girls; women curled or braided their hair and wore it with a headdress. Here, the queen's loose hair, along with the arrow-pierced heart motifs that pattern the gentleman's doublet, suggest that this is an allegory of courtly love. The man's hair is fashionably cut in a "pudding-basin" style that accommodates his rising doublet collar.

Crackowes/Poulaines, 1360s

Paired buttons fasten and decorate an otherwise plain red doublet; further visual interest comes from black and red mi-parti hose that are soled on the bottom, making separate shoes unnecessary. The extraordinarily long, pointed toes, known as crackowes in English and poulaines in French, were described by one moralist in 1362 as "more suitable as claws of devils than as the apparel of men."

Queen Iseult and a Knight of the Garter, c. 1380

A mythical figure from Arthurian times, Queen Iseult wears a figured gown with tight, elbow-length sleeves revealing the longer sleeves of the underdress beneath. Racinet identified her companion as a Garter Knight of Arthur's contemporary, King Marc of Cornwall; he wears the garter of his order prominently below his left knee. The Order of the Garter, founded by Edward III of England in 1348, is said to have been inspired by the Arthurian legends but it does not actually predate the mid-14th century.

Padded Chest, 1360s

The "A" motifs embroidered on this rich, golden doublet suggest that its wearer is the legendary King Arthur. The doublet's rounded chest, slender skirt, and prominent buttons recall a surviving silk doublet or jacket associated with Charles of Blois (d. 1364) that is cut in thirty-two pieces to ensure its close fit to the body.

Headwear
- crowns
- hats
- hoods

Hairstyles
- long, curled or braided
- "pudding-basin" style

Dress
- close-fitting, buttoned, padded

Upper Garments
- doublet
- gown
- jacket
- mantle
- undergown

Lower Garments
- hose

Accessories
- belt

Footwear
- long, pointed toes (poulaines/ crackowes), soled feet, in one piece with hose

Italy, *11th–15th Century*

Venetian Ducal Dress

Given the Venetians' keen interest in dress and the strict laws that governed what could and could not be worn by civil servants by the end of the Middle Ages, it is unsurprising that the dress of the doge, head of the Venetian government, came to be codified both in color and in form with rules for official and unofficial clothes. By the end of the 15th century, standard ducal official dress had evolved into a long gown, usually with open sleeves, a mantle, and a fur shoulder cape. The doge could wear only four colors—white, gold, crimson, and scarlet—but most used a wide range of velvets, silks, and damasks to vary the quality of the garments in their extensive wardrobes. By far the most distinctive ducal garment was the *corno*, a cap with a large point curving up at the back of the crown, which probably developed from the fashionable hood of the 13th and 14th centuries and evolved into official dress.

▶ Two Doges, 15th Century

The kneeling doge is in ceremonial armor (most were well past combat age by the time they were elected). The other is in "civilian" dress, in a gown with the kind of large sleeves described by a contemporary German visitor to Venice as "narrow at the hand but behind they hang down about an ell wide, like a sack."

▶ Laborers, 15th Century

Here is a glimpse of how people interacted with their clothes. The reaper (*center back*) has no hose, only a long shirt under a loose doublet, probably to keep cool and to facilitate movement. The gravedigger (*far right*) has partly untied his cloth hose from his doublet to loosen them enough so he can bend over without tearing either hose or doublet.

See also
Italy, 14th Century,
pages 82–83
Italy, 1400–50,
pages 84–85

Doge's Trumpeter

Racinet dates this trumpeter to the 14th century but his overall silhouette and the position of his waist, the suggestion of pleats down the front of his tunic, and, most of all, the style of his elaborate mi-parti hose—which may be part of his ducal livery—suggest the 15th century.

Doge and Attendant, 14th Century

The several parts of the doge's official dress can clearly be seen here: the open-sleeved robe worn under a gold brocade mantle and a fur cape. In the 14th century ducal headgear was still not entirely codified, but this one is shown wearing the familiar corno over the customary white linen coif. His attendant's garments are similar, but the colors differ, as does the hat or hood, over his coif.

Ducal Attendant, 14th Century

Like those above right, this man derives from a painting, either from St. Mark's Basilica or from the Doge's Palace. He wears the crimson or scarlet gown prescribed for members of the Venetian Senate on special occasions, plus a shoulder cape. His hood, with its short liripipe flipped forward, may be the style from which the ducal corno developed.

Doge, 11th Century

Although identified by Racinet as a 9th-century doge, this image, from a mosaic in St. Mark's Basilica in Venice, dates him to the 11th century. It is clear that his dress has not yet settled into the uniform of later centuries. He wears a belted tunic beneath a mantle fastened on one shoulder in typical knightly style, and the shape of his conical cap suggests the helmets of the period.

Headwear
• cap (corno)
• coif
• conical cap
• linen coif

Hairstyles

Dress
• loose and stately

Upper Garments
• doublet
• long gown
• long shirt
• mantle
• open-sleeved robe
• tunic

Lower Garments
• hose

Accessories
• belt

Footwear

Italy, *14th Century*

Florentine, Milanese, and Sienese Dress

Italy's well-established silk-weaving industry and the involvement of several key Italian cities in international trade made it an important center for the development and spread of new fashions during the 14th century. Indeed, some contemporary English and French chroniclers attributed to Italy the fashion for shockingly shorter and tighter men's tunics that emerged about 1340—although some Italians preferred to blame the Spanish and the Greeks. By the late 14th century, although there is relatively little evidence of it in these images, dress in Italy was showing the influence of the French International Gothic style, which emphasized elongation of the body and flamboyant decoration.

Italian Styles, Mid-14th Century

The man on the left wears one of those shorter, tighter tunics so enthusiastically adopted by young Italians during the mid-14th century; his slashed sleeve could presumably have been worn normally, as it is here, or as a hanging sleeve as the wearer preferred. His companion, according to Hottenroth, is a Florentine woman, although the source of the image is not specified. Both wear long, open-sided mantles, his with a hood, hers without.

See also
England, 14th Century, *pages 52–53*
France, 13th and 14th Century, *pages 60–61*

Turbanlike Hoods

Toward the end of the 14th century people started wearing their hoods (*cappucci*) in ways that made them look more like turbans. The edges of the face opening were rolled up and placed on the crown of the head, while the hood's shoulders and liripipe were often wound around the head. Italians also developed a smaller, neater version, worn here by both men.

Hooded Mantle, Later 14th Century

Hoods were often separate garments during the 14th century, but this man's splendid, gold-embroidered cloak is still connected to its hood. The hood has a long liripipe, the tail extending from the top of the crown, which here falls free but which in this era was also often worn wrapped around the head.

Long Gown, Late 14th Century

The long gown worn by the woman in this group was called a *pellanda* in northern Italy, a *cioppa* in Tuscany, and a *houppelande* in northern Europe. The rising collar and waistline, along with the long, full sleeves and slight train, are hallmarks of the International Gothic style of the later 14th century.

Headwear
• hood (cappuccio)

Hairstyles

Dress
• flamboyant, with elongation of the body

Upper Garments
• cloak
• long gown (pellanda, cioppa, or houppelande)
• open-sided mantle
• tunic

Lower Garments

Accessories

Footwear

Italy, *1400–50*

Florentine, Milanese, and Sienese Dress

In the 1400s Florence, Milan, and Siena were all centers of fashion—the Sienese were especially noted for the extravagance of their dress. Rich fabrics, furs, embroidery, and pearls were worn by those who could afford them. The era was particularly noted for its voluminous sleeves, and all over Italy sumptuary laws were passed to prevent women from such sartorial excess (men, although equally guilty, were not subject to the same legislation). In 1427 the Sienese friar San Bernardino preached against the wearing of sleeves so big that they used more material than the rest of the costume. Predictably, neither laws nor sermons had much of an effect.

Men's Headwear

The two men on the right wear the larger hood that developed during the 14th century. It continued to be worn into the 15th century, but other styles, such as the *beretta*, a rounded or semiconical cap with a turned-up brim or no brim at all, grew in popularity. An example of the former is worn by the falconer on the left.

Florentine Man

Sadly, Hottenroth does not cite his source for this image, but the size of his sleeves dates him to the second quarter of the 15th century. They appear to be hanging sleeves, which are slit from the hem to reveal the man's doublet-clad arm. There would doubtless be a decorative lining.

Headwear
• headdress
• hood
• rounded cap
(beretta)

Hairstyles

Dress
• layered

Upper Garments
• chemise
• doublet
• sleeved silk dress
(cotta)
• sleeved woolen
dress (gamurra)

Lower Garments
• hose

Accessories

Footwear

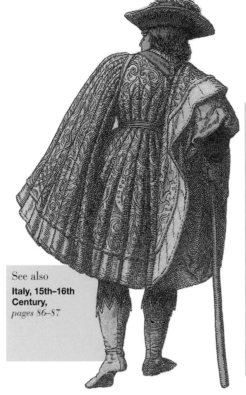

Sienese Style, 1443

This fashionably dressed young Sienese man is from a 1443 painting by Domenico di Bartolo, although Hottenroth added the walking cane. His splendid, wide-sleeved pleated gown is made of gold brocade, lined and bordered in gray fur. One large sleeve is stylishly turned back over his shoulder, toga-style. His motley stockings are gray above the calf and red and white below.

See also
Italy, 15th–16th Century,
pages 86–87

Layers of Dress

Two women in the center wear the *gamurra*, a simple, sleeved woolen dress laced up the front or side, or the similar but grander silken *cotta*. Both were most often worn as the middle layer, over the chemise and below the overgown. The overgowns worn by the others here show the passion for enormous sleeves and sweeping trains. Tall headdresses, such as the one at far left, were in fashion in the 1430s and 1440s.

Italy, *15th–16th Century*

Men's Dress

The evolutionary pattern of an under garment gradually becoming an outer garment is a standard one in dress. In this example, the fashion for short, tight, revealing clothes of the last quarter of the 15th century resulted from fashionable young men with good figures omitting the customary concealing gown or tunic and going about in their doublet, sometimes alone, sometimes—particularly in Venice—with an equally closely fitted belted tunic on top. When a gown was worn it was often loose, the better to contrast with the tight clothes beneath. The figures here demonstrate the long, luxuriant hair, the arched back, and the emphasis on the leg that characterized the fashions favored by Italy's young male elite between c. 1490 and 1505.

See also
Italy, 1450–1500,
pages 104–05

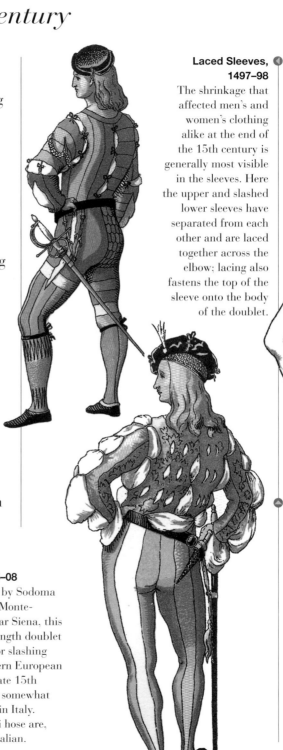

Laced Sleeves,
1497–98
The shrinkage that affected men's and women's clothing alike at the end of the 15th century is generally most visible in the sleeves. Here the upper and slashed lower sleeves have separated from each other and are laced together across the elbow; lacing also fastens the top of the sleeve onto the body of the doublet.

Fashionable
Venetian, 1496
This stylish man is in the background in Gentile Bellini's *Procession of the Reliquary of the Cross*. His rounded torso is typical of Venetian styles of the 1490s that may have been produced with padding. His small, round cap, sporting a feather aigrette, is also typically Venetian.

Young Man, *c.* 1505–08
Taken from a fresco by Sodoma at the monastery of Monte-Oliveto Maggiore near Siena, this gentleman's waist-length doublet shows the passion for slashing that overtook northern European fashion during the late 15th century, but made a somewhat belated appearance in Italy. His striped, mi-parti hose are, however, typically Italian.

Livery

Elaborate hose were worn by servants as livery, as well as by the fashionable, and it can be difficult to distinguish between them. Here, since the pages are dressed in identical short-skirted doublets and three-tone hose, the identification of their costume as livery is clear.

Codpieces

Up until the late 15th century each leg of a man's hose was separate. However, once doublets shrank to waist length, the two legs needed to be joined together, rather like panty hose. The gap between them over the crotch was filled in with a separate piece of cloth called a codpiece, which was modest in size at first, but grew to substantial proportions over the next century.

Flemish Nobleman, 1470–71

This man, identified by Racinet as a Flemish nobleman, is King Herod, from a painting by Hans Memling. Unfortunately, his clothing, especially his furred gown of brown-and-gold figured Italian velvet, has lost much of its impact in redrawing.

Headwear
• round cap

Hairstyles
• long

Dress
• tight-fitting, flamboyant

Upper Garments
• belted tunic
• gown
• short doublet

Lower Garments
• codpiece
• hose

Accessories
• aigrette

Footwear

Spain, *13th Century*

Men's and Women's Dress

The surviving visual sources suggest that Spanish dress in the late 1200s was similar to that of the rest of western Europe at the time. Both sexes wore basic tunics, long or short for men and long for women, under a variety of supertunics, surcoats, and cloaks. The tapering sleeve often seen in Europe at this time is not apparent here, but neither are some of the elements known from other Spanish manuscripts of the period, such as tight-fitting tunics with prominent lacing down the sides and the sleeves. The most distinctively Spanish aspect shown here is the headgear. These images, dated 1275–1284, are taken from the *Cantigas de Santa Maria*, compiled by King Alfonso X, "El Sabio" of Castile.

Male and Female Costume

The man wears the loose surcoat and pillbox-shaped headdress found in other contemporary Spanish manuscripts, but the styles the two women are wearing are much more unusual. Racinet commented that they are similar to the headdresses worn by Venetian women, and, indeed, they bear a resemblance to the corno worn by the doge in the 14th century.

Royal Procession

King Alfonso himself, accompanied by a bishop, leads this procession. The king is dressed in much the same fashion as his courtiers, in a plain short tunic underneath an open cloak. His legs are covered with cloth hose and he wears a pair of elaborately decorated, slightly pointed shoes. His rank is suggested most by the shoes, and by the gold circlet that he wears on his head. The bishop wears the miter and gloves that are part of his processional insignia.

See also
France, 12th–13th Century, *pages 58–59*
Spain and Portugal, 14th–16th Century, *pages 90–91*

Towering Headdress

This upper-class couple are dressed largely alike, in solid-color tunics beneath contrasting surcoats slit at the neck. Both wear long cloaks fastened at the neck with double ribbons, the lady's possibly lined with ermine. Noblewomen in other Spanish manuscripts of this period are often shown wearing distinctive tall, tapering headdresses over their loose, flowing hair, but this bejeweled headdress widens as it rises.

Huntsmen

These three riders are dressed for hunting, although they do appear to be wearing the kind of mail hose (chausses) also worn by knights. The rider on the left wears a gray supertunic and sleeveless surcoat, and the central figure wears a simple long-sleeved tunic; his gloves suggest he is hunting with a falcon or a hawk. King Alfonso is the lead rider, wearing a loose gown with a button-trimmed cape. Their tall, flat-topped coiflike headdresses are distinctively Spanish; the coat of arms on the king's identifies him.

Headwear
• pillbox-shaped headdress
• tapering headdress

Hairstyles

Dress
• loose and layered

Upper Garments
• cloak
• supertunic
• surcoat
• tunic

Lower Garments
• hose (chausses)

Accessories
• gloves

Footwear
• pointed shoes

Spain and Portugal, *14th–16th Century*

Men's and Women's Dress

Spain achieved considerable wealth and political prominence in the 16th century and was at the peak of its influence on European fashion. Spain was credited with the era's somber and rather rigid grandeur. One characteristic Spanish garment was the farthingale, a cone-shaped, hooped petticoat to hold out the skirts in the stiff triangle so typical of the period. Farthingales appeared at the Spanish court in the 1460s and 1470s; Palencia, a contemporary chronicler, believed that their original purpose was to conceal Queen Juana's unintended pregnancy. The style caught on, and had spread all over Europe by the early 16th century.

Eleanora of Portugal, Early 16th Century

She is drawn from a painting by Pintoricchio depicting her marriage to Frederick III, Holy Roman Emperor. The marriage took place in 1452 but the painting dates from 1505–07 and the clothes she is wearing are those of a high-ranking Spanish or Portuguese lady from that later period.

Henry II of Castile

This figure is probably drawn from a 14th-century manuscript illumination portraying Henry's execution of his half-brother Pedro of Castile in 1369. The shape of his doublet and his low belt are of the period and appear in the original manuscript, but the hood does not.

Order of Santiago, 15th Century

The central figure is dressed as a knight of the Order of Santiago (a military order founded in Spain in the 12th century). He wears white robes with a red Cross of Saint James (in which the lower leg is a sword blade) and a red cap.

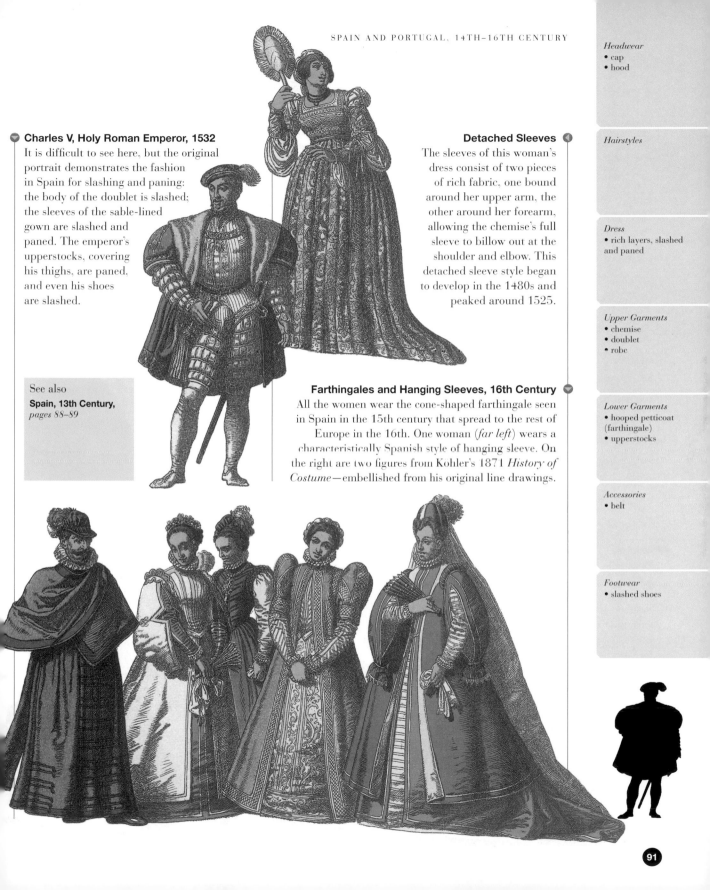

Headwear
• cap
• hood

Hairstyles

Dress
• rich layers, slashed
and paned

Upper Garments
• chemise
• doublet
• robe

Lower Garments
• hooped petticoat
(farthingale)
• upperstocks

Accessories
• belt

Footwear
• slashed shoes

Charles V, Holy Roman Emperor, 1532

It is difficult to see here, but the original portrait demonstrates the fashion in Spain for slashing and paning: the body of the doublet is slashed; the sleeves of the sable-lined gown are slashed and paned. The emperor's upperstocks, covering his thighs, are paned, and even his shoes are slashed.

See also
Spain, 13th Century,
pages 88–89

Detached Sleeves

The sleeves of this woman's dress consist of two pieces of rich fabric, one bound around her upper arm, the other around her forearm, allowing the chemise's full sleeve to billow out at the shoulder and elbow. This detached sleeve style began to develop in the 1480s and peaked around 1525.

Farthingales and Hanging Sleeves, 16th Century

All the women wear the cone-shaped farthingale seen in Spain in the 15th century that spread to the rest of Europe in the 16th. One woman (*far left*) wears a characteristically Spanish style of hanging sleeve. On the right are two figures from Kohler's 1871 *History of Costume*—embellished from his original line drawings.

Ecclesiastical Dress, *9th–18th Century*

Church Vestments

Vestments, the characteristic garb of Catholic clergy worn during Mass and at other ceremonial times, developed from the secular dress of the Roman Empire. According to contemporary chroniclers, it had emerged as distinct from everyday dress by the middle of the 3rd century. It was codified during the several centuries immediately following into a formal system of garments associated with specific ranks of the clergy. Although they were originally simple garments, as the centuries passed vestments became progressively grander and more elaborate, and often acquired sacred or mystical associations.

Maniple

Originally, the maniple was a white linen handkerchief; it developed into this purely ornamental narrow, fringed strip after the 10th century. It is worn on the left forearm by bishops, priests, deacons and subdeacons.

Miter

The miter developed from a simple, conical, white linen cap into this distinctive gabled hat worn primarily by bishops. This elaborate example is embroidered and set with jewels.

Ordinary Canonical Dress

This canon of the order of St. Sepulchre in Poland wears the ordinary dress of the order prior to the 17th century: a cassock (long, nonliturgical tunic) under a hip-length surplice and sleeveless rochet. Both surplice and rochet developed from the alb; the rochet, which may be sleeved or sleeveless, was originally intended as a dustcoat.

See also
Monastic Dress, Middle Ages–17th Century, *pages 94–95*

Tonsured Monk

This Polish monk is tonsured: his crown is shaved, leaving only a circular fringe of hair remaining below. Tonsures were adopted during the 5th century throughout the Church as a sign of ordination and a symbol of affliction and suffering.

Alb and Cope

This priestly figure dating from 1450–1500 appears to be wearing only an alb under a richly decorated red cope. Copes—semicircular capes—are processional garments with no liturgical significance, adopted for use by all ranks of clergy during the 11th and 12th centuries.

Headwear
• miter

Hairstyles
• tonsure

Dress
• liturgical

Upper Garments
• alb
• amice
• cassock
• chasuble
• cope
• dalmatic
• rochet
• stole
• surplice

Lower Garments

Accessories/
Marks of Office
• crosier
• maniple

Footwear

Flemish Deacon

He wears a rich cloth-of-gold dalmatic with its characteristic side slits clearly visible above a white alb. This combination had become the characteristic dress of both bishops and deacons by the 4th century; this figure dates to *c.* 1460.

Chasuble

The chasuble is the principal vestment worn by a priest celebrating Mass; this Venetian priest from *c.* 1460 wears a blue one trimmed with a gold-embroidered, cross-shaped red orphrey. This capelike chasuble reflects its origins as a Roman traveling cloak. In the Renaissance, as its materials became richer and stiffer, the chasuble's sides were routinely cut away to allow its wearer to move his arms freely.

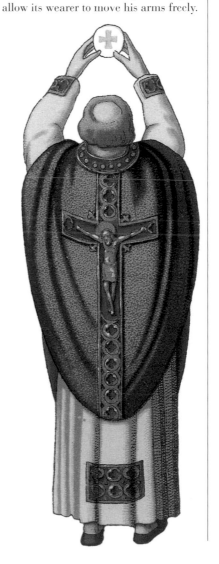

Bishop in White

White, the color of most vestments in the early Church, connotes purity; it is now one of four principal groups of liturgical colors. Although color subsequently crept into other vestments, the alb—the vestment worn next to the skin—generally remains white, although it is often trimmed at the hem with apparels—rectangular panels of embroidery or figured fabric. This bishop is attired in a full suit of vestments: from bottom to top, alb, amice, stole, dalmatic, maniple, and green-lined chasuble. The miter on his head is one distinctive mark of his rank; the crosier in his hand is another.

Monastic Dress, *Middle Ages–17th Century*

Monastic Austerity

The monastic movement began during the 3rd century and by the 6th century its dress had been codified in the guide to monastic life known as the Rule of St Benedict. The Rule of St. Benedict did not prescribe color but it was understood that a monk's habit was to be austere, so its colors were commonly inconspicuous and its materials made locally and inexpensively. Most orders of nuns were women's divisions of the male orders and wore a feminized version of the monk's habit for their particular order.

See also
Ecclesiastical Dress, 9th–18th Century, *pages 92–93*

Abbot and Nun

The abbot is a Benedictine and wears its characteristic black habit. The nun is in a white habit, which suggests that she may be a Cistercian, a reformed order of Cluniacs. However. Cistercian nuns commonly wear white veils, and hers is black.

Mendicant Franciscan

Franciscans took vows of poverty and served poor populations. When the order was founded early in the 13th century the monks wore gray, but eventually the brown shown here came into use. Note his characteristic rope belt holding his rosary, his hooded cloak and his lack of shoes.

Cloistered Nuns

These nuns include a Poor Clare (*center*) and a Brigittine (*right*). The Poor Clares were founded in Assisi in Italy in 1212, the Brigittines by St. Bridget of Sweden in 1344, but their habits are very similar.

Dominican

The monk on the right belongs to the Dominicans, a mendicant order founded in Spain in 1215. He is dressed characteristically in a white wool robe and scapular under a black mantle and sporting the order's distinctive pointed hood.

Carmelites

The first Carmelite habit was the brown-and-white striped cloak shown here. It was abandoned in 1287 in favor of a white mantle over a brown robe.

Indoor Habit

This nun hospitaler of St. Catherine in Paris wears her standard white indoor habit girdled with a long black belt, and a black veil over her wimple.

Choir Habit

This is an older form of choir habit, the dress worn by clerics and religious followers when they are sitting in the congregation or during non-Eucharistic public prayer. Her veil, which is lined in white, hangs far enough forward to obscure her face.

Choir Habit

The nun on the right is an abbess of the military order of St. Stephen wearing choir habit: a loose white robe emblazoned with the eight-pointed star of the order.

Headwear
• hood
• veil
• wimple

Hairstyles

Dress
• austere

Upper Garments
• cloak
• habit
• mantle
• robe
• scapular

Lower Garments

Accessories
• belt
• rosary

Footwear

Renaissance Europe

The Renaissance touched all aspects of art and culture in Europe, including, inevitably, dress. Scholars generally agree that it began in Italy, in Florence, during the 15th century and gradually spread to the rest of Europe. In art it is characterized by a heightened sense of realism, the development of perspective and, most crucially for dress, changing ideas in the representation of human anatomy that are based on the rediscovered ideals of ancient Greece. Historian Margaret Scott, in her study of dress in northern Europe during the 15th century, described the Renaissance body as "muscular, broad-shouldered men and full-breasted women with discernible waistlines and short, full hips." This departure from the linearity of Gothic style brought about a revolution in the depiction of the clothed body in art that, in turn, influenced fashion.

Fashion leadership during the Renaissance was centered in the growing splendor of Europe's courts, in Italy, France, Germany, and particularly Spain, which was dominant during the 16th and early 17th centuries. Distinctive elements of national style, while harder to discern now, were obvious to contemporaries and, according to Baldassare Castiglione, whose *Book of the Courtier* was published in 1528, were attractive to courtiers who sought to vary their dress according to the manner of other nations. This was especially true in England, where Elizabeth I's court (1558–1603) was renowned for this.

Europeans' fascination with the dress worn by themselves and others shows in the development of the costume book. A dozen were published between 1560 and 1601, in Italy, France, Flanders, and Germany. These were collections of woodcuts and engravings that portrayed the typical garb of a wide range of classes and nationalities. Many were European but some went considerably farther afield to depict the clothes worn in the Near East, Africa and even the New World. Some images clearly were drawn from life and some just as clearly were based either on previously published plates or purely on imagination. Sixteenth-century authors copied liberally from each other, and their plates were subsequently consulted and copied by scores of authors down the centuries, including both Hottenroth and Racinet.

Northern Europe, *15th–16th Century*

Upper-Class and Mourning Dress

This was a transitional period in northern Europe as the Renaissance finally took hold. The French court was influenced by the cultural and artistic ferment in Italy and nearby Burgundy, and became, in turn, the model to which King Henry VIII aspired. These images, most derived from Flemish tapestries, offer a mix of upper-class fashionable dress and imaginary or exoticized elements or garments. They demonstrate the changes in silhouette from the elongated Gothic ideal of the late 15th century to the broader lines of the early Renaissance and, in their depictions of surface decorations and fur linings, hint at the splendor that would characterize dress in the 16th century.

White Mourning

White has a long history in both Western and non-Western cultures as a mourning color. Pleated white barbes like the one this woman wears beneath her chin were mourning garments for upper-class women from the late 14th century into the 16th century. Were she properly dressed in mourning, however, the rest of her clothes would normally have been plain black or white.

Late Medieval Contrasts

This couple are from the early 15th century. He has a high-collared houppelande with a turbanlike hood; she, a low-necked surcoat with a high waistline. Their silhouettes, neckline shape, and headdress styles are in contrast with the later styles shown on these pages.

See also
Northern Europe, 1485–1510, *pages 100–101*

Real and Imaginary

This couple are a mixture of the real and the imaginary. Her bodice, with its low, square neckline and big sleeves, is based on fashion, but the length of her dress seems an exaggeration. His dress is harder to read, but the sleeveless mantle is probably modeled on a real garment, reflecting the fashion for spotted furs. His headdress is plainly fanciful.

Hoods

In France, at the very end of the 15th century, hoods began to move toward the back of the head, to reveal center parted hair. The woman on the left has a hood with slightly longer lappets at the sides and the back curtain folded up and pinned on top.

Felt Caps,

Both early 16th-century men wear caps or bonnets of blocked felt over shoulder-length hair that is brushed under. The cap on the right has a split or slashed brim that is turned up all the way around the crown, while the other appears to be turned up only at the back, its corners joined with a red band. Their low-necked doublets reveal shirts gathered into wide decorative bands.

Northern Europe, *1485–1510*

Male Figures from Tapestry

It is curious that Racinet identified the images on these two pages as French, because all but one is drawn from Flemish tapestry. The two moving figures, one on this page, the other on the facing page, were originally figures in a winter interior from a set of tapestries depicting the seasons. Three of the others are background figures taken from a tapestry series that Racinet identified as depicting the *Triumph of Beatrice* from Dante's *Divine Comedy*. The remaining image, at the bottom of this page, derives from a painting and it is easy to see the difference in the style and accuracy of the delineation of the dress.

Gentleman of Leisure, Early 16th Century

In the original tapestry this man is playing cards with the lady of the manor, but he is not further identified. The enveloping drapery of his mantle or gown makes the actual details of his clothing difficult to discern, but his overall silhouette suggests a date in the first quarter of the 16th century.

Historic or Oriental Figure

He wears the wide, slashed shoes of the early 16th century and his long, draped, figured mantle is probably loosely based on a man's gown, but its construction details are so vague that it does not seem to be a direct depiction of a real garment. His turban and long beard also mark him as an historic or Oriental figure.

Maximilian I von Habsburg, Late 15th Century

He wears the jeweled collar of the Burgundian Order of the Golden Fleece (founded in 1430), which may have been conferred on him when he married Mary of Burgundy in 1477. The collar consists of firesteels in the shape of the letter B (for Burgundy) linked with flints, holding the order's badge, a golden sheepskin.

Lord of the Manor

A figure in the Winter tapestry, he has just walked into the Great Hall of the house and is laying his gloves on a table. He appears to be wearing a jerkin with a knee-length, pleated skirt beneath a sleeveless or short-sleeved blue gown. Peeking below the jerkin skirts may be an early example of trunk hose.

Torchbearer

Of all the figures on these pages that derive from tapestries, this man's dress is perhaps the easiest to read. His shirt rises to the base of his neck above the low neckline of his doublet, which in turn seems to be worn beneath a knee-length jerkin. The outer garment is a gold-embroidered gown lined in spotted fur, which was popular for men in the early 16th century.

See also
France, 16th Century, *pages 108–09*
France, 1550–1600, *pages 110–11*

Messenger

Racinet identified this figure from the *Triumph of Beatrice* as a messenger who is either receiving or delivering a sealed letter, and likened his dress to the sleeved tabards worn by heralds. Most of the imagery on his tabard is floral but there does seem to be a central motif that could be heraldic.

Headwear
• turban

Hairstyles

Dress
• broad Renaissance lines

Upper Garments
• gown
• jerkin
• mantle
• shirt
• skirt
• tabard

Lower Garments
• hose
• trunk hose

Accessories
• gloves

Footwear
• slashed shoes

France, *1485–1510*

Women's Headwear

Hoods and hats were an important part of dress for both sexes in the Middle Ages and the Renaissance. The 15th century, just prior to the beginning of this period, saw some of the most elaborate versions of veils, caps, rolls, nets, and hoods in the history of Western women's fashion. Styles ranged from simply wrapped headcloths to intricately wired, winglike veils worn over bulbous padded supports, steeples, or small undercaps. Keeping one's head covered was not merely a matter of fashion, it was an outward show of virtue and honor. Married women's headdresses completely concealed their hair through most of the second half of the 15th century; it was not until the beginning of the transition from medieval to Renaissance in northern Europe, in the 1490s, that styles changed to an occasional glimpse of hair. The hoods and hats that carried forward into the 16th century, while perhaps less *outré* than those of the period immediately prior to it, remained extremely elaborate.

See also
**Northern Europe,
15th–16th Century,**
pages 98–99

France, 1550–1600,
pages 110–11

Head to Toe

Both women are court ladies from a Flemish tapestry, *The Triumph of Beatrice*. The one on the left wears a hood with curved sides that are probably wired. The hood's back curtain is turned up and pinned on top of her head. Her companion wears a jeweled net combined with a bourrelet. While these dresses seem somewhat longer at the back than was usual at the time, extralong trains were a feature of 15th-century upper-class dress. Women of sufficient rank could command the services of a train bearer, a clear indicator of status.

Red Lining
The heavy, dark hoods of this period were often lightened with a strip of contrasting material around the face. This one has a gold-edged veil over a matching undercap that is turned back to reveal a red lining.

Jeanne de France
Racinet identified this picture as Jeanne de France (b. 1464), first wife of Louis XII, who had their marriage annulled in 1498. Her horned headdress and veil indicate the second and third quarters of the 15th century, not the last.

Squared Hood
This simple, rather loose-fitting squared hood is drawn as if it has no undercap, but it is quite likely that there would have been one. The curtain of fabric at the back is considerably longer than the lappets at the side.

White Lining
The hood shown here appears to be in the same style as the example next to it, although without the undercap. Its side lappets and back are pinned up to show a contrasting white lining.

Two-Piece Headdress
This was a popular style of hood in France and elsewhere in the late 14th and early 15th centuries. It is probably formed of two pieces: a striped headcloth over a jeweled or embroidered undercap that frames the face.

Catherine of Aragon
Racinet claimed that this was Catherine of Aragon, although it does not correspond to any currently known portraits of her. Her headdress seems more akin to the styles of the second and third quarters of the century.

Italy, *1450–1500*

Milanese and Venetian Men's Dress

Milan and Venice, in the north of Italy, were far more open to fashions from other countries during the 15th century than cities in the south. Geographical proximity and trading patterns opened Venice to influences from Germany and several eastern countries, and Milan to ideas from Burgundy and France. There was also a strong Spanish influence in Milan, due in part to the Aragonese women who married into Milan's ruling Sforza clan. The fact that Italians were interested in the clothes worn by other peoples is evident in the number of foreigners who appear in Quattrocento paintings and drawings. The adoption of what were perceived as foreign styles did, however, cause some anxiety, as shown by the Venetian sumptuary laws of around 1500 that strove—no doubt fruitlessly—to prevent young men from wearing the tight and revealingly low-cut doublets then fashionable in Germany.

See also
Italy, 1450–1500, *pages 106–07*
Italy, 16th Century, *pages 116–17*

▶ Long Gowns, *c.* 1490
Long gowns continued to be worn in the later 15th century by older men and as official or ceremonial dress. The central figure may come from a betrothal scene of around 1490. In the original his rust-brown damask gown has narrow contrasting revers and is open to the waist over a black doublet. The belt is slightly lower in front than at the back to emphasize the fashionable arched-back stance, a detail omitted in the reproduction.

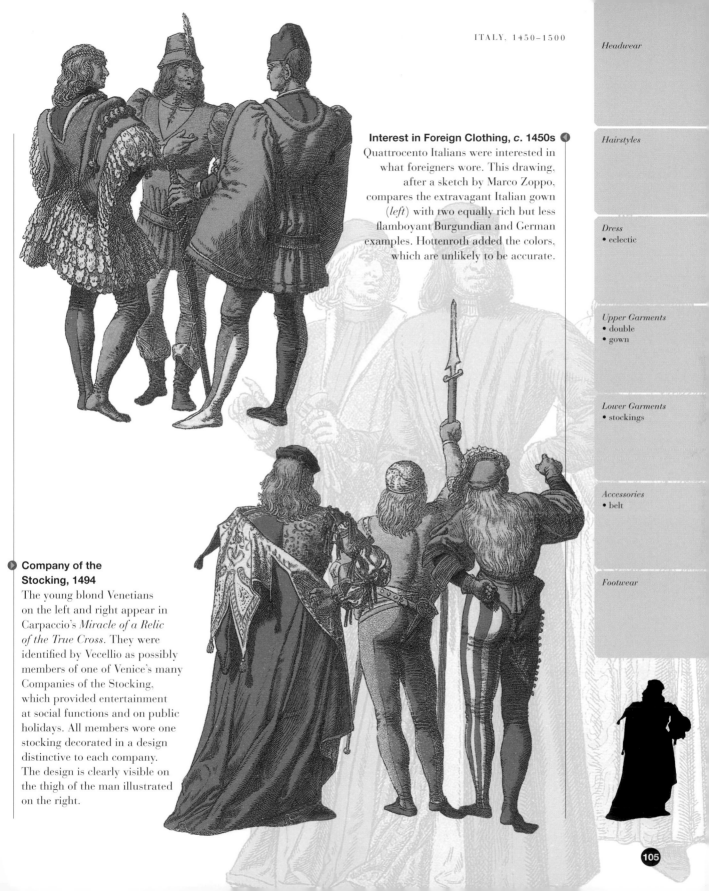

Interest in Foreign Clothing, *c.* 1450s
Quattrocento Italians were interested in what foreigners wore. This drawing, after a sketch by Marco Zoppo, compares the extravagant Italian gown (*left*) with two equally rich but less flamboyant Burgundian and German examples. Hottenroth added the colors, which are unlikely to be accurate.

Company of the Stocking, 1494
The young blond Venetians on the left and right appear in Carpaccio's *Miracle of a Relic of the True Cross*. They were identified by Vecellio as possibly members of one of Venice's many Companies of the Stocking, which provided entertainment at social functions and on public holidays. All members wore one stocking decorated in a design distinctive to each company. The design is clearly visible on the thigh of the man illustrated on the right.

Headwear

Hairstyles

Dress
• eclectic

Upper Garments
• double
• gown

Lower Garments
• stockings

Accessories
• belt

Footwear

Italy, *1450–1500*

Women's Dress in Florence, Venice, and Mantua

As with men's dress, women's fashions at this time tended more to extremes in the north of Italy, where foreign influences were more evident, than in the south. At the end of the 15th century, Venetian women, perhaps because of their geographical isolation, wore high-waisted, low-cut styles that look nothing like what was being worn in the rest of Italy. Beatrice and Isabella d'Este, the daughters of the Duke of Ferrara, are considered among the great fashion innovators of the time. Beatrice was said to have amassed no fewer than eight-four new dresses by 1493, while Isabella, who was married to the Marquis of Mantua, was willing to go into debt to keep pace with her fashionable younger sister.

Isabella d'Este, Marchioness of Mantua, 1505–06
This image comes from an allegorical portrait of Isabella's court painted by Lorenzo Costa. The fine, probably silk, chemise, trimmed with blackwork embroidery, and her dress, with its dogale sleeves and low, square neckline, are characteristic Italian styles of the era.

See also
Italy, 1450–1500,
pages 104–05

Sleeves, Late 15th Century
The three women on the right illustrate three different sleeve styles. The wide, flowing sleeves (*left*), called *dogale* because they resembled the style worn by the doge, were fashionable during the 1490s. The long, snug sleeve (*right*) was in fashion in the 1470s, and the split and slashed sleeve (*center*) dates to *c.* 1485–90. It is probably drawn from a Ghirlandaio portrait of Giovanna degli Albizzi, a member of a prominent Florentine family.

Layers, c. 1470 ◀

The three layers that women commonly wore are shown in this picture of a Florentine woman. At the bottom is a white linen *camisia* (chemise). Next is the gamurra, the basic dress, laced closed across the camisia. The *giornea* (overdress) is open down the front to allow the gamurra to be seen.

Braided Hair, Late 15th Century ▲

Long braids were popular in Italy. Two braids, as depicted here on a woman who is getting dressed, are unusual: the vast majority that appear in paintings of the period are single braids, usually encased in a cloth tube or wrapping that is attached to a cap or caul.

Venetian Woman, 1495

The Venetian woman far left is adapted from a pen-and-ink drawing by Albrecht Dürer. Hottenroth's version reflects the era's fashionable hair color—blonde—and the stylish chignon on top of the head, but fails to capture other key details, including the true split construction of the sleeve that allows the chemise sleeve to billow out at wrist and elbow, and the tiny, high-waisted, off-the-shoulder bodice. The original sitter has caught up the long train of her overdress, missing here, to reveal a damask or brocade skirt beneath.

Headwear
• cap
• caul

Hairstyles
• braided
• chignon

Dress
• flowing yet fitted

Upper Garments
• bodice
• chemise (camisia)
• dress (gamurra)
• overdress (giornea)
• skirt

Lower Garments
• hose

Accessories

Footwear

France, *16th Century*

Guards and Soldiers

Prior to the Thirty Years' War in the 17th century, European armies were raised as needed. They comprised mostly mercenaries who served alongside nobles, personal bodyguards and retainers, and local militia. The French were frequently at war in the 16th century (in the futile hope of establishing dominion over Italy and breaking the Habsburg Empire), and François I and his successors made ample use of hired professional soldiers, both for war and as bodyguards. The company of Swiss Guards, known as the *Cent-Suisses*, who protected the king himself, was formed by Charles VIII in 1496. The images here are a sampling of 16th-century French, Swiss, German, and Scottish professional soldiers who served France during the 16th century.

Soldiers, 1548–60

These soldiers include a pikeman, an arquebusier, a Swiss Guard and three mercenaries: a Swiss captain, a landsknecht, and a Scottish archer. The first two are in battle armor; the others wear noncombat garb. According to Racinet, Swiss troops came into the service of the French around the time the Swiss Guard was formed; they and the landsknechts formed a considerable part of the French infantry. The Scots joined the French in the mid-15th century and the regiment's archers became part of the king's guard.

Headwear
• plumed hat
• toque

Hairstyles

Dress
• heavily slashed

Upper Garments
• doublet
• shirt
• tunic

Lower Garments
• slashed hose

Accessories

Footwear
• slashed shoes

Soldiers, 1520–34
Left to right, these images show a landsknecht captain, a Swiss Guard, an infantry drummer, and a halberdier. Landsknechts are usually depicted in the kind of tight, slashed clothing worn by the Swiss captain (*see left*), so it is unusual to see one wearing an unslashed knee-length tunic. The Swiss Guard is identically dressed to the Swiss captain, the only differences being that he is wearing his plumed hat and instead of a long sword he is holding a halberd, which was the weapon he carried when on guard duty.

See also

Germany, 15th–16th Century, *pages 120–21*

Europe, 16th Century, *pages 136–37*

Captain, *c.* 1520
The above figure is splendidly dressed in a doublet that is half cloth of gold and half crimson velvet, slashed to reveal the white shirt beneath, and matching slashed hose and shoes. His plumed red toque is behind him. The source for this image was a bas-relief in Rouen that depicted the Field of the Cloth of Gold, a meeting between François I and Henry VIII and their retinues for two weeks of feasting, jousting, music, and display of the finest clothes that each could muster.

France, *1550–1600*

Middle Class and Professionals

Racinet notes in his introduction to the original plate that these people are dressed in the styles of *c.* 1560–74, during the reign of Charles IX. Dress at the highest levels, as depicted in contemporary paintings, retained a certain splendor and was becoming more exaggerated: the ruff grew steadily in size, the torso lengthened, and men's doublets were stuffed and padded to form the peascod belly. Around 1580, women began to wear the wheel or French farthingale. But here few extremes are to be seen: surface decoration is relatively modest, colors are somber, the ruff remains small, the farthingale is the familiar, cone-shaped Spanish style and men's torsos, while plainly padded, have not yet developed the characteristic curve of the peascod.

Spanish Influence, 1560s

The Spanish taste for black permeated French style, as this woman's relatively severe dress shows. Her turned-back gown sleeves were a fashion of the earlier part of the century but her ruff and puffed shoulders place her firmly in the 1560s. She wears a *bongrace* over her French hood—a projecting detached brim that was worn to protect the face.

Middle-Class Man

This man, dressed well but not extravagantly, wears figured onion-shaped trunk hose beneath a plain gray jerkin, or doublet, with a skirt finished in *pickadil* (cut into small, stiffened tabs). His single-layer ruff is also plain. He wears his hair quite short but he has a full beard and mustache, and he holds a jaunty plumed bonnet in his hand.

Mourner

This man wears the long-sleeved, black robe worn by male mourners at funerals in the 16th century. The hood, which is drawn well over the face, was separate and often had a long liripipe, although those traits are not visible in this image. This style of mourning for men had been in use prior to the 16th century and was worn at least until 1590.

University Rector

The Rector of the University of Paris was originally in charge of the faculty; the office is elective and still exists. He wears academic dress: a pale-blue gown, buttoned down the front, trimmed with ermine and a shoulder cape, and belted. His hat is a four-cornered biretta.

See also
France, 1550–1600,
pages 112–13
Europe, 1500–1600,
pages 114–15

Jean Guillemer, 1586

Jean Guillemer was a doctor; Racinet describes him as being soberly dressed in a sort of short *soutane* buttoned down the front, with stockings and a mantle to match. He is also wearing a biretta. Doctors commonly wore gowns as a mark of their profession, but the style varied from country to country.

France, *1550–1600*

Kings, Noblemen, and Courtiers

Even so grand a personage as Henry VIII of England envied the magnificence of the early 16th-century French court—a grandeur not lessened later in the century during the bloody religious wars that threatened the stability of the country and of the monarchy. Racinet attributed the splendor of the court to Catherine de' Medici, powerful widow of Henri II and regent during the minority of her son Charles IX, who remained politically active throughout her life. Racinet's opinion may stem from the contemporary chronicler Pierre de Brantôme's report that Catherine dressed beautifully and had high standards for court dress, although she herself wore mourning during the entirety of her widowhood. The sumptuousness of the court dress in the original paintings is only hinted at in the versions on these pages.

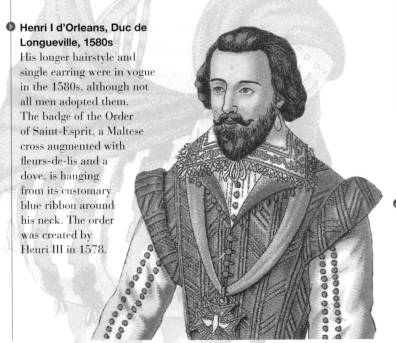

Henri I d'Orleans, Duc de Longueville, 1580s
His longer hairstyle and single earring were in vogue in the 1580s, although not all men adopted them. The badge of the Order of Saint-Esprit, a Maltese cross augmented with fleurs-de-lis and a dove, is hanging from its customary blue ribbon around his neck. The order was created by Henri III in 1578.

Courtier, 1560–74
Black and white was a favorite color combination in this period. The artfully draped black cloak obscures some of the details of the dress, but not its richness. Both the doublet and the onion-shaped trunk hose are made of white satin embroidered or brocaded in black, while his legs are encased in knitted silk stockings, a luxury in this period. His tall-crowned hat has a jeweled band and a jaunty black ostrich plume.

Headwear
• bonnet
• tall-crowned hat

Hairstyles
• long

Dress
• richly decorated

Upper Garments
• cloak
• doublet
• gown

Lower Garments
• hose
• silk stockings
• trunk hose

Accessories
• carcanet
• ruff
• single earring

Footwear

François, Duc d'Alençon and Duc d'Anjou, c. 1572

Elizabeth I's one-time suitor wears a rich doublet with a lace-trimmed ruff and jeweled carcanet around his neck, and a jeweled band on his feathered bonnet. This drawing resembles a portrait from the early 1570s by François Clouet, in which his ermine-lined cloak is worn slung across his left shoulder.

Charles IX, c. 1570–75

The drawing of Charles IX on the left could be based on one of several portraits. He wears a white silk doublet and trunk hose embroidered in gold and slashed, with matching shoes. The collar identifies him as a knight of the Order of St. Michel, the oldest French chivalric order. His companions are both French statesmen from earlier in the century, in long, furred gowns.

See also
Italy, 16th Century,
pages 118–19
Germany, 1578,
pages 126–27
Europe, 16th Century,
pages 136–37

Europe, *1500–1600*

Queens and Noblewomen

European courts drove fashion in the 16th century, and monarchs and courtiers strove to be dressed in the most ostentatious and up-to-date clothes. Social advancement for the gentry, including good marriage prospects for women, often lay in service to the court, so it was vital to be well dressed. Honor Lisle, who was maneuvering for a place for her daughter Anne at Henry VIII's English court in 1537, was warned that Anne must have "double gowns and kirtles of silk, and good attirements for her head and neck."

Luxurious Textiles

The silhouette differences between the cone-shaped Spanish farthingale and the wheel-shaped French farthingale on the far right are easy to see. These women also wear luxurious textiles and jeweled ornaments; even the woman in black wears silk satin or taffeta banded with velvet for contrast.

See also
Italy, 16th Century, *pages 116–17*
Europe, 16th–17th Century, *pages 138–39*

Diane de Poitiers

Diane de Poitiers, mistress of Henri II of France, is on the left, dressed in a gold-trimmed pink dress with wide oversleeves lined in ermine. These are odd colors, however, since Diane was reputed to wear only black, white, and gray.

Headwear
• gabled hood

Hairstyles

Dress
• low-necked and wide sleeved

Upper Garments
• gown
• long-sleeved tunic (kirtle)

Lower Garments
• cone- or wheel-shaped petticoat (farthingale)

Accessories

Footwear

English and Spanish Queens, *c.* 1530–65

The three English queens on the left date probably to the 1520s and 1530s. They wear the gable hood with low-necked, wide-sleeved dresses. The different headdress, neckline, and sleeves of the Spanish queen on the right are attributable both to her nationality and the date: 1560s.

Catherine de' Medici, Mid-1550s

Catherine de' Medici, a member of the family that had long ruled Florence, is on the far left. She is said to have brought a variety of Italian fashions to France with her when she married the future Henri II of France in 1533, among them the custom of wearing drawers. The source for this image is unknown but it probably dates to before 1559, when she was widowed and donned mourning dress for the rest of her life.

Italy, *16th Century*

Noblewomen and Courtesans

Italian women were frequently the target of sumptuary legislation during the 15th and 16th centuries. Lawmakers targeted specific styles that they didn't approve of, such as large sleeves, overlong trains and excessive expenditure on luxurious fabrics. However, there is little evidence to suggest that any of this was effective. In many cases, prohibitions were simply ignored, and they must have been difficult, if not impossible, to enforce. Also, the styles that the authorities railed against were often on their way out of fashion by the time the laws were enacted. Some laws specifically targeted courtesans. One oft-cited example, enacted in 1543 in Venice, forbade prostitutes to wear silk (other than coifs), precious metals, or pearls and other jewelry, because they were so well dressed that noble and middle-class women were often mistaken for them.

Courtesan, *c.* 1590s
The source for this drawing was Vecellio's *Habiti Antichi et Moderni di Tutto il Mondo* of 1590, in which this woman is identified as a courtesan from a brothel. Indeed, she is much more simply and less richly dressed than the woman pictured below. Her high-soled shoes are *chopines*, which were particularly popular in Venice. Hers are crudely boxlike, in contrast to the more graceful—and taller— ones seen below.

See also
Italy, 16th Century,
pages 118–19

Venetian Courtesan, 1591
There is evidence that Italian women were wearing underpants or drawers by the early 17th century, and it is thought that the practice may have started there with courtesans. In this plate from *Diversarum Natium Habitus* by Pietro Bertelli, the courtesan's skirt is printed on a separate piece of paper attached to the ground sheet with a hinge so it can be flipped up to reveal the lady's naughty secret. The horned hairstyle is associated with Venetian courtesans but contemporary portraits confirm that gentlewomen wore it, too.

Two Noblewomen, *c.* 1530–50

Portraits by Bronzino and Andrea del Sarto were the models for these two drawings. The woman on the right, probably dating from around 1530, wears a low-necked dress with billowing sleeves that are tight from elbow to wrist. The woman on the left, probably from the 1540s, sports a high collar open in front and narrower, slashed sleeves with puffs at the shoulders.

Laura da Pola, 1543

The original portrait, by Lorenzo Lotto, contrasts the sitter's snow-white chemise with the heavy, tasseled gold partlet filling in her neckline and her figured black velvet dress. The gold chains around her waist add extra richness.

Hairstyles
• center-parted
• tall horns over the temples (Venetian)

Dress
• elaborate silks and brocades

Upper Garments
• chemise
• dress
• yoke-piece (partlet)

Lower Garments
• drawers
• skirt

Accessories
• gold chain worn as belt

Footwear
• high-soled shoes (chopines)

Rich Cloth, *c.* 1575–85

Paolo Veronese painted this group of women in gorgeous Italian polychrome silk brocades and velvets, figured in the large, symmetrical motifs fashionable at the time. Their finery contrasts sharply with the monochrome senatorial gowns of the two men. The Italian textile industry eventually lost its preeminence, but at this time it was still the source of some of the most desirable silks in Europe.

Italy, *16th Century*

Venetian, Paduan, and Milanese Men's Dress

Italy's production of highly desirable textiles continued in the 16th century, although her influence on fashion waned as Spain's waxed, politically and economically. Elements of Spanish, French, and German styles were seen in Italian fashion at the end of the 15th century and Spain's influence became marked after her victory in the Italian wars of 1521 to 1526. This resulted in more use of somber colors, in northern Italy especially. Brighter shades did linger in southern Italy, and Venetians, whose civic dress was strictly controlled, retained their distinctive gowns well into the 1500s.

**Man of Quality,
c. 1530s**
The combination of a bright pink, deep-skirted jerkin and orange hose may not be true to life but both colors appear individually in Italian portraits of the early and middle 16th century. The lower sash, just above the prominent codpiece, would probably have held his sword or a dagger.

Senator
He wears the official Renaissance-era Venetian toga, or *vesta*—an ample, long robe—purplish damask in this instance—with a standing collar and wide ducal sleeves that reveal a spotted fur lining. The stole on his left shoulder is a *becho*, a vestigial remnant of the long, hanging end of the rolled hood popular in the 14th and early 15th centuries. It was peculiar to Venice.

Middle-Class Merchant and Upper-Class Gentleman, Mid-16th Century
The merchant (*left*) and gentleman (*right*) offer few obvious differences other than the extensive slashing on the gentleman's suit contrasting with the plainer clothes of the merchant. Both wear the knee-length breeches called "Venetians" by the English.

Headwear
• tall-crowned hat

Hairstyles

Dress
• rich but somber

Upper Garments
• doublet
• jerkin
• long robe
(toga, or vesta)
• sleeved cloak

Lower Garments
• breeches
• codpiece
• hose
• trunk hose

Accessories
• sash
• stole (becho)

Footwear
• low boots

Equerry

Equerries were attendants responsible for the horses of persons of high rank; this man's occupation is suggested primarily by his low, brown boots. He wears a paned doublet with narrow skirts and round, puffed and paned trunk hose that show a prominent codpiece. His short gown is turned back to reveal a contrasting lining, and his tall-crowned hat is set at an angle and trimmed with feathers.

Togati, Late 15th to Early 16th Century

This man wears the black toga assumed by Venetian noblemen and ordinary citizens after they reached the age of 25. His very full *comeo* sleeves, tightly gathered at the wrists, are a holdover from the International Gothic style of the late 14th and early 15th centuries.

See also
Italy, 11th–15th Century,
pages 80–81

Milanese Gentleman

The colors worn by this gentleman would have been an unusual combination in the 16th century and are likely to be Hottenroth's additions. His rounded chest is plainly padded but he is not wearing the exaggerated, pointed peascod belly that developed during the 1570s. His cloak appears to be of the sleeved variety that was popular in this century.

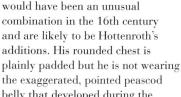

Germany, *15th–16th Century*

Plate Armor

Plate armor began to develop in Europe around the early 13th century with the appearance of the coat of plates, a cuirass reinforced with steel bands shaped to the torso. By the mid-14th century, a fully armored knight wore plate armor shielding his limbs, a coat of plates over a mail hauberk, worn in turn over a padded aketon. By 1425 a solid-plate cuirass had replaced the coat of plates and the limbs, hands, and feet were encased in plate. Later refinements consisted mainly of small changes to improve articulation and protective capabilities. Decorative techniques, such as etching, chasing, damascening, and embossing, also blossomed. The finest armor of the period came from northern Italy and southern Germany.

See also
Germany, 1500–50,
pages 122–23

Landsknecht, Early 16th Century

Landsknechts were Swiss and German mercenaries, famous for their slashed and highly colorful clothing. This one has diagonally slashed breeches, mi-parti hose, a two-tone codpiece and striped shoes. Under his fluted German cuirass, his doublet is most probably slashed as well.

Poleyns and Haute-Pièces, Early–Mid-16th Century

This beautiful etched and gilded armor is striking for its gothic poleyns, which protect the knees, and its *haute-pièces*, the flanges that extend the *pauldrons* (shoulder guards) to protect the wearer's neck. Instead of a helmet, he wears the sort of broad-brimmed feathered hat often seen in depictions of landsknechts (*see above right*).

Costume Armor, c. 1515–35

This striking suit of armor essentially reproduces certain fashionable men's garments of the period in steel, and its helmet has a distinctive visor in the form of a grotesque human face. So-called costume armor like this was made primarily in Germany.

Heraldic Jerkin, 15th Century

This foot soldier wears combination armor of plates and mail and a close-fitting heraldic jerkin laced up the center front. Armor was often embellished with textiles, and heraldic devices were among the most popular forms of decoration.

Armor, 15th Century

The soldier on the right wears individual pieces of armor rather than a full suit, and although it is decoratively quite simple, it appears to be partly gilded. His breastplate, greaves (shin guards), and vambraces (arm protection) are augmented with a mail apron, and he wears a long mail coif under his helm.

Tournament Armor, Late 15th Century

Tournament armor is essentially field armor with extra reinforcement; which parts are reinforced depends on the type of tournament. This suit is for the German joust; its characteristics include a reinforced breastplate, a heavy frog-mouth helm with a high, narrow eye slit, and the stiff gauntlet with a shell protecting the elbow on the left arm. There is no gauntlet on the right arm since that hand would be protected by the lance shield.

Knight, Mid-15th Century

This knight has full armor embellished with etching and gilding over a red doublet. He wears a light helmet, or sallet, and his face is protected with a beaver, covering his neck and chin. His long, piked sabatons date him to the mid-15th century; their plate toecaps were removable.

Headwear
- broad-brimmed hat
- fur hat (beaver)
- helm
- light helmet (sallet)
- mail coif

Hairstyles

Dress
- plate armor
- slashed clothing

Upper Garments
- arm guards (vambraces)
- cuirass
- doublet
- jerkin
- shoulder guards (pauldrons)

Lower Garments
- hose
- knee guards (poleyns)
- mail apron
- shin guards (greaves)

Accessories

Footwear
- long, armored shoes (sabatons)

Germany, *1500–50*

Men's Dress

Germany was in religious turmoil during the first half of the 16th century. In the Reformation, many German princes saw the opportunity to advance their own narrow political and economic interests, which in turn led to frequent internal conflict. That, combined with the decline of the Holy Roman Empire, left Germany a divided society. In terms of dress, Germany was left relatively powerless to influence international fashion, apart from the style for slashing that had begun at the end of the 15th century and continued through much of this period. The regional character of much 16th-century German dress, particularly for women, is also a mark of Germany's internal divisions.

Peasants
The dress of these three reveals a much stronger resemblance to fashionable dress in the 15th century than in the 16th and is quite ill-fitting, suggesting that perhaps some or all of the clothes were obtained secondhand. The cloth hose worn by the man on the right have visible seams up the back of the leg.

Scholars, 1500–50
The first German universities were founded late in the 14th century and by 1502 there were eleven of them. There, as elsewhere in Europe, students and faculty wore gowns that would later evolve into a distinctive academic dress based mainly on styles of the 15th and early 16th centuries. Hanging sleeves and four-cornered birettas are among its features.

See also
Germany, 1500–50,
pages 124–25

Cloak and Gown
Beneath his cloak the man on the right wears a waist-length doublet, cut low to reveal an expanse of pleated, gold-embroidered shirt. Gowns were more popular than cloaks in this period; that worn by the man on the left has hanging sleeves with a slit large enough to allow a large puffed doublet or jerkin sleeve to emerge.

Landsknechts
These landsknechts wear their typical parti-colored slashed clothes. One is armed with a pike, their preferred weapon. Landsknechts might be of questionable utility in battle, but they were always eyecatching!

Short Gown
This short, fur-lined gown was largely a middle-class garment. The leather purse reinforces the impression. His tall fur hat is in a style more often found in summer straw hats.

Headwear
• four-cornered cap (biretta)
• tall hat

Hairstyles

Dress

Upper Garments
• cloak
• doublet
• gown
• jerkin
• shirt

Lower Garments
• hose

Accessories
• leather purse

Footwear

Germany, *1500–50*

Women's Dress

Germany was out of the fashion mainstream in the 16th century, save for the German passion for slashing that spread all over western Europe at the end of the 1400s. German clothing in the 16th century retained a more Gothic flavor than fashion did elsewhere, and developed a strong regional character—particularly in women's headdresses. Although Germany was politically fragmented at this period, it was not completely insular. Cities in southern Germany, especially the prosperous commercial center of Nuremberg, traded actively with Asia and Italy and their dress did show some Italian influence, while that of northern Germany retained a strong Netherlandish character.

● Regional Dress

This is regional rather than fashionable dress, as evidenced by the unusually short skirt, and the serviceable apron and linen headdress. The large leather bag hanging from her waist is very similar in style to several surviving examples, which suggests that it is rendered accurately.

● Curious Sleeves

The source for this figure is unknown but there are some features that suggest artistic license. Particularly curious are the sleeves: the forearm of the green sleeve appears on the left arm to be fastened over a billowing chemise sleeve of an unlikely pink shade, while on the right arm the pink sleeve is a large, open oversleeve.

● Gold Trim, 1504

This image derives from a portrait of Margaret Stalburg by the Swabian painter Jörg Ratgeb. In the original, her slender bodice visibly laces closed over a rich gold-trimmed chemise. Gold trim was used lavishly in much of the dress that appears in surviving portraits of the early 16th century. Not only is her chemise trimmed with gold, the tall cap set back on her head is embroidered with a gold sawtooth pattern.

Headwear
• large headdresses

Hairstyles

Dress
• full, high-waisted and low-necked

Upper Garments
• bodice
• chemise
• cloak
• gown

Lower Garments
• apron
• skirt

Accessories
• leather bag

Footwear

Missing Chemise

This figure seems to derive from a line drawing in Carl Köhler's 1871 *History of Costume*. In that version, she is properly wearing a chemise that covers her shoulders; inexplicably. Hottenroth omitted it. Contemporary images do not bear out his bare-shouldered vision; even the widest, lowest-cut German necklines sit just on the shoulder and most are worn in tandem with a visible chemise.

See also
Germany, 1578,
pages 126–27

Women's Dress, *c.* 1500–10

These five dresses show some specifically German elements: pleated skirts and aprons, extralong, tight sleeves, waistlines above natural level, and wide necklines filled with modesty pieces. The three women on the left are based on drawings made in 1500 by Dürer of Nuremberg women dressed for different occasions. The central woman is dressed for a dance in a fur-trimmed green velvet gown with hanging sleeves. On her left is a housewife dressed for indoors. On the far left is a woman dressed for church in an enveloping cloak and an enormous linen headdress.

Germany, *1578*

Regional Style

The images here are drawn from Abraham de Bruyn's *Imperii ac sacerdotii ornatus*, published in Cologne in 1578. The attire worn by both sexes points to German dress retaining its strongly regional character throughout the 16th century. Fynes Moryson, a young Englishman who traveled extensively in Germany in the early 1590s, was not impressed by German dress. He noted that Germans were "of all… Nations least expencefull in apparrell… Citizens and men of inferior ranke, weare coarse cloth of Germany, and only the richer sort use English cloth; and this cloth is commonly of a blacke or darke colour, and they think themselves very fine, if their cloakes have a narrow facing of silk or velvet."

See also
England, 1550–1600,
pages 134–35

◉ Wadded Sleeves

The man on the right is a courtier belonging to the household of a nobleman or prince. He wears a doublet fastened with a column of tiny buttons and decorated with embroidered or braid crosses; its large sleeves are padded with wadding or horsehair. Racinet did not care for the sleeves, stating that they were an unattractive style that went out of fashion quickly.

Courtier

His short, Spanish-style cloak is satin-lined velvet or damask. His doublet is violet, and his paned trunk hose, with their lining pulled through in large puffs, are distinctively German. His codpiece is similarly decorated, so much so that it resembles a large bow, and his silk stockings are tied with sashes.

Women from Augsburg

Three of these women are from Augsburg: the two on the left are noblewomen wearing winter clothes, and the similarly dressed woman second from right is middle class. All have high-cut bodices, small plain ruffs, striped skirts under fine, long white aprons, and overgowns with puffed sleeves or shoulder welts. The differences lie in the short trains and gold necklaces worn by the noblewomen, and the various styles of headdress.

Doctor and Gentleman

The doctor, on the left, is from Cologne; he wears a long black cloak with a distinctive wired standing collar. De Bruyn described the other man as a *civis honestus* (respectable citizen); Racinet imagined him to be a politician or financier. His loose, fur-trimmed gown has large puffed sleeves, and his full beard is particularly long.

Hairstyles
• full beard and mustache for men

Dress
• full, wadded clothes

Upper Garments
• bodice
• cloak
• doublet
• gown
• overgown

Lower Garments
• apron
• codpiece
• silk stockings
• skirt
• trunk hose

Accessories
• gold necklace

Footwear

Netherlands, *15th Century*

Men's and Women's Dress

Netherlandish dress was portrayed by some of the finest artists of the 15th century: Jan van Eyck, for instance, worked in Bruges, as did Petrus Christus and Hans Memling (Memlinc). Rogier van der Weyden operated from Brussels and later in the century Hugo van der Goes worked in Ghent and Brussels. These Flemish artists had local patronage plus an international reputation, and frequently painted works for wealthy foreign patrons. Unfortunately, these images fall short of the best of Flemish representation. Some are drawn from bronze tomb sculptures, which may account for the dark colors; others are from an engraving by the German artist Israel van Meckenem and seem, unsurprisingly, more Germanic than Dutch. Perhaps the problem lies in the redrawing by Hottenroth himself. Whatever the reason, there is an odd, gnomelike quality to these people that does not serve the dress well.

Scalloped Sleeves

This drawing recalls one of John, Duke of Brabant, *c.* 1420, in a houppelande with heavy folds, a lowered waist, and scalloped bombarde sleeves. The wider shoulders may be Hottenroth's additions, or indicate a slightly later date.

Fantastical Headgear

All but one of these figures were mourning statues or weepers that stood around the tomb of Isabella of Bourbon, erected in Antwerp in 1476. Their elegant Dutch gowns are more somber than their fantastical dagged hoods and varied hats.

Weeper, 1476

Her bodice opens over a chemise or modesty piece; her skirt is held up to emphasize the fashionable swell of the stomach. Her headdress has an understructure to support a veil that was deliberately pressed into folds to ensure that it held just the right angle when in place.

See also
**Netherlands,
1480–1580,**
pages 130–31

Deep Pleats

In the middle of the century men's doublets and gowns began to be cut flat at the sides but with deep pleats massed in the front and back, an effect that van Meckenem has underscored by showing a loose belt hanging below. In reality, the belt is likely to have been firmly at the waist, helping to control the pleats.

Lacing, *c.* 1470s

The man and woman on the left, from van Meckenem's *Feast of Herod,* show the fashion for visible lacing, but this is not simple fashionable dress. A broad, waist-length laced gown opening was briefly in style for adults in the 1470s, but it would not have extended to thigh level nor have been worn twisted around the body. However, the lappet that is pinned up on top of the steeple headdress is definitely a fashionable touch.

Netherlands, *1480–1580*

Men's and Women's Dress

Teasing out the background to several of these figures by Hottenroth, which he identified as late 15th- or early 16th-century Netherlandish people of different classes, underscores the problems in using them as fashion examples. Take the woman facing forward at the top of page 131: Hottenroth copied her from Racinet but altered the colors of her gown, added stripes, and redesigned her headdress. Racinet had identified her as French, but admitted that he sourced her from a Flemish tapestry. While Hottenroth's identification may be closer than Racinet's, one must question her accuracy, and ask whether, as a figure in an allegorical tapestry, she was ever a completely straightforward example of fashionable dress.

Fashionable Gentleman, 1560s

This fashionably dressed man wears a plain, tight-fitting doublet over paned trunk hose and cloth netherstocks, and with a prominent codpiece. His soft, flat leather shoes are slashed. The ruff, still quite small, perches atop the high collar of his doublet. His curly-brimmed, tall-crowned hat is called a *capotaine*.

See also
Netherlands, 15th Century,
pages 128–29

Male and Female Costume

All the figures on these pages were drawn from 16th-century costume books depicting people of different classes and nations. Their accuracy varies tremendously since few artists worked from direct observation. Most artists were French, German, or Italian, so it is hard to gauge their familiarity with Flemish dress.

Headwear
• headdress
• tall-crowned hat
(capotaine)

Hairstyles

Dress
• many-layered

Upper Garments
• bodice
• doublet
• gown
• yoke-piece
(partlet)

Lower Garments
• codpiece
• netherstocks
• trunk hose

Accessories

Footwear
• flat, slashed shoes

Square Neckline

The woman on the left is discussed briefly on the opposite page; although it is not possible to trust the accuracy of the textiles she wears or the style of her headdress, features such as her low-cut, square neckline filled in with a white partlet seem grounded enough in real turn-of-the-16th-century dress.

Orientalism

Hottenroth took this man from Racinet, who had found him in the *Triumph of Beatrice* tapestry. He is unlikely to be a Dutchman: the turban, long beard, and mustache were used by Western artists to suggest exotic or historic figures.

Figures from Vecellio

All three figures are from Vecellio's 1590 costume book. The one in the center was first drawn by the Italian artist Enea Vico and published between 1540 and 1560. She was then copied for the first costume book, published in France in 1562. Over the years, many other artists copied her for their costume books, changing a few details each time. Vecellio seems to have added the ruffs around her neck and wrists, and the scalloped trim on her bodice. The coloring is Hottenroth's addition.

England, *1500–50*

Elaborate Clothing

Dress in England in this period reached new levels of magnificence and exaggeration. Led by the burly Henry VIII, men began to dress in rich fabrics with brocaded, embroidered, slashed, jeweled, furred, and braided surfaces. By mid-century their heavily padded silhouettes had become wider than ever before or since. Women's clothes were equally fine if less wide, their silhouette being marked by increasing rigidity. By the 1530s women were wearing stiff bodices that shaped the torso into a flattened, inverted cone, and from about 1545 they also adopted the farthingale, the cone-shaped, hooped petticoat that originated in Spain.

Royal and Noble Women, 1540s

The figure on the left comes from a 1546 portrait of the future Elizabeth I painted when she was thirteen. She wears a magnificent gown of crimson cloth-of-gold damask ornamented with jewels and embroidery and a curving French hood. The woman behind her wears a bodice with a stiffened, turned-out collar, a popular style in the 1540s, and the English version of a French hood, with a wider, flattened crown.

Nobleman, *c.* 1548

This well-known but anonymous portrait shows men's dress at its maximum width. The subject is, unusually, dressed entirely in red—jerkin, short gown with enormous sleeves, flat cap, trunk hose, stockings, and even his codpiece—which contrasts sharply with his white linen shirt. The blackwork embroidery, worked in black silk on a white ground that decorates the shirt, is particularly associated with England in this period but it, too, may have originated in Spain.

Headwear
• flat cap
• French hood
• gable headdress

Hairstyles

Dress
• unusually ornate

Upper Garments
• bodice
• gown
• jerkin
• shirt
• short gown

Lower Garments
• codpiece
• hooped petticoat (farthingale)
• stockings
• trunk hose

Accessories

Footwear
• duckbill shoes

Slashing and Shoes, Early 16th Century

The man in the red-and-black doublet and red hose is most likely one of the Landsknechts, the mercenaries whose elaborately slashed clothes influenced 16th-century fashionable dress. The silhouettes of the three standing men are narrow compared with the figure on the opposite page (*top*), showing they date from earlier in the century, but their duckbill shoes reflect the era's widening line.

Hoods, Early 16th Century

The two standing women appear to be wearing variations on the gable hood, a distinctive, arched headdress favored by Englishwomen. That worn by the woman on the left covers her hair completely and so probably dates to after 1525; the one in the center is in an earlier style.

See also
Spain and Portugal, 14th–16th Century, *pages 90–91*
England, 1550–1600, *pages 134–35*

England, *1550–1600*

Spanish Influence

The somber colors of Spanish styles and the use of paning (vertical slashing) enjoyed a vogue in England during the 1550s, as did garments such as the hip-length, hooded Spanish cloak. Brighter colors and busier surfaces returned with Elizabeth I in 1558, who presided over one of the most richly attired courts in Europe. Men's dress lost width in the second half of the century but was exaggerated in other ways, notably the protruding peascod belly, fashionable between the 1570s and the 1590s. Women began to swap the Spanish farthingale for the wheel-shaped French one in the 1580s, while both sexes adopted the ruff, a stiff, pleated collar that had developed from the ruffle attached to the neckline of the shirt or chemise into a separate item.

Smocklike Doublet

The smocklike shape of this man's doublet or jerkin suggests he may be working class, but the rest of his clothing announces he is well-off. His baggy Venetians meet ribbon garters at the knee, and he wears a short cloak with a stand collar. Tall felt hats were popular, and his has a flat crown and a wide band.

See also
**Spain and Portugal,
14th–16th Century,**
pages 90–91

Furred Gown, 1560s

This man wears the long gown of the professional; his is brocaded and lined with a rich brown fur. Portraits from the 1550s and 1560s often feature gowns with a contrasting fur lining, although the fur is often white against the gown's dark material, rather than the tones of puce lined in brown chosen by Hottenroth. The rising collar that extends to form revers appears in portraits around 1560.

Peascod Belly, 1580s–90s

This doublet is extensively padded to curve down over the wearer's body into the extraordinary shape called a peascod belly. It is most frequently seen paired with short, puffed trunk hose, but this one is worn with Venetians, which, unusually, appear to have been unlaced from the doublet to reveal the shirt.

Furred Gown

The calf-length red brocade gown hides all but the satin sleeves of the doublet beneath. The gown is lined with gray fur and has hanging sleeves slit in two places, so the wearer may choose how much of the sleeve covers his arm. The gown's collar is turned down beneath a small, plain linen ruff that cushions the wearer's chin.

Gentlewomen, c. 1550–1600

In a fur-lined gown and underskirt of gold-braided silk, the woman in the center is richly dressed. A Spanish farthingale gives her skirt its cone shape; the woman to her right wears either a small, round French farthingale or hip pads that mimic its shape.

Slashed Suit, c. 1580s

This well-dressed gentleman wears a matching doublet and narrow Venetians of slashed white silk embroidered with gold. The gold-lined short cloak slung over his shoulder is in the Spanish style that was popularized in England in the 1540s. His wide, starched, single-tier ruff is unornamented and matches the small ruffs at his wrists.

Headwear
• tall felt hat

Hairstyles

Dress
• full, with exaggerated padding

Upper Garments
• cloak
• doublet
• gown
• shirt

Lower Garments
• cone-shaped or hooped petticoat (farthingale)
• hip pads
• narrow breeches (Venetians)

Accessories

Footwear

Europe, *16th Century*

Armor and Military Dress

During the 16th century armor styles diversified and types were developed for different uses: battle, jousting, tournaments, ceremonial, and parade. Infantrymen might be armored differently from cavalrymen, but for the most part these were variations on a theme, and many armorers made interchangeable parts that could be configured as required. Particular troops might use specific types; for instance, brigandines (sleeveless fabric jerkins armored with small plates) were generally worn only by foot soldiers, or as parade dress. Armor for parade might be lighter than battle dress, more ornate, or both.

Company Clerk, Late 1580s
Racinet presented this dapper figure as a French infantryman in uniform, but in reality he is a well-dressed company clerk in the Dutch army, a fact Racinet was almost certainly aware of. Racinet sought to illustrate the lack of uniformity in military dress and argued that the differences between French and Flemish uniforms of the period were so slight as to make one serve as an example of the other, but the misrepresentation is nonetheless unfortunate.

Infantry Captain, 1572
He wears only a steel cuirass and gorget, which suggests that he is dressed for parade, not for battle. He carries a pike—an infantry spear with a leaf-shaped head and a shaft that ranged in length from 16 to 22 feet (5 to 7 meters). Pikes were in use from the 15th to the 17th century.

François, Duc d'Alençon, c. 1572–84
The son of Catherine de' Medici and brother of Henri III of France wears parade armor with gilded, etched motifs on a blackened ground. Armorers often used Italian grotesques as motifs; a similar suit made for Henri II has dense Italianate foliate scrolls.

See also
France, 16th Century, *pages 108–09*
France, 1550–1600, *pages 112–13*
Germany, 15th–16th Century, *pages 120–21*

Composite Armor, Mid-16th Century

"Composite" armor is a full suit of plate armor with mail. Many features are common to cavalry battle dress—asymmetric pauldrons, lance rest and visored helm—but he carries the round shield (targe) used primarily in tournaments.

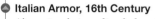

Italian Armor, 16th Century

Above is a brigandine belonging to Francesco Maria I della Rovere, Duke of Urbino. It was made by Filippo Negroli in Milan in around 1532. The Negroli family were among the finest armorers working in Italy. They may also have been responsible for the beautifully embossed armor next to it, although other Italian armorers were also working in this style.

Half Armor, *c.* 1540s

This is lighter armor than the full suit on the right: it consists of a skirted cuirass with tassets to protect the thighs, pauldrons to protect the shoulders, a gorget covering the neck, and an open helmet, probably a burgonet. His flag has a white cross on a red ground, which Racinet identified as the flag of the Picardy regiment founded in 1479.

Headwear
• helmet
• throat guard (gorget)

Hairstyles

Dress
• elaborate surface decoration

Upper Garments
• cuirass
• overtunic with metal plates (brigandine)
• shoulder guards (pauldrons)

Lower Garments
• shin guards (greaves)
• thigh guards (tassets)

Accessories
• round shield (targe)

Footwear

Europe, *16th–17th Century*

Women's Collars and Ruffs

Developed from the ruffle trimming the high collar of a mid-16th-century shirt or chemise, the ruff became the most distinctive accessory of its era. Its spectacular growth for both men and women was enabled by the discovery in the 1560s of a method of extracting starch from wheat. Starch burns easily and stiffens as it cools, so it was as challenging to produce as it was to arrange the increasingly unwieldy ruff at the correct angle on its wire support (the *underpropper*, or *supportasse*). No doubt many admired the wealth, status, and skill of those who mastered the art of ruff-wearing, but moralists such as Philip Stubbes were outraged. In his 1583 *Anatomie of Abuses*, he claimed "the devil... first invented these great ruffes" and that ruff wearers' efforts would be wasted if they were caught in the rain, as their ruffs would "goe flip flap in the winde, like rags flying abroad, and lye upon their shoulders like the dishcloute of a slut."

Marie de' Medici
In the original portrait by Franz Pourbus in 1611, the queen wears a fan-shaped *reticella* lace ruff wired to stand up behind her head. In Racinet's drawing, however, it looks more like a *rebato*, an unpleated but similarly shaped and wired collar.

See also
**Europe,
1600–50,**
pages 142–43
**Netherlands,
1600–50,**
pages 144–45

Small Ruff
Infanta Isabella Clara Eugenia's cutwork and needle-lace trimmed ruff in de Llano's 1584 painting is more modest than many from the 1580s. Smaller ruffs were popular during the last fifty years or so that ruffs remained in fashion.

Cartwheel Ruff
In this anonymous portrait a lace-edged cartwheel ruff is positioned almost vertically on its underpropper, as if it were literally a frame for the face. Both its large size and steep angle were popular in the 1580s and 1590s.

Triple Ruff
This anonymous woman wears a magnificent triple-tiered cutwork ruff that is tilted up behind her head and covering her shoulders. The ruff's width and depth visually divorce her head from her body.

Headwear
• head rail

Hairstyles

Dress
• elaborate

Upper Garments

Lower Garments

Accessories
• collar
• ruff
• wire support
(underpropper
or supportasse)

Footwear

Princess Orsini

This portrait of an early 17th-century Princess Orsini features a double-tier lace-edged ruff that is relatively narrow beneath the chin but widens as it rises around the back of her neck and beside her ears.

Fan-Shaped Ruff

The sitter wears a lace-edged, fan-shaped, wired standing collar paired with a soft lace-trimmed collar that accents her *décolletage*. Racinet dates this German portrait to 1555, but clothes and hairstyle suggest the later 16th or early 17th century.

Embellishment

Lace developed during the 16th century from openwork embroidery techniques to become the most important and expensive trimming of the era. This ruff is trimmed with a cutwork band and edged with spiky needle- or bobbin-lace points.

Plain Ruff

In the 1590s, an English traveler commented on the plainness of Dutch dress, a view borne out by this soberly dressed Dutch widow. She wears a modest version of the plain white linen ruff characteristic of the Netherlands.

Multilayered Ruff

The unknown sitter in this portrait by Paulus Moreelse wears a deep, multilayered, lace-edged ruff that has a much shallower tilt than many of the others from the same period shown here.

Elizabeth I

In the original painting by Gheeraerts, *c.* 1592, Elizabeth wears a large, fan-shaped ruff, but here it is incorrectly drawn as two separate pieces. The heart-shaped head rail behind looks like a collar but is in fact part of her headdress.

Europe, *1600–50*

French Influence on Men's Dress

During the early 17th century, the flamboyant men's fashions of the late 16th century developed a slimmer, more elegant line—particularly in the 1630s, when a rising waistline elongated the silhouette. Surface decoration, rich and busy at the beginning of the century, was simplified in the 1620s, slowly swinging back toward elaboration a decade later. French influence on style and demeanor was strong, accounting for such innovations as bucket-topped boots and slashed or paned doublets, as well as the carelessly romantic habit of wearing the doublet unbuttoned to reveal yards of white linen shirt.

▶ Puritan, 1640s

Puritans, also known as Roundheads for the short hair some wore, were radical English Protestants who controlled the English government during the Commonwealth period (1649–60). Soberness or flamboyance in Puritan dress was more a matter of class than religious conviction, and was never legislated. This man's black clothes and plain linen are simply examples of normal middle-class dress for the era.

▶ Standing Band, *c.* 1615–30

This Dutchman is wearing a standing band, a transitional collar between the late 16th-century ruff and the falling band that became popular in the late 1620s. Standing bands were closed linen collars, often trimmed with lace. Starch and a metal underpropper held them parallel to the shoulders. The startling effect was of the head set out on a platter.

See also
Netherlands, 1600–50,
pages 144–45
France, 1600–50,
pages 146–47

Bucket-Topped ◀ Boots, *c.* 1630s

The man to the left is wearing a typical example of leather boots with stiff, bucket-shaped tops. Most commonly, a second pair of stockings, often lace-trimmed, was also worn with bucket tops, and these sat decoratively just inside the boot top. Spurs, another standard accompaniment, were usually attached to the boot with butterfly-shaped leather straps.

Dutchman, 1620s–30s

Spain continued to influence Netherlandish dress at this period, which is less heavily decorated than French examples. This man wears a buff leather jerkin over full black breeches; the plainness of his clothes is offset by the deep lace trim on his falling-band collar.

Fashionable Frenchman, c. 1645

Men's doublets got progressively skimpier during the first sixty-five years of the century, a fashion that originated in France. This man's doublet is no longer long enough to cover his shirt at the waist, and is worn unbuttoned. More shirt is visible through and below his slashed and shortened doublet sleeves.

Fashionable Frenchman, Late 1630s

In contrast to the figure above right, this man wears a doublet that covers the waist of his breeches, which have not yet shortened and widened into the petticoat style. The falling-band collar is still broad enough to cover his shoulders.

Frenchman, c. 1640

France produced some of the most elaborate clothes in Europe at this time. This man's doublet and breeches are trimmed with lace and ribbons, while his cloak appears to be either embroidered or appliquéd in gold, and his hat sports several ostrich plumes.

Headwear
• plumed hat

Hairstyles

Dress
• French-influenced

Upper Garments
• doublet
• jerkin
• shirt

Lower Garments
• breeches

Accessories
• falling-band collar
• standing-band collar

Footwear
• bucket-topped boots
• spurs

141

Europe, *1600–50*

Women's Dress

Although the first great age of the costume book is considered to have ended with the 1601 publication of Jean de Glen's *Des Habits, mœurs, ceremonies, façons de faire anciennes et modernes du monde*, artists continued to illustrate the clothes worn in many countries. Greater travel opportunities meant that 17th-century costume plates were more likely to be based on direct observation. Bohemian artist Wenceslas Hollar, whose engravings of Englishwomen are highlighted on pages 148–49 and who is the origin of several of these figures, is an excellent example. His detailed costume plates demonstrate first-hand knowledge.

Englishwomen, 1643–49

Hollar identified the central figure as a noblewoman. His original drawing shows clearly that both the lace-trimmed kerchief and the collar worn over a long-waisted bodice are transparent. The woman on the left is a lady mayoress of London, England, wearing a very similar dress, albeit with a ruff (now old-fashioned), and a black felt hat with a tapering crown.

Spanish Woman

The plain, millstone ruff (*see page 144*) remained in fashion longer in both Spain and the Netherlands than elsewhere in Europe. This woman's shaped hanging sleeves are also typically Spanish, as is the triangular line of her skirt, probably worn over a farthingale. Spanish-style bodices were usually cut high; the V-neck on this one may or may not be due to Hottenroth's deployment of color.

Headwear
• felt hat with tapering crown

Hairstyles

Dress
• keenly observed

Upper Garments
• bodice
• overgown

Lower Garments
• hooped petticoat (farthingale)
• skirt

Accessories
• collar
• fur muff
• kerchief
• ribbon belt
• ribbon ornament
• ruff

Footwear

Formal Dress, 1630s

A noblewoman's dress: a stiff, slightly high-waisted bodice and skirt with overgown. The materials used would have been rich and probably brocaded or embroidered, and there would have been a ribbon sash at the waist. There is a ribbon ornament at the center of her low-cut neckline, and more ribbon ties her paned, padded virago sleeves into their characteristic double puff.

Wheel Farthingale, 1643

On the right is a merchant's wife from Frankfurt, Germany. Both women wear the French, or wheel, farthingale, which entered fashion in the 1580s and was long out of mainstream fashion by 1643, although it is here seemingly retained in regional dress. The woman on the left, as was typical, rests her arms on it.

See also
Europe, 16th–17th Century, *pages 138–39*
England, 1642–49, *pages 148–49*

English Gentlewoman, 1643

This woman is wearing winter outerwear. Most striking are her large, fashionable fur muff and her skirt, which is pinned into a bustle shape. Over her shoulders she wears a linen collar over a kerchief. The triangular point between the layers, which Hottenroth has colored black, belongs in fact to the linen collar, not the kerchief. He has also elongated her train.

Netherlands, *1600–50*

Urban Dress

Racinet identified the plate from which these images come as representing urban dress in the Netherlands from 1630 to 1660. Spanish styles were strong in the Netherlands in the 17th century among the Dutch ruling class; this translated into relative plainness in surface decoration, a strong preference for black contrasted with white, and a somewhat more rigid, more exaggerated silhouette for women than was fashionable elsewhere. The large, platter-like ruffs that appear time and again in Netherlandish paintings of the early to mid-17th century are especially characteristic; these ruffs remained in fashion in the Netherlands far longer than anywhere else in Europe.

Millstone Ruff

A broad, two-tier millstone ruff dominates this cloaked woman. Such ruffs were made of widths of linen stitched onto a neckband in a figure-of-eight pattern, and stiffened with starch.

The Merry Company, 1626

This rendering of Dirk Hals's painting shows both the muted Dutch palette and a variety of neckwear: the large millstone or cartwheel ruff, plain and lace-edged; the soft, falling ruff; the stiffened, platelike standing band worn by the woman in the right foreground; and the coming style, the lace-edged falling band worn by the seated man at left.

Soldier's Dress

This man is dressed like a soldier, with a sleeveless leather jerkin over a white-sleeved doublet, and with tapering breeches tucked inside leather boots with wide tops that have not been folded over. The crenellated edge of his falling band and cuffs suggests a lace trim, although he would be unlikely to wear lace into battle.

Influence of French Fashion, *c.* 1660

This man sports a short doublet open at the center front. The slashed sleeves show plenty of billowing linen shirt and he has petticoat breeches. Both doublet and breeches are trimmed with knots of ribbon called "fancies." The breeches are drawn as if they were a skirt, but the few pairs that survive do have separate, albeit extremely wide, legs.

See also
Europe, 1600–50,
pages 140–43

Virago Sleeves, 1630s

Double-puffed or virago sleeves, the puffs defined with tied ribbon, were in fashion in the late 1620s and 1630s. This formal dress of high-waisted bodice and petticoat with contrasting overgown suggests a date in the first half of the 1630s.

Sloping Shoulders, 1650s

The deeply sloping shoulders here suggest the 1650s, when the bodice neckline had moved off the shoulder and the sleeves were cut so far into the back of the bodice that women raised their arms above shoulder level with difficulty.

Musician, *c.* 1630

The violoacellist wears a paned, skirted doublet that fastens down the front with prominent buttons, an important fashion feature from around this date, and the wider breeches called "slops." The spiky, Italian needle lace that edges his falling band suggests that he is a man of some means.

Headwear

Hairstyles

Dress
• quite plain, but with an exaggerated silhouette

Upper Garments
• bodice
• doublet
• jerkin
• overgown
• shirt

Lower Garments
• breeches
• petticoat breeches
• wide breeches (slops)

Accessories
• decorative ribbon knots (fancies)
• prominent buttons
• ruffs

Footwear
• wide-topped boots

France, *1600–50*

Fashionable Frenchmen

A cloak was an indispensable gentleman's accessory in the first half of the 17th century, and Racinet intended these figures, drawn from Abraham Bosse's *Le Jardin de la noblesse française* (1629), to demonstrate the various ways in which they were worn. Cloaks are often depicted in contemporary paintings and engravings slung over one shoulder and underneath the opposite arm, then tied across the chest; occasionally they are shown sitting atop both shoulders. These figures also suggest the sweeping gestures men made with their cloaks to call attention to their fine clothes.

Across the Shoulder

This gentleman's cloak is slung under his left arm, revealing a full doublet sleeve and what is probably the shoulder wing and hanging sleeve of a jerkin, a doubletlike garment sometimes worn over a doublet until about 1630. Instead of boots, this man wears shoes that fasten with large ribbon rosettes.

Matching Breeches

Not content to leave his cloak simply covering both his shoulders, this man has swept its fullness across his chest and left shoulder, nearly obscuring his face in the process but revealing that the cloak's spotted lining matches his breeches.

Folded Cloak

This man's wide, feathered hat, full, paned doublet sleeves, and the cloak he has folded back over his forearm so he can reach his sword, give him the impression of tremendous upper-body bulk. His doublet fastens down the center front with numerous small buttons, and his breeches, too button down the outseam, highlighting the importance of buttons as a fashion feature at this period. His sword hangs from the baldrick buckled diagonally across his chest.

Waist-Length Cloak

The graceful folds of a waist-length, circular cloak are displayed by its wearer's stance. It balances his long, full breeches, trimmed at the knee with loops of ribbon, and his wide, bucket-topped boots —one of the period's most fashionable forms of masculine footwear.

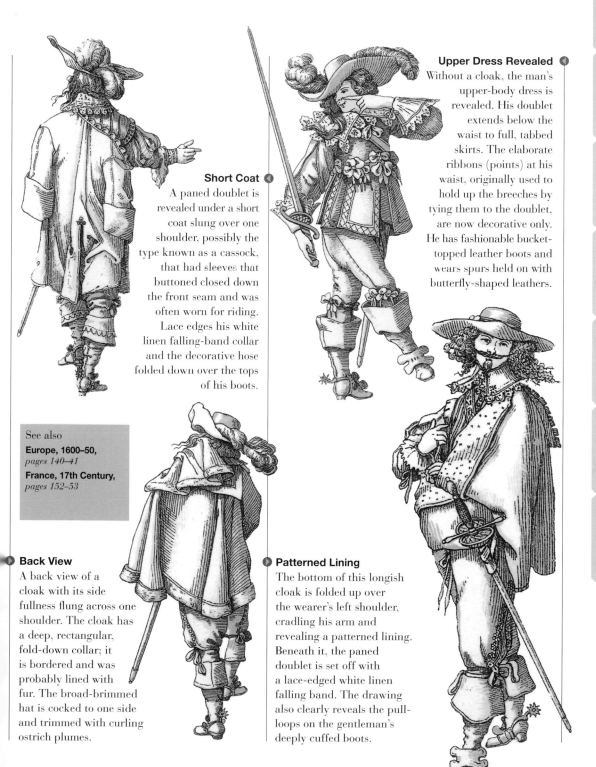

Short Coat
A paned doublet is revealed under a short coat slung over one shoulder, possibly the type known as a cassock, that had sleeves that buttoned closed down the front seam and was often worn for riding. Lace edges his white linen falling-band collar and the decorative hose folded down over the tops of his boots.

Upper Dress Revealed
Without a cloak, the man's upper-body dress is revealed. His doublet extends below the waist to full, tabbed skirts. The elaborate ribbons (points) at his waist, originally used to hold up the breeches by tying them to the doublet, are now decorative only. He has fashionable bucket-topped leather boots and wears spurs held on with butterfly-shaped leathers.

See also
Europe, 1600–50,
pages 140–41
France, 17th Century,
pages 152–53

Back View
A back view of a cloak with its side fullness flung across one shoulder. The cloak has a deep, rectangular, fold-down collar; it is bordered and was probably lined with fur. The broad-brimmed hat is cocked to one side and trimmed with curling ostrich plumes.

Patterned Lining
The bottom of this longish cloak is folded up over the wearer's left shoulder, cradling his arm and revealing a patterned lining. Beneath it, the paned doublet is set off with a lace-edged white linen falling band. The drawing also clearly reveals the pull-loops on the gentleman's deeply cuffed boots.

Headwear
• broad-brimmed hat

Hairstyles

Dress
• easy-fitting, high-waisted

Upper Garments
• cassock
• cloak
• doublet
• jerkin

Lower Garments
• breeches

Accessories
• baldrick
• buttons as feature
• falling-band collar

Footwear
• bucket-topped cuffed boots
• shoes with rosettes
• spurs

England, *1642–49*

Women's Dress

These five images are drawn from a series of engravings of 17th-century women's dress by Bohemian artist Wenceslas Hollar in his *Theatrum Mulierum* (1643–44). Hollar created some of the most important visual records we have of the dress of European women of the upper and merchant classes in the 1640s. Although Racinet recorded the dress of women from a number of different countries, he chose to focus on his drawings of Englishwomen. These images highlight the line and features of women's dress in the mid-1640s. In particular, they record the change in proportion from the high-waisted styles of the 1630s to the more balanced silhouette of the mid-1640s, with its waistline at natural level at sides and back and extending to a point at the center front. Decorative emphasis was provided by moderately full skirts, often worn looped up over a contrasting petticoat (intentionally revealed); by modest ribbon trim; and by the collars and kerchiefs, either plain or edged with lace according to the occasion and the wearer's means, that fill in or accentuate the neckline.

Gentlewoman

Drawn in 1644, Hollar's English gentlewoman wears a heavy bodice cut long in front and rising to the natural waistline at the sides and back, and a matching skirt worn elaborately looped up over a contrasting petticoat. The bodice neckline is concealed by a white linen collar edged with scallops of lace, and her hair is hidden under a black hood. Her large fur hand muff was a popular winter accessory for well-to-do women.

Noblewoman

Hollar entitled this "An English Noblewoman in Winter Clothes." It is a rare back view that clearly shows how the pinned-up skirts were looped or clasped back into a bustlelike shape and how the square, white linen collar that she wears over a warm kerchief was folded over her shoulders. Racinet copied Hollar quite closely; Hottenroth's slightly different version of this same figure appears on page 143.

See also
Europe, 1600–50,
pages 142–43
Netherlands, 1600–50,
pages 144–45

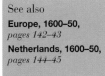

Headwear
• hood

Hairstyles
• chignon
• curled at sides

Dress
• long, tight bodice
and full skirts

Upper Garments
• bodice
• stomacher

Lower Garments
• petticoat
• skirt

Accessories
• collar
• fur muff
• kerchief
• pearls
• ribbon ornament

Footwear

Fashion for the Court
The wealth and standing of this
fashionable lady of the English
court are suggested by the string
of pearls around her neck, the
jewel pinned at her low neckline,
and her deeply lace-edged linen
collar and cuffs. Her hair, pulled
smoothly back from her forehead
into a high chignon, and curled
and shoulder-length at the sides,
is as fashionable as her dress.

Day Dress
The figure on the right
wears daytime dress of
1643; the one on the left,
drawn in 1644, is wearing
more formal clothing. Both
wear long bodices with
long, stiff stomachers. The
double sleeve, shown in a
tight version on the right
and a more elaborate,
paned version on the left,
was new in fashion in the
mid-1640s.

Modern Europe, 1650–1840

Clothing styles, especially women's, underwent many changes in this period, but the changes in the clothing industry itself were nothing short of cataclysmic. The Industrial Revolution began in 18th-century Britain in the textile trades, with the invention of tools such as the flying shuttle (1733) and the spinning jenny (*c.* 1764) that enabled cloth to be woven far quicker than ever before and boosted overall production levels tremendously. These developments helped to promote rapid urbanization as the locus of production shifted from cottages to factories, and brought profound changes in the tenor of life and work. One such change that had a lasting effect on dress was the reimagining of gender roles within society, which now assigned to women primary responsibility for the consumption of fashion.

Increased production went hand in hand with increased consumption and new or expanded fashion-related industries. The ready-made garment trade, which had begun in the 16th century with accessories, now included full garments, such as men's coats and uniforms, and women's outerwear. The popular serial fashion press also evolved in this period, and as a result fashion cycles, especially in women's dress, speeded up. France's lead in the luxury textile trades and its dominance as a fashion center were established by the mid-17th century and maintained—as far as women's dress is concerned—throughout this period, but by the end of the 18th century the center of influence for men's dress had shifted to Britain.

Modern men's dress began its development around 1666, when both the English and French courts adopted what would eventually become the three-piece suit: coat or jacket, vest, and breeches (later pants). The new styles were favorably commented upon by those invaluable diarists of the day, Samuel Pepys and John Evelyn. Soon thereafter, women's dress began to evolve in ways that separated it visually from men's dress even more than before. Previously, male tailors had commonly made clothes for both sexes, but after about 1670 the making of women's clothes, with the exception of riding habits, increasingly fell to women, and both the 18th and early 19th centuries saw marked contrasts between male and female silhouettes and use of fabrics and trims.

France, *17th Century*

Military dress

Armor was worn less during the 17th century as the use and efficacy of guns on the battlefield increased. With the exception of some heavy cavalry, most soldiers discarded everything but a simple cuirass, helmet, and perhaps gauntlets, and most wore plain pieces of relatively low quality that were mass produced. As the nature of warfare changed, tournaments also ceased and the demand for tournament armor disappeared all over Europe. Decorative suits of armor did survive in the 17th century for parades and ceremonies, and continued as an artistic convention in 17th-century portraiture.

Cavalry Officer, *c. 1640*

A sleeveless version of the buff coat pictured below. Its shoulders are trimmed with small wings, and it laces closed up the center front; decorative metal clasps and plain hooks and eyes were also popular fastenings. The broad sash around his waist is decorative only and would not have appeared on the battlefield. Buff coats gave effective protection against sword cuts, but not against gunfire.

Braid-Trimmed Coat, *c. 1620s*

The stylization and odd use of colors in the drawing make it difficult to tell exactly what is being worn. Most likely, it is a buff coat under the cuirass, with sleeves that are decorated with braid applied in horizontal bands. Surviving coats, such as one in the Museum of London's collection in England dating from the 1620s, prove that this form of decoration did indeed exist.

Musketeer, 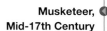 Mid-17th Century

This rifleman wears a long-sleeved buff coat without any armor protection at all. Buff coats were made of heavy, stiff leather, often ox hide, and could be either long-sleeved or sleeveless, plain or embellished with embroidery or applied braid. They first came into use in the 16th century and were worn throughout the 17th century.

Siege Armor, Early 17th Century

This is an example of the reduced armor that some cavalry continued to wear in the 17th century. Made of blued steel, it features a cuirass with no tassets, elbow-length pauldrons, and a morion helmet. A protective buff coat is visible beneath. His stiff, bucket-topped boots were common riding wear during this period.

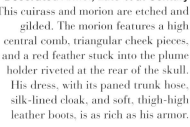

Decorated Armor, Late 17th Century

This cuirass and morion are etched and gilded. The morion features a high central comb, triangular cheek pieces, and a red feather stuck into the plume holder riveted at the rear of the skull. His dress, with its paned trunk hose, silk-lined cloak, and soft, thigh-high leather boots, is as rich as his armor.

Musketeer, Early to Mid-17th Century

Rather than a buff coat, this soldier protects himself with a buff jerkin worn over a plain steel breastplate. His plain steel morion was the style of helmet most frequently used in the 16th and 17th centuries by cavalry and light infantry, particularly archers and musketeers.

See also
France, 1724–86, *pages 168–69*

France and Germany, *1650–1700*

Women's Dress: Ladies of Quality

Louis XIV and Jean-Baptiste
Colbert, his Chief Minister,
recognized the importance of
textiles as an engine for economic
growth and prosperity. In the 1660s
they enacted legislation designed
to greatly expand and improve
France's silk, wool, and linen
weaving industries, to serve both
domestic and foreign markets.
Some of Colbert's achievements
were undone by the Edict of Nantes
in 1685, which drove large numbers
of French Protestant weavers out
of France and into the arms of
her competitors. Nonetheless, by
the early 18th century France's
superiority, especially in figured-
silk weaving, was established.
French fashion also began its rise
to dominance in this period, which
was initially linked to the prestige
and power of Louis XIV's court at
Versailles but later shifted to Paris.

Duchesse d'Orléans, 1670s

This depiction of the
duchess in her riding
clothes appears to be
loosely based on a 1673
portrait. Riding habits
for women were a new
development in the 17th
century, and, since they
were made by tailors, not
dressmakers, they strongly
resembled men's suits.
The masculine effect
is heightened by her
mannish full-bottomed
wig and feathered
tricorn hat.

Long Bodice, 1660s

In the 1660s and 1670s women were encased
in stiffly boned bodices that extended to a point
well below the waist; the bodice, which was
accompanied by a separate full skirt, became so
long and stiff that women eventually were forced
to sit with their legs apart to accommodate it.
That is the style the woman on the right is
wearing; it was superseded in the 1670s
by the one-piece, unboned *mantua*.

See also
**France,
1680–1700,**
pages 160–61
**Western Europe,
18th Century,**
pages 166–67

Headwear
• full-bottomed wig
• tall headdress
(fontange)
• tricorn hat
• veil

Hairstyles

Dress
• moving from
the very stiff and
structured to the
more relaxed

Upper Garments
• bodice
• one piece unboned
dress (mantua)
• riding habit

Lower Garments
• full skirt
• petticoat
• train

Accessories
• lace apron

Footwear
• low-heeled

**Renée du Bec-Crespin,
Maréchale de Guébriant,
and Her Niece,** *c. 1660s–70s*
Both women are in the stiff-bodied
gown and full skirt of the 1660s
and 1670s; however, Mme du
Bec-Crespin is wearing mourning,
signified both by her black dress
and her long widow's veil. Her
niece's dress is both more colorful
and more richly decorated.

Marie-Thérèse of Austria, 1660
Marie-Thérèse is in formal dress,
whose characteristic tight bodice,
full skirt and train, short sleeves,
and elaborate decoration evolved
into French court dress, the *grand
habit*, of the 18th century
(worn then with a large
hoop to spread the skirt).

Duchesse d'Aiguillon, After 1675
She wears one of the new
mantuas, the one-piece unboned
dress that superseded the stiff-
bodied gown; hers is of mauve
silk, banded with silver, worn
over a blue silk petticoat trimmed
with silver braid and tassels. Both
her dress and her *fontange* are
sprinkled with pearls. Despite the
richness of her overall dress,
Racinet called attention to her
metallic lace apron, describing it
as "the most luxurious object."

155

Northern Europe, *1650–1700*

Men's Dress

These illustrations show the significant transformation made in men's dress in this period, from the suit of doublet and breeches to one of coat, vest, and breeches. The proportions of men's garments also changed. The shrinking doublet in the 1650s and 1660s was dwarfed by the billowing shirt and wide breeches, whereas the coat and vest concealed most of the shirt and virtually all of the breeches. Lingering styles of surface decoration, such as the bunches of ribbon trim that had been a feature of men's dress since the 1630s, helped to bridge the gap between old and new, and it is certain that the new styles took time to become widespread.

▶ **Petticoat Breeches,
c. 1660**

Ribbon-trimmed petticoat breeches, their wide legs resembling a skirt, were a French fashion that spread throughout Europe, despite their effeminacy. The legs on a surviving English pair made in 1660 are each 62 inches (1.6 m) in circumference and trimmed with 475 ft (145 meters) of different-colored satin, taffeta, and silk ribbon. The matching doublet and shirt pale in comparison.

▶ **Wigs, Late 17th Century**

These four Germans all wear long, heavily curled, full-bottomed wigs, the latest style in men's hairdressing. Wigs were an all-or-nothing proposition, since one's head had to be shaved in order to wear one. Samuel Pepys wrote in 1663 of having the wigmaker cut off his hair, saying that it "went a little to my heart at present to part with it."

See also
France, 1650–1780,
pages 158–59
**Western Europe,
1700–50,** *pages 162–63*

Early Three-Piece Suit, Late 1660s– Early 1670s

The man on the right wears the earliest version of the coat and vest that was adopted in both England and France in 1666. The coat has very short sleeves (in reality probably a little longer) that reveal his billowing shirt, and a long, fairly straight cut. It is worn with a sash at the waist. Gauntlets and bucket-topped boots complete his ensemble.

Braid-trimmed Vest and Steinkirk, c. 1690–1700

Coat decorations were often subordinate to a vest lavish with braid or brocade in contrasting colors and fabrics. He wears a steinkirk, a cravat whose long ends are loosely twisted several times and thrust through a buttonhole on the chest of a coat. His fashionable leather high-cut shoes have long tongues curling back at the ankle.

Gentleman of Quality, 1694

The man on the right is from a costume plate by J.D. de St. Jean. In the twenty years since the figures above were drawn, the coat has become more fitted to the body. Here it is worn open except at the waist, to show off the vest and cravat. Instead of a sash, this man sports a huge muff slung on a belt around his waist.

Headwear
• full-bottomed wig

Hairstyles
• shaved, under wig

Dress
• transition from doublet and breeches to coat, vest, and breeches

Upper Garments
• coat
• doublet
• shirt
• vest

Lower Garments
• breeches
• petticoat breeches

Accessories
• decorative ribbons
• gauntlets
• long cravat (steinkirk)
• muff
• sash

Footwear
• bucket-topped boots
• high-cut shoes

157

France, *1650–1780*

Early Three-Piece Suits

The first three-piece suits, adopted in the mid-1660s, consisted of a knee-length, close-fitted sleeved vest worn over wide petticoat breeches and under a looser-fitting coat of similar length. Early versions often had a belt or sash around the waist over the vest, although those soon disappeared. By the end of the 1670s, although the coat remained knee-length it was more fitted to the body and flared below the waist; the vest was slightly shorter, and the breeches narrower. Men's neckwear changed, too, from the collarlike falling band to the rectangular cravat, the forerunner of the modern neck tie. In the late 17th and early 18th centuries, French men's styles strongly influenced menswear throughout the rest of Europe.

Undress Cap

Wig-wearers shaved their heads and often wore decorative undress (i.e., informal) caps like this indoors when not wearing their wigs. Such caps might be brocaded, quilted, or embroidered; this one appears to be of white silk with floral embroidery worked in colored silk thread.

Ribbon-Trimmed Coat

In general, coats had become more fitted by the 1670s, although this one fits fairly loosely through the torso. Its fullness is gathered into stiffened side pleats below the waist. The contrasting facings on the pockets, cuffs, and front edges match the prominent trimming of ribbons on the right shoulder, a holdover from the mania for ribbon trims in the previous decade.

Full-Skirted Coat

Dating from the 1690s and probably based on a French costume plate, this fashionable man's braid-trimmed coat is open above his waist to show off a loosely tied lace-trimmed cravat and blue silk baldrick. From the waist down, his clothes are dominated by a huge fur muff hung from a brocade sash. The feather-edged tricorn hat was a new fashion at the time.

Nightgown

As an informal alternative to the three-piece suit and heavy, full-bottomed wig, men often wore loose, T-shaped robes over a shirt and breeches. Called nightgowns in the 17th century, they were comfortable and practical. This one may have been made of Chinese silk or Indian cotton chintz. It is topped off with a turban-like undress cap.

Headwear
• campaign wig
• cocked hat
• tricorn hat
• undress cap

Hairstyles
• shaved, under wig

Dress
• moving from doublet and breeches to three-piece suit

Upper Garments
• coat
• loose robe (nightgown)
• vest

Lower Garments
• petticoat breeches

Accessories
• baldrick
• belt or sash
• cravat
• muff

Footwear

Campaign Wig

There were many fashionable variations on wig styles in the late 17th and early 18th centuries; this one is a campaign wig, in which the hair is divided into three sections with one or both of the long front locks tied into a knot or caught with a ribbon.

Brocade Nightgown

This gentleman has retained his large wig, although he has shed his coat in favor of an informal brocade nightgown over his vest, shirt, and breeches. The painterly gesture with which he holds the nightgown around himself emphasizes the rich drape of the silk.

See also
Northern Europe, 1650–1700, *pages 156–57*
France, 1670–1790, *pages 164–65*

Fashionable Sash

The broad sash tied around this gentleman's hips over his coat was a fashion of the 1680s. In this image it is possible to see that his sword, hung from a blue ribbon, passes through the stiffened side pleats in his coat skirts and out through the vent at center back. His feathered tricorn is tucked under his arm rather than perched on his head.

Lavishly Trimmed Coat

This man wears a blue coat open over a gorgeous silver and gold brocade vest. The coat is lavishly trimmed with silver braid, not only on the pockets and cuffs as usual, but also around the armscye and down the sleeve and side seams. Under a befeathered cocked hat his full-bottomed wig is tossed back over his shoulders.

France, *1680–1700*

Women's Dress

In contrast to the stiff, long-waisted bodices and separate skirts of the formal styles for women in the third quarter of the 17th century, the mantua was a one-piece dress with an unboned bodice and a long, trained skirt worn caught back over a decorative petticoat. It developed in the mid-1680s from a loose, informal gown and swiftly became the prevailing style. The fontange (or "commode" in English) was a towering headdress made of wired tiers of linen or lace and ribbons that appeared in the 1680s and finally fell out of fashion in the 1710s. It was named after a Mlle de Fontange who was said to have invented it—and enchanted Louis XIV—when she tied her hair up with her garter after losing her cap while out riding one day. The fontange rose and fell in height over the years.

Lace-Trimmed Mantua, *c.* 1695

Mantuas had become formal wear by the late 17th century; this example is expensively trimmed with lace robings on the bodice, loose sleeves, and skirt, the latter swept back to reveal a petticoat covered with flounces of gold and silver lace, called *falbalas*. Her face is rather too lavishly adorned with patches—small, stiffened pieces of black velvet or silk worn by both sexes to highlight their good features, or to conceal blemishes.

Winter Town Dress, *c.* 1695–1700

This gentlewoman is in winter town dress, with a black taffeta scarf worn covering her head like a hood and concealing the bodice of her mantua. Her fontange is low, jutting out nearly horizontally. In addition to the scarf, her essential accessories include a small, beribboned muff, lavender kid elbow-length gloves, a decorative lace apron and a fan, to keep herself cool indoors and for purposes of flirtation.

Cap and Lappets

As well as wired tiers, the fontange included a cap trimmed with pendant lappets to cover the back of the head. This is Mme de Maintenon, second wife of Louis XIV, her cap trimmed with ribbon.

Hooped Petticoats, c. 1710

Both women wear hooped petticoats under their outer, decorative petticoats, which gives the mantua a wider silhouette and the bustle created by its pinned-back skirt more prominence. Although the hoops are relatively modest in size, they caused much negative comment among contemporary moralists and satirists.

Tall Fontanges, c. 1700

The Loison sisters wear their very tall fontanges pushed well back on their heads to reveal artfully arranged curls over their foreheads. Fontanges were often satirized because they made women look taller than men.

Comtesse de Montfort

The Comtesse de Montfort in undress—a striped bathrobe over an embroidered and fringed petticoat and bodice. Her fontange is of moderate height, its cap pulled forward to cover her ears completely.

See also
France and Germany, 1650–1700, *pages 154–55*
Western Europe, 18th Century, *pages 166–67*

Headwear
• cap
• scarf
• tiered headdress (fontange)

Hairstyles

Dress
• mantua becomes more formal

Upper Garments
• bodice
• bathrobe
• mantua

Lower Garments
• flounces of lace (falbalas)
• petticoat

Accessories
• apron
• elbow-length gloves
• fan
• muff

Footwear
• shoes with pointed toes

Western Europe, *1700–50*

Formal and Casual Dress

Nowadays a man might remove a garment such as his suit coat or his neck tie to mark a less formal occasion, but in the 18th century gentlemen did not, as a general rule, appear in public in their shirt-sleeves or with their collars open. The differences between formal and casual dress then often lay in the fabrics used, and how lavish the trimmings were, if any. Men commonly reserved their most lavish brocades, embroideries, laces, and velvets for the most formal occasions. However, there were also specific styles that were reserved for daytime or sporting dress only.

See also
France, 1650–1780,
pages 158–59
France, 1670–1790,
pages 164–65

◗ Frock Coat

The man in the center appears to be wearing a frock coat, which in the 18th century denoted an informal single-breasted coat with a turn-down collar and small cuffs or no cuffs at all. Frock coats first appeared in the 18th century as military and riding coats, and crossed over into general daywear soon thereafter.

Undress ◖

This *banyan*, or bathrobe, worn over a shirt and breeches is typical undress for the 18th-century gentleman; writers and artists also often chose to be painted wearing it. This man's black stockings suggest that he is a professional. Even with undress there were degrees of formality and casualness, and this ensemble is on the formal side. He is wearing a wig rather than an indoor cap, and proper shoes instead of mules.

Suit, c. 1730

The open coat and vest buttoned only at the waist offer a look at a man's shirt of the period, made of white linen and trimmed with a narrow ruffle along the center-front placket. Instead of a cravat, this man wears a stock—a stiffened fabric band that tied or was buckled around the neck, which was in fashion from the 1720s until near the end of the century.

Matching Suit, c. 1725

This man wears a matching three-piece cloth suit; its modest gold-braid trim renders it relatively informal. His coat has stiffened side pleats and is only slightly longer than his vest, and his large, turned-back cuffs, called "boot cuffs," are in the latest style.

Bag Wig and Solitaire, c. 1725

These gentlemen illustrate the front and back of the bag wig that came into fashion in the mid-1720s. The long ends of the silk bow that conceals the bag's drawstring were sometimes brought around the neck to tie in a large bow at the base of the throat in a style called a *solitaire*.

Contrasting Vest, c. 1715

This man's semiformal red silk suit, embroidered or braided in gold, contrasts with a vest of yellow satin with similar trim. The shorter coat sleeve with its deep, rounded cuff evolved in the next decade into a longer sleeve with an even deeper "boot" cuff (*see above*).

France, *1670–1790*

Male Dress with Chivalric Orders

Orders of chivalry developed in Europe during the Middle Ages. Some, like the Order of Malta, originated during the Crusades as quasimilitary religious organizations that protected pilgrims traveling to the Holy Land, or guarded a hospital or monastery. Later orders, like the Order of the Holy Ghost, were created by monarchs to strengthen the aristocracy's loyalty to the Crown as the feudal system declined. Their size was generally limited—one hundred knights or fewer was common—and their members were nobles. The Order of Saint Louis, founded in 1693 by Louis XIV, was, by contrast, an order of merit, the first of its kind. There was no limit on the number of men who could be made knights and no requirement that they be of noble rank. The process, however, was a lengthy and expensive one, as was the cost of the necessary equipment.

See also
France, 1724–86,
pages 168–69

◗ Knight of the Two Swords (reign of Louis XVI)

The lack of surface decoration on this gentleman's slender coat, short vest, breeches, and accessories shows the 18th-century evolution of men's dress towards plainness and somber colors. His striped stockings and shoe buckles are his only decorative touches.

Knight of the Hospital of Aubrac, Early 1700s ◖

The medieval Hospital of Aubrac was on a pilgrimage route through France to Santiago de Compostela in northwest Spain. The knights protected the hospital and may also have contributed financial support. This knight's insignia is the large Maltese Cross emblazoned on his coat.

Knight of Saint Louis, 1787 ◗

This plate shows the badge of the order, a gold Maltese Cross edged in white with fleurs-de-lis between the arms, suspended from a red ribbon rosette.

◗ Knight of Saint Louis (Paris, 1784)

This gentleman's excessively large fur muff, as well as his striped stockings, suggest that he was an *élégant*, one of a group of young men who tended toward fashion extremes.

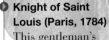

Knight of Malta, 1678

This is an early version of the male three-piece suit, first adopted in France around 1666. His breeches are full and beribboned, and his Maltese Cross badge is pinned at his waist.

Commander of Saint Louis, 1693

There were three ranks in the Order of Saint Louis: knight, commander, and grand-cross. Commanders wore the badge of the order on a red ribbon around their necks.

Knight of Saint Louis, 1693

This plate offers a rare back view of the decorative sashes, or baldricks, from which 17th-century gentlemen sometimes hung their swords. His wig, worn with one long curl knotted up, is topped by a cocked hat trimmed with braid and long ribbon loops.

Knight of the Star, Late 1680s

This probably dates to the 1680s, when vertical, button-trimmed coat pockets were especially in vogue. The flowing, curly, full-bottomed wig, feather-trimmed beaver hat, and fringed sash are equally fashionable.

Knight of Malta, 1678

This knight stands fashionably posed: right hand thrust into his coat at mid-chest and large, cocked hat tucked under his arm. His coat, which is open to below the waist to reveal a contrasting vest, has the badge of his order pinned through an unused buttonhole.

Headwear
- beaver hat
- cocked hat
- wig

Hairstyles

Dress

Upper Garments
- coat
- vest

Lower Garments
- breeches
- stockings

Accessories
- chivalric insignia
- muff
- sash or baldrick

Footwear
- buckled shoes

Western Europe, *18th Century*

Women's Dress

Several different styles of dress were worn
during the 18th century: important ones were
the mantua, the *robe à la française* and the
robe à l'anglaise. The mantua from the previous
century was in fashion until the 1730s, when
it fossilized into very formal and court dress.
It was supplanted by the robe à la française, or
sack dress, which developed in the 1720s and
remained in fashion for fifty years. The sack,
usually worn over hoops, had a flowing back
and a distinctive triangular silhouette. The robe
à l'anglaise had a fitted bodice that was thought
to set off the figure in a
particularly English way.
It was especially popular in
the mid-18th century, and
again in the 1770s and 1780s.

▶ Mantua, 1730s

The small shawl, which Racinet
called a *mantilla* and described
as a small scarf with pointed ends
that was popular in spring and
fall, obscures its bodice,
but the dress may be a
mantua, dominated by
its brocade petticoat
worn over the large,
bell-shaped hoops
of the late 1720s
and 1730s.

▶ Polonaises, c. 1776–78

The woman second from left
is drawn from an engraving
after Moreau le Jeune
entitled *Le Rendez-vous
pour Marly* of c. 1776.
She and the woman to her
right are wearing the popular
polonaise, an open robe
whose skirt is outfitted with
internal ties or hooks to
allow it to be drawn up
into three distinctive
puffs. The towering
coiffures of all four
women date them to
the late 1770s, when
hair was at its highest.

Informal Dress, 1729

Jacket and petticoat combinations were popular in the 18th century; this comes from Hérisset's *Recueil des différentes modes du temps à Paris*. The fitted, hip-length jacket is called *casaquin* in French. The fur tippet was a fashionable accessory, as was a knotting bag (knotting was popular with women of leisure).

Formal Dress, c. 1765

The sitter is Maria Louisa, wife of Leopold II, Grand Duke of Tuscany. Her dress is dominated by its silk brocade skirt, stretched over the wide hoops that were fashionable in the 1740s and remained de rigueur at court long after they were no longer worn for less formal occasions. Her stomacher is trimmed with *échelles*, a column of graduated bows.

See also
France, 1680–1700,
pages 160–61
France, 1785,
pages 170–71

Robe à la Française

This drawing shows the flowing back of the robe à la française, although it incorrectly features a gathered neckline instead of the dress's characteristic double box pleats. The robe à la française was in fashion from the late 1720s to the 1770s.

Day Dress, 1760s

This woman is a *bourgeoise*, or possibly a very fashionably dressed servant. The skirt of her gown is pinned up to reveal a contrasting petticoat, but is otherwise largely concealed beneath an apron. A yellow kerchief fills in her neckline and her forearms are encased in mitts.

Headwear

Hairstyles
• very tall (1770s)

Dress
• fitted (robe à l'anglaise, mantua) and flowing (robe à la française)

Upper Garments
• fitted jacket (casaquin)
• jacket
• open robe (polonaise)
• robe à l'anglaise
• robe à la française
• stomacher

Lower Garments
• apron
• hoop
• petticoat
• skirt

Accessories
• kerchief
• knotting bag
• mitts
• small shawl (mantilla)
• tippet

Footwear

France, *1724-86*

Military Uniform

The modern army—a national standing
force composed of regiments tied to a
leader or locale, raised and paid by the
state—developed in Europe during the
17th century. Along with the modern army
came the modern uniform. Uniforms were
initially based on civilian fashions but later
developed specific identifying styles and
color combinations that served the dual
purpose of giving soldiers a visible symbol
of their allegiance and making it easier for
them to distinguish between friend and foe
in the thick of battle. The 18th century,
when monarchs began to regard their
standing armies not just as fighting units
but as vehicles for the impressive display
of ritual ceremony and power, was the great
age of uniform development. It culminated
during the Napoleonic period, just beyond
the years illustrated here.

▶ Trumpeter

Musicians were non-
combatants, armed
with swords but not
guns. Their dress was
intended to identify
them as such in battle.
The trumpeter wears
French royal colors:
a blue-and-white
striped coat faced
in red. His tasseled,
fur-trimmed *bonnet
à flamme* is particular
to his regiment.

See also
**France, 17th
Century,**
pages 152–53

Infantry Officer and ◢
Grenadier, 1724

The mounted officer is
dressed like any infantry
officer, except for his
dragoon-style riding
boots. White became
the color of the French
infantry, beginning in
the late 17th century;
the color of the cuffs
and linings varied,
depending on
the regiment.

Grenadier and Fusilier Corporal
Not all French soldiers wore the same uniform colors, but these two are both in the popular combination of blue coat with red cuffs and collar, trimmed in white and worn over a red vest and white breeches. The long white gaiters were for parade or battle wear. The bearskin hat identifies its wearer as a grenadier.

Officer of the French Guard, c. 1757
The protective gorget around his throat and his officer's tricorn, cocked higher in front than at the back, are typical of French uniform.

Coast Guard Officer
The Coast Guard belonged to the Royal Marine Corps and wore green uniforms, here pictured as a green vest and breeches under a blue coat with green facings. The bicorn, here with a feather aigrette, replaced the tricorn as standard military headgear in the mid-1780s.

Military Wigs, 1786
Powdered wigs, with curls over the ears and a long queue, were standard military accoutrements until the French Revolution.

Headwear
- bearskin hat
- bicorn hat
- bonnet à flamme
- tricorn hat
- wig with queue

Hairstyles

Dress
- coats with contrasting trim, facings, and cuffs

Upper Garments
- coat
- gorget
- vest

Lower Garments
- breeches
- gaiters

Accessories
- aigrette

Footwear
- riding boots

France, *1785*

Fashionable Day Dress

These images all come from a plate that was Racinet's tribute to the early French fashion periodical *Cabinet des modes*. It was, according to Racinet and later scholars, the first magazine that was dedicated solely to fashion news. Its hand-colored plates covered clothing and hairstyles for both sexes, and scholars surmise that it was probably aimed at those supplying the clothes rather than those who wore them. Racinet crammed all the figures published by the magazine during its first year (October 1785–September 1786) into the plate and reproduced some of the original commentary in his text, making it a valuable record of a journal that is now scarce.

Beribboned Hat

This hat of pink taffeta with green stripes is trimmed with gauze, artificial flowers, and double-faced blue silk ribbon. The brim is bound in black ribbon and the whole is trimmed with red, pink, blue, and white plumes, and a tufted aigrette of black coq feathers.

See also
Western Europe, 18th Century, *pages 166–67*

Redingote

This fitted *redingote* (coatdress) is made of amethyst Louviers cloth (a high-quality wool fabric) accented with white buttons. The sleeves end in little cuffs of muslin or batiste, and her bodice and petticoat are of lemon-yellow taffeta. On her head is a hat à l'anglaise, its crown trimmed with a black velvet band fastened with a worked steel buckle. Her shoes match her redingote.

Grande Parure

This woman in full dress wears a bonnet of puffed gauze à la Figaro, trimmed with two white plumes and a flower garland. Her satin pelisse is trimmed with marten and conceals a blue satin dress worn over a white satin petticoat and white shoes. Her muff is of white angora.

Fashionable Young Man

He wears a round, high-crowned hat and his hair is plaited and tied into a Cadogan wig. His double-breasted frock coat is of green cloth and his vest is striped. His very tight, sulfur-colored breeches are molded to his thighs, his stockings are white with amethyst stripes, and his shoes are tied with shoelaces.

Overcoat

This man wears a wool cloth overcoat trimmed with mother-of-pearl buttons. His vest is of striped black silk strewn with green flowers and fastened with embroidered buttons, his breeches are sulfur-colored and his stockings are blue-and-white striped.

Riding Dress

This man wears a coat of dragoon-green wool cloth. The revers, pockets, and naval-style cuffs have mother-of-pearl buttons. His vest has gold and green stripes, and his riding breeches are of light yellow suede.

Wig

This man wears a Cadogan wig (popular in the 1770s and 1780s) with a bristly toupet and a bundle of hair at the back, dressed with two buckles (curls) over each ear, one above the other.

Wig

This magistrate's wig has a square crown and chestnut curls massed over the ears and tumbling down the back. The linen bands around his neck were common among the legal profession and the Protestant clergy.

France, *1780–1820*

Cashmere and Other Shawls

Shawls were the ideal complement to the lightweight, often light-colored muslin and silk dresses that dominated early 19th-century fashion. Wool shawls were beautifully warm, and their rich colors set off plain, white dresses perfectly. The best and most costly came from Kashmir, woven from *pashmina*, a rare wool spun from mountain-goat hair that is exceptionally soft, light, springy, and warm. Pashmina shawls were a must-have accessory and feature prominently in the portraiture of the period. European manufacturers were swift to imitate the Indian shawls but failed to reproduce their seductive texture and feel.

Developing Style, 1787
Despite its date, the clothing in this drawing is more in keeping with the styles of the early 19th century.

Family Group, 1800
At right, a large square shawl is worn folded diagonally. At left, a rectangular shawl is worn folded asymmetrically, showing a wedge of the center medallion near the hem of the dress, and a corner of the border folded back like a collar.

Outdoor Dress
Most cashmere shawls were quite large, but these two women dressed for outdoors are sporting long shawls that are narrow enough to be worn as scarves.

Contrasting Shawls, 1799

These are typical of the cashmere shawls of this period: large rectangles with solid central fields—often white or a rich red, green, or brick yellow—and decorative end borders woven, or sometimes embroidered, in contrasting colors.

See also
France, 1794–1804,
pages 174–75
France, 1802,
pages 178–79

Fashion Plate, 1811

Although here dated 1811, the spotted shawl worn by the figure on the left is similar to one depicted in a 1798 French fashion plate.

Evening Shawls

Shawls also accessorized evening dress, folded and draped around the shoulders or across the elbows in endless graceful ways. The togalike drapery of the shawl on the far right is very much in keeping with the period's Neoclassical taste.

Headwear

Hairstyles

Dress
• plain white or pale silk or muslin dress with contrasting shawl

Upper Garments
• Empire-line dress

Lower Garments

Accessories
• cashmere shawl
• shawl

Footwear

France, *1794–1804*

The Muslin Dress

The rise of the high-waisted, puff-sleeved, slender white muslin dress began in the early 1780s when Marie Antoinette's adoption of its precursor, the T-shaped, white muslin chemise dress, scandalized many who thought a queen should not appear so lightly dressed. But the new style of dress perfectly fitted Republican politics and the culture of the 1790s, and the Neoclassical mode blossomed. These clothes, echoing the drapery-clad sculpture of ancient Greece and Rome, were comparatively revealing, although they required proper underpinnings to maintain the fashionable shape. To preserve the illusion of nudity, some women wore tight, flesh-colored knitted stays.

Sleeve Detail

Instead of a seam, the sleeves of this dress are caught together with small clasps or buttons at intervals along the top of the arm, one of the construction techniques that were used in women's dress in both ancient Greece and Rome. The narrow twin stripes adorning the hem mimic the decoration on a Roman tunic.

Changing Waistlines

These three dresses date from 1794, 1798, and 1799 respectively. They reflect a radical change in the waistline and silhouette between the middle and the end of the decade. The robe à l'anglaise on the far left has a natural waistline and a curvaceous skirt worn over pads or a bum roll. The two others have waistlines directly under the breasts and full, yet columnar, skirts that extend to trains.

Round Gown, *c.* 1798

The fashion both for spotted shawls and for the crisscrossed ribbons decorating the bodice and long sleeves of this round gown date to about 1798. Red ribbons were known as *croisures à la victime*; they are a rather gruesome reference to victims of the guillotine during the Terror of 1793–94. This woman also carries a large *réticule* (handbag), necessary because Empire dresses were too narrow and diaphanous for pockets.

See also
France, 1780–1820, *pages 172–73*
Greece, 500–300 BC *pages 26–27*
Rome, *pages 36–37*

Low-Cut Bodice

The ball dress on the right appeared in the *Journal des dames et des modes* in 1800. In the original, although not in Racinet's version shown here, the bodice is cut so low that the wearer's nipples are (discreetly) revealed. The dress on the left is similarly styled, with a colored tunic overskirt above a white muslin skirt, but with a seemingly higher-cut neckline.

Fashion Plate, 1800

According to the original caption for this fashion plate from *Modes et manières du jour*, this woman wears a "short tunic" and a "transparent skirt." The flat slippers with ties represented Classical footwear styles. The plate, entitled "The Pretext," suggests that the need to retie a sandal provides a perfect excuse for showing off one's ankles.

Headwear
• bonnet

Hairstyles

Dress
• Empire-line dress

Upper Garments
• dress with fitted bodice (robe à l'anglaise)
• knitted stays
• overskirt
• slender muslin dress

Lower Garments

Accessories
• decorative ribbons
• handbag (réticule)
• shawl

Footwear
• flat shoes with ribbon ties

Western Europe, *1790–1815*

Men's Day Dress and Outerwear

Beginning in the mid-18th century, leadership in men's fashion shifted from France to England at essentially the same time that Enlightenment thought drew the interest of many Europeans, particularly the French, to the English social and political systems. English aristocratic life was more rural than urban, and by the end of the century the sartorial ideal of the informal English country gentleman, which for many symbolized the comparative freedom of the English political system, had eclipsed that of the French court exquisite. What we think of as classic tailoring for men developed according to this English esthetic in the period between 1780 and 1820. Its standard of a perfectly fitted body relied on breakthroughs in the art of tailoring achieved in this period.

Frock Coats, 1790s
Two different styles of frock coat—men's coats with turn-down collars and small or no cuffs that became fashionable in the 1720s—are shown here. The coat on the left fastens with one button high on the chest and slopes away toward the hem. The other is slightly cut across at the waist, a style that first appeared around 1790 and became prevalent in the 19th century. Frock coats began as informal crossovers from sporting styles, but by this time had become acceptable formal wear.

English Style, 1790s
This portly gentleman is wearing the English-style dress that swept Paris: tight-fitting coat and vest, cravat, buff leather breeches, and jockey boots. There is a degree of exaggeration in his dress—the oversized lapels of his striped vest, bulky cravat, unkempt hair, tall cocked hat, and posturing stance resemble caricatures of "Jessamies" (a contemporary term for a fop) from the 1790s. The late 18th century was a tremendous age for caricature.

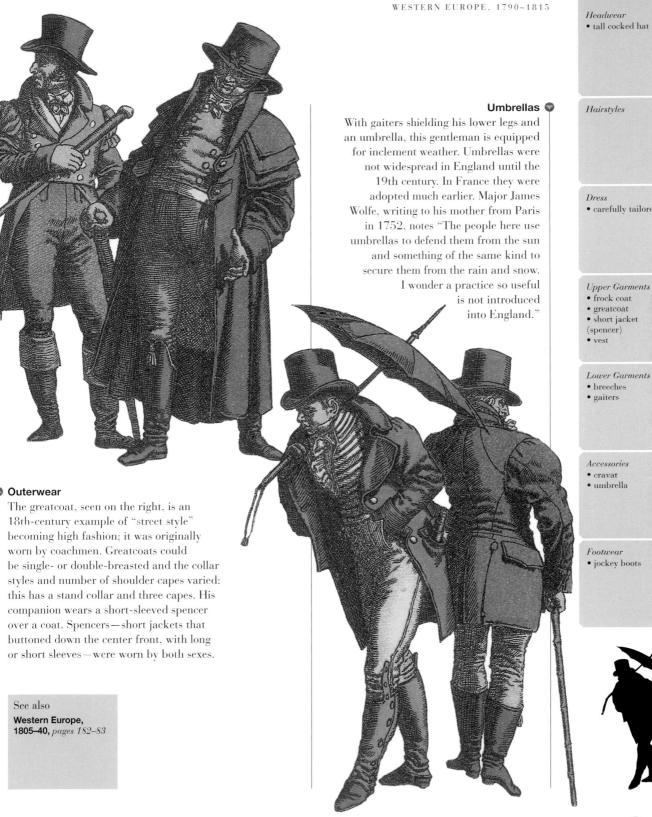

Headwear
• tall cocked hat

Hairstyles

Dress
• carefully tailored

Upper Garments
• frock coat
• greatcoat
• short jacket
(spencer)
• vest

Lower Garments
• breeches
• gaiters

Accessories
• cravat
• umbrella

Footwear
• jockey boots

Umbrellas

With gaiters shielding his lower legs and an umbrella, this gentleman is equipped for inclement weather. Umbrellas were not widespread in England until the 19th century. In France they were adopted much earlier. Major James Wolfe, writing to his mother from Paris in 1752, notes "The people here use umbrellas to defend them from the sun and something of the same kind to secure them from the rain and snow. I wonder a practice so useful is not introduced into England."

Outerwear

The greatcoat, seen on the right, is an 18th-century example of "street style" becoming high fashion; it was originally worn by coachmen. Greatcoats could be single- or double-breasted and the collar styles and number of shoulder capes varied: this has a stand collar and three capes. His companion wears a short-sleeved spencer over a coat. Spencers—short jackets that buttoned down the center front, with long or short sleeves—were worn by both sexes.

See also
**Western Europe,
1805–40,** *pages 182–83*

France, *1802*

Neoclassical Men's Dress

In the early 19th century, men, as much as women, were intent on seeing and being seen in Paris's fashionable haunts, and the Promenade de Longchamp in the Bois de Boulogne had long been such a locale. In 1886, London's *Gentleman's Magazine* deemed it one of the "universally favoured places for parading most of the pretentious outdoor vanities of Parisian society," an assessment that seems borne out by the strutting figures on this page, even though they date from eighty years earlier. All are drawn from a single fashion plate published in 1802, and together they offer a representative sampling of turn-of-the-century men's fashions. France and Britain had been at war for a decade but, save for the man in uniform, these Frenchmen have adopted the British country style. French appreciation and knowledge of English modes and fabrics received a boost in this year because British tourists, who had been unable to visit France since 1793, flocked to Paris in 1802 and 1803 during the short-lived Treaty of Amiens.

The Figure of a Man

The ideal figure for snug-fitting Neoclassical menswear was tall and well-proportioned. These styles were not kind to stout men, as the ungainly-looking gentleman in the buff breeches, red coat, and chin-swallowing cravat attests. Indeed, the *Taylor's Complete Guide* (1796) warns of the pitfalls tailors face in fitting "swag-bellied" men.

See also
France, 1794–1804, *pages 174–75*
Western Europe, 1805–40, *pages 182–83*

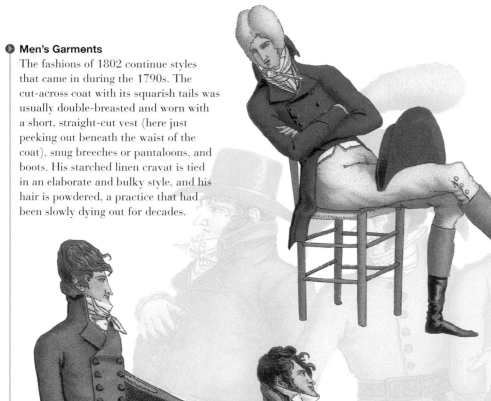

Headwear
• bicorn hat (chapeau-bras)

Hairstyles
• occasionally powdered

Dress
• English-influenced

Upper Garments
• cut-across coat
• double-breasted vest

Lower Garments
• breeches
• pantaloons

Accessories
• cravat

Footwear
• military-style riding boots (Hessians)
• top boots

Men's Garments

The fashions of 1802 continue styles that came in during the 1790s. The cut-across coat with its squarish tails was usually double-breasted and worn with a short, straight-cut vest (here just peeking out beneath the waist of the coat), snug breeches or pantaloons, and boots. His starched linen cravat is tied in an elaborate and bulky style, and his hair is powdered, a practice that had been slowly dying out for decades.

Military Style

Military styles often cross over into civilian clothes. The large bicorn (called a *chapeau-bras* in this form) carried tucked under the arm of the man on the left is of military origin, and his tasseled Hessians are distinctive military riding boots that curve up toward the knee in front. His companion is wearing top boots, a popular country style with a distinctive, buff-colored turn-down top.

Western Europe, *1805–40*

Women's Dresses and Outerwear

In 1805 women's fashions still reflected the high waists, pale cottons, slender lines, and unadorned surfaces of Neoclassicism. But during the 1810s, Classically inspired purity waned as fashion took up printed cottons and brightly colored silks and satins trimmed with puffs and frills. During the 1820s the waistline finally returned to its natural level. At the same time, both hemline and shoulderline broadened, creating a shapely hourglass silhouette.

Spencers and Pelisse, *c.* 1820

The central woman wears a pelisse, a long fur-trimmed overcoat that follows the line of her dress and shows a nascent leg-of-mutton sleeve. Her companions both wear short-waisted spencers that sport elaborate trim on the shoulders and sleeves. All three women wear Elizabethan-inspired rufflike collars.

Day and Evening Dress, Mid-1830s

The woman in evening dress, her hair in a tall, elaborate Apollo knot, wears leg-of-mutton sleeves whose width may be supported by down sleeve puffs worn underneath. Her companion dates from around 1836 and exhibits a more sloping shoulderline, emphasized by her *pèlerine* collar and her sleeves, whose fullness has slid toward the elbow.

Evening Dresses

The trim waistline at its natural level, coupled with the relatively small puffed sleeves, suggests that these dresses date from *c*. 1825–27. The woman on the right wears a "Mary Stuart" bonnet, so called because its dipped brim and wide sides recall the French hood of the mid-16th century.

Outerwear, Late 1830s

Both women wear their bonnets pushed back on their heads, revealing smooth bands of center-parted hair and ruffled caps. Mantles and shawls or scarves were popular outer garments since they could accommodate the era's large sleeves. Their full skirts are probably supported on multiple petticoats, including a crinoline, which at this period was a petticoat stiffened with horsehair.

Outerwear, Late 1820s

This woman is dressed for winter in a blue, fur-lined caped mantle and tan leather gloves. The beribboned confection perched on her head is typical of the almost comically large hats of the late 1820s that developed to accommodate the period's tall hairstyles and counterbalance the width of the sleeves.

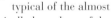

See also
France, 1794–1804,
pages 174–75

Headwear
• bonnet
• wide-brimmed hat

Hairstyles
• Apollo knot
• center-parted

Dress
• dropping waistline creating hourglass silhouette

Upper Garments
• mantle
• overcoat (pelisse)
• short jacket (spencer)

Lower Garments
• petticoat
• skirt
• stiffened petticoat (crinoline)

Accessories
• gloves
• rufflike collar
• scarf
• shawl

Footwear

Western Europe, *1805–40*

Men's Tailored Day Dress and Outerwear

English styles continued to dominate men's fashions after the end of the Napoleonic Wars. Men strove to achieve an elegance in their dress that relied as much on precise cut and fit as it did on somber colors and fine materials. There were several key developments in tailoring at this time, such as the invention of the tape measure early in the 19th century, which allowed tailors to fit clothing to the body more closely than before. The development of the "waist seam" cut for the coat, which appeared in England around 1810 and became an emblem of English style all across Europe by 1820, was also significant. Coats cut this way had short, closely fitted and lightly padded bodies and tight sleeves, and were designed to reveal, and sometimes augment, the natural curves of the body.

▶ Winter Attire, 1830–40

This man is dressed for outdoors in a long winter frock coat, gloves, and top hat. By about 1830, the frock coat had replaced the caped greatcoat, fashionable during the previous generation. Shown hanging loosely open, it masks the almost feminine silhouette—rounded chest and hips and relatively narrow waist—emphasized by the cut of his tail coat and pants.

● Caped Cloak, 1820–40

A caped cloak was a viable alternative to a greatcoat, frock coat, or paletot during the first half of the 19th century, but coats were in general preferred to cloaks. This cloak is of brown wool lined with black, with a broad black turn-down collar and revers. Walking canes, such as the one he carries in his right hand, were fashionable accessories for men throughout the century.

See also
Western Europe, 1790–1815, *pages 176–77*
France, 1802, *pages 178–79*

Pants or Pantaloons, 1830–40

Pantaloons, the tight-knitted or doeskin nether garments of the Neoclassical era, predated pants as fashionable clothing by a few years, but from about 1807 to mid-century both were worn. Pants initially were acceptable only on casual occasions, but by 1825 most men used them for general day wear, reserving their pantaloons for evening.

Frock Coat, c. 1840

The frock coat of the 19th century was different from that of the 18th century. The later version was full-skirted and cut with a seam at the waist, and could be either single- or double-breasted. It appeared in fashion in the 1810s and continued to be worn into the early 20th century.

Foot Straps, 1830–40

The combination of a black or dark coat and light pants for daywear was popular in this period; here a long-tailed black coat sets off taut white pants strapped under the instep. These pants are notched over the instep so that the shoe does not interfere with the pants' smooth line.

Headwear
• top hat

Hairstyles
• short, with long sideburns
• mustaches and occasionally beards

Dress
• English-influenced

Upper Garments
• caped cloak
• frock coat
• greatcoat
• paletot
• tail coat

Lower Garments
• pantaloons
• pants

Accessories
• gloves
• walking cane

Footwear

East and Southeast Asia

The dress of China, Japan, Thailand, and Laos shares a single common denominator: the most basic garments for men and women (the robe in China, the kimono in Japan, the upper- and lower-body wrappers of Southeast Asia) are based on a width of cloth as it comes off the loom. Bast fibers (such as ramie and hemp) were used in the earliest times and in some areas continued to be used for specific types of garments and for summer wear for the élite. Silk—the great discovery of China, approximately 5000 to 8000 years ago—was the material for the upper classes. It was also used in festival dress for commoners, and became a coveted trade commodity throughout the region and as far away as Europe. Cotton, native to South Asia, spread to Southeast Asia and China and eventually to Japan by the 17th century, where it largely replaced bast fiber in the daily clothing of the lower classes.

In China and Japan the main garment was the robe of varying lengths, with a front overlap and with either a belt or a loop-and-button closure. For warmth and modesty, multiple layers of almost identically cut robes were worn. In China, women also wore jackets and pants, either alone or under a skirt, depending on social class. In Japan, both farming men and women and the military élite wore pants, although of different styles. Dress in Japan was relatively consistent stylistically, but in China there were many ethnicities and dress varied considerably, although the dominant styles were urban Han (indigenous), Chinese, and Manchu (Manchurian) dress of the ruling Qing Dynasty (1644–1911).

Loom widths were used either untailored or cut and sewn, but fabric was never wasted. The basic elements of male dress throughout mainland Southeast Asia consisted of either wide, Chinese-style pants or a hipwrapper, worn with bare chest, jacket, or shirt. Women wore a hipwrapper (of varying lengths) or, less commonly, pants, with bare breasts or a breastwrapper. In some minority communities, women also wore a T-shaped jacket and leggings. Given the hot, humid climate in this region, minimal daily dress is not surprising. Locally produced cottons and silks were worn by the majority of the population in Laos and Thailand, but the nobility wore imported luxury textiles from India, China, Cambodia, and Malaysia.

China, *1850–1900*

Imperial Dress

Imperial dress of the Qing Dynasty (1644–1911) maintained a strict ranking system that was restricted to important court functions. The imperial court consisted of nine civil and nine military ranks, each assigned its own attire. The jeweled finial on top of the court hat and the *buzi* (a square insignia badge) attached to both the front and back of a *bufu* (court surcoat) were essential marks of court rank. Buzi depicting birds and animals indicated ranks for civil officials and military officers respectively. The court dress of female family members of a government official also corresponded to the rank of the official, and the types of bird or animal patterns, the number and posture of dragons, the color, material, and accessories were all indications of rank.

Liangmao (Summer Hat)

A low-level government official in a plain robe, accessorized with a summer hat and a fan. Summer hats were usually made of bamboo or rattan covered with silk fringes. The finial on top of his hat indicates his low court rank. Holding a fan in the summertime was customary both within and outside of the court.

Women's Court Attire

An imperial wife, adorned in court attire. Her costume consists of a *chaopao* (court robe) and *chaoqun* (court skirt). The pattern for her robe depicts a four-clawed dragon, which is called *mang* (python). The lower portion of the court skirt, exposed under the hem of the robe, is embroidered with exquisite rank-specific patterns. Smoking pipes was a widespread fashion for both male and female courtiers.

Headwear
• bamboo or rattan summer hat (liangmao)

Hairstyles

Dress
• strictly defined according to rank

Upper Garments
• court robe (chaopao)
• shoulder cape
• surcoat (bufu)
• yellow riding jacket (huang mangua)

Lower Garments
• court skirt (chaoqun)

Accessories
• court necklace (chaozhu)
• fan
• insignia badge (buzi)

Footwear

Bufu of a Military Official

This military bufu features an animal pattern that depicts rank. Rank is denoted by the *chaozhu* (court necklace), too, plus the number of eye-shaped motifs on the peacock feather attached to the hat.

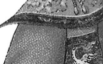

Emperor and Empress

The emperor and empress are both wearing ceremonial costume, which has a similar form for men and women and is heavily decorated with dragon patterns. The five-clawed dragon pattern is reserved for the emperor and his immediate family. The emperor's throne is adorned with a three-layered finial, indicating his majestic status as the "son of heaven."

Huang Mangua (Yellow Riding Jacket)

Only the top-ranking ministers and the emperor's relatives were entitled to wear the yellow riding jacket, which was bestowed upon the wearer by the emperor. It symbolized the highest honor.

See also
China, 19th Century, *pages 190–91*

Bufu of a Civic Official

A civic official is shown adorned in Qing Dynasty court attire, which constitutes several garments to create a layered look. The shoulder cape suits the formality of an important occasion. Underneath the bufu is a long robe with *matixiu* (horse-hoof cuffs). The bird pattern on the buzi is the mark of his position and rank.

China, *1850–1900*

Manchu and Han Women's Dress

Manchu and Han women in the Qing Dynasty had distinctive dress forms. Manchu women generally wore a floor-length robe with two side slits, which covered a pair of loose pants underneath. Skirts were an element of court dress, worn by Manchu women on rare occasions. The common dress for Han Chinese women featured a jacket (approximately knee-length, padded for winter) worn over floor-length skirts. Upper-class Manchu and Han women sometimes imitated each other's silhouettes, especially toward the mid to late Qing Dynasty. Manchu and Han women also wore different hairstyles and shoes.

Manchu Women's Dress

The Manchu woman here is dressed in a typical long robe. The soft long scarf is worn as a substitute for a collar. The robe features an asymmetrical closure, side slits, and banding around the edges of the garment. The headwear is called *dalachi* (big stretchy wing), and has a stiff board inserted to give it a horizontal shape on top.

Han Women's Dress

All of the women in the picture are wearing long jackets with asymmetrical closures. The jackets are trimmed with embroidered banding insertions. Reflecting upon the notion of modesty, the entire garment has a very copious cut to conceal the shape of the body. Headbands (*doule*) attached with flowers, worn around the forehead, were prevalent.

Headwear
• Han: decorated headband (doule)
• Manchu: board-topped headdress (dalachi)

Hairstyles

Dress

Upper Garments
• double-tabard (xiapei)
• Han: knee-length jacket
• Manchu: long robe

Lower Garments
• Han: skirt
• Manchu: pants

Accessories
• fan
• scarf

Footwear

Mamian Qun (Horse-face Skirt)

Skirts constituted part of everyday wear for Han women. The change in skirt style reflected the relatively dynamic fashion changes during the Qing Dynasty. The woman is wearing a "horse-face skirt" with a rectangular sash draped down from the waist as an integrated section of the skirt. Other popular skirt styles included *baizhe qun* (skirt with a hundred pleats), *fengwei qun* (phoenix-tail skirt), *yunlin qun* (fish-scale skirt) and *yuehua qun* (moonlight skirt).

Plain Dress

Compared to the rich, who were able to afford lavish embroideries and other trims, the relatively poor majority wore clothes with fewer embellishments. The clothes of this woman are trimmed with mostly plain banding insertions. She is holding a folded fan, which was popular among men and women as both a functional and decorative object.

Xiapei (Rosy-Cloud Cape)

Both women are adorned in ceremonial dresses consisting of a chaopao (court robe), a chaoqun (court skirt), and a *yunjian* (cloud collar). The woman to the right is also wearing a *xiapei*, which consists of two long, separate teal tabards, suspended down over the neck. The patterns on the xiapei were important symbols of court rank.

See also
China, 1850–1900, *pages 186–87*

China, *19th Century*

Dress of the Chinese Opera

During the early to mid-19th century, *Jingju* (Beijing Opera) arose and soon gained popularity with the imperial court. Beijing Opera dress incorporated elements from many older schools of Chinese opera, such as *Kunqu* and *Yiqiong*. The costumes come in five general categories: *mang* (python robe for royal families or high-ranking officials), *pi* (casual robe with a symmetrical neckline for the upper class), *kao* (stylized form of armor), *zhe* (casual robe, usually with a slanted neckline), and *yi* (varied forms symbolizing special roles). These forms reflected various roles and they function as a visible mark of social hierarchy. There are four corresponding types of headgear: *guan*, *kui*, *mao*, and *jin*. The chief roles are *sheng* (main male role), *dan* (female role), *jing* (painted-face male role), and *chou* (male crown role).

Kao Qi (Armor Flags)

Four triangular flags are attached to the back of the armor, which indicates that the character has been fully equipped for battle. The use of the flags originates from the command flags of ancient military officers. The design of these flags usually matches the color of the armor and features dragon-pattern embroidery. The character's movements are enhanced by the motion of the flags, which adds to the drama of battle scenes.

Qing Military Armor

Sleeveless, multilayered armor includes symmetrical units to protect vital body parts. The helmet is made of either leather or metal materials and divided into many sections in order to provide full protection all around the neck. The ornaments on top of the helmet, the materials used, and the embroideries on the armor signify different military ranks. Embroideries feature animal or plant themes.

Yunjian (Cloud Collar)
Adapted from everyday women's dress, the yunjian (cloud collar) is a cape attachment worn over the shoulder. The yunjian is used in Chinese opera to express the formality of the occasion and to enhance the beauty of the female role. It is often embroidered and trimmed with fringes.

Female Armor
Female armor is similar in shape to the male armor, but displays more vivid colors and decorative trim, such as fringes and many soft streamers hanging down from the lower portion of the armor. Female armor depicts a phoenix pattern. The matching headgear is decorated with two colorful features. Female *ying kao* (hard armor) also uses armor flags.

Headwear
• ornamental helmet

Hairstyles

Dress
• hard armor (ying kao)
• soft armor (luankao)

Upper Garments
• military armor
• cloud-collar cape (yunjian)

Lower Garments
• skirt
• pants

Accessories

Footwear

Japan, *19th Century*

Standard Dress

The standard dress for both men and women in Japan in the 19th century was the kimono, called a *kosode* in the premodern era. This robelike garment was tied at the waist with a sash (*obi*). For formal or outdoor activities, the split skirt (*hakama*) was worn by men of the warrior class (*samurai*), and leggings (*kyahan*) by men and women while traveling or doing physical labor. A short coat (*haori*) added warmth and protected the kosode fabric from the weather. Outdoors, both sexes wore raised wooden clogs (*geta*) when streets were muddy. Alternatively, thong sandals (*zori*) of a variety of materials, or straw sandals (*waraji*), could be worn, depending upon the formality of one's dress. The feet could be protected additionally by split-toed socklike covers (*tabi*).

Fireman in Street Dress

This young man is dressed for cool weather, with a padded haori over layers of kosode. The markings on the haori make it appear to be a deerskin fireman's jacket for formal wear by a samurai. This man wears white tabi and wooden geta.

See also
Japan, 19th Century, *pages 194–95*

Samurai

During the Edo Period (1615–1868), society was divided into four classes, each with distinctive clothing: warriors (samurai, the highest), farmers, artisans, and merchants. Here, three samurai wear kosode with hakama. Two have hunting helmets; all carry swords at the obi. Tabi are worn with zori. Their garments would generally be of silk, wool, or ramie (a plant fiber), but leather and cotton coats were also worn.

Middle-Aged Samurai

A samurai wearing kosode tucked into hakama, belted by an obi, sports a typical male hairstyle with shaved pate and a double-looped twist to his oiled hair. The hakama has two sets of elongated ties. Both sets are wrapped around the body and tied in front. A sword (*katana*) is secured at the man's waist by being inserted through the obi.

Buddhist Priest

The priest wears a formal robe (*koromo*) over a *kesa*, a vestment sewn from patches of used clothing. This is a long rectangular piece that wraps around the body and over the shoulder, and is knotted at both ends through a ring. His skirt (*mo*) reveals that he wears tabi and geta. He carries a bag (*atozukegori*) for texts and personal effects.

Pilgrim

A pilgrim wears a bamboo hat (*ajirogasa*), a kosode, and obi, usually of ramie, the sleeves of the kosode tied out of the way with a tasseled cord. He has leggings (kyahan) and waraji sandals. He uses a staff to aid his journey and to startle insects to prevent them from being crushed. Lay people wore this costume, its uniformity uniting all classes in their faith.

Warm-Weather Clothes for a Townsman

In the premodern era, shaven hair was indicative of a lay Buddhist priest, but in the Meiji Period (1868–1912) men began to shave their hair short as a sign of modernity. This man carries a bamboo hat (ajirogasa) and wears a kosode, haori, obi, tabi, and geta. He is dressed with few layers and light fabrics for warm weather, and carries a decorated fan.

Headwear
• bamboo hat (ajirogasa)
• hunting helmets

Hairstyles
• short, crown shaved

Dress
• layered garments

Upper Garments
• formal robe (koromo)
• leather and cotton coat
• robe (kosode)
• short coat (haori)
• vestment (kesa)

Lower Garments
• leggings (kyahan)
• skirt (mo)
• split skirt (hakama)

Accessories
• bag (atozukegori)
• sash (obi)

Footwear
• clogs (geta)
• split-toed socks (tabi)
• straw sandals (waraji)
• thong sandals (zori)

Japan, *19th Century*

Women's Dress: Kosode

The kimono with a small sleeve opening, in the premodern era called a kosode, was standard outerwear for women of all classes by the beginning of the Edo Period (1615–1868). The kosode evolved from an undergarment first used in the Heian Period (794–1185), and eventually worked its way to the surface as costume styles developed, becoming the primary garment by the end of the 15th century. The woman's sash (obi) progressed with time from a narrow belt tied at the hips in the 15th century to a wide brocade panel tied at the waist in the late 18th and 19th century. To complement the wide obi, kosode fabric of the 19th century was often patterned with plaids, stripes, or small repeat patterns woven or dyed over the entire surface, or there might be motifs at the base of the skirt or the lower edges of the sleeves.

Samurai Woman
Samurai women's outfits were assembled from the same components as those of women of all classes. What distinguished the samurai wife's clothing was the quality of the fabric, which was often silk or ramie patterned and colored with expensive dyes and techniques, sometimes incorporating metal-wrapped threads.

Street Wear
The kosode was a flexible garment, soft enough to tuck up into the obi for walking out of doors, or allowing multiple layering in cold weather. A haori (short coat) was worn over the kosode to guard from the elements. Like men, women wore geta or zori (wooden clogs or thong sandals) for walking out of doors, and went barefoot or wore tabi (foot covers) indoors.

Headwear
• square cap for children

Hairstyles

Dress
• layered garments

Upper Garments
• knee-length jacket (haori)
• kimono with short sleeve openings (kosode)
• kimono with long sleeve openings (furisode)
• under kimono (nagajuban)

Lower Garments

Accessories
• sash (obi)

Footwear
• clogs (geta)
• split-toed socks (tabi)
• thong sandals (zori)

Merchant-Class Woman

Checked, plaid, or striped kosode became fashionable in the late 18th century, when government rules about dress restricted the showiness of townspeople's apparel. Townspeople (*cho-nin*) included members of the artisan and merchant classes, who ranked low in the official class system of warrior, farmer, artisan, and merchant.

See also

Japan, 19th Century,
pages 192–93

A Mother and Child

By the time of this illustration, women were wearing Western make-up, and no longer shaved their eyebrows or blackened their teeth, as would have been done in the Edo Period (1615–1868). Under her kosode, layered with a haori, this woman wears one or more under-kimono (*nagajuban*) for warmth. Her baby's kimono is also layered for warmth, and he wears a squared cap.

Young Women

Kosode with long sleeve openings (*furisode*) were worn by single women, seen most easily here on the dancer. The patterns for tying obi varied with fashion and the age of the wearer, but the underlying principle remained that the older one became, the less elaborate the method of tying.

195

Laos and Thailand, *19th Century*

Male and Female Dress

Racinet illustrates a mix of social classes and professions, generally taken from mid-19th-century photographs. Both Lao and Thai clothing were primarily based on an untailored loom-width, wrapped around the loins or the upper body in a variety of distinctive ways depending on social status, geographic origin, or ethnicity. Garments were held in place by knotting, tucking, metal belts, or, sometimes, interlocking metal buttons or fabric loops and ball buttons. In contrast to daily dress, the formal attire of royalty and dancers was elaborately embroidered with gold thread (often stiffened with thick paper to form fantastic shapes). It was embellished with precious stones (royalty) or glass imitations (dancers), and used lavish lengths of silk (imported for royalty, domestically woven for dancers). The multitiered metal headdresses are made of gold and gemstones for royalty, base metals and glass for dancers.

Lao Woman

From Muang Payap in northern Thailand, this Lao woman wears a typical Lao hipwrapper (*phasin*) divided into three parts: a waistband or "head," a midsection or "body," and a border or "foot." The wearer steps into the phasin, which is sewn into a tube, then folds the sides to the front, forming a diagonal line. The waistband is folded over a narrow, fringed belt just visible under her basket.

Thai Dancer

She wears a high headdress and a tight-fitting, long-sleeved, metallic brocade bodice under stiffened epaulets embellished with couched metal embroidery and glass stones. A long rectangular skirt (*chongkraben*) is pulled between her legs and tucked into a belt; a brocaded sash hangs down in front. She wears metal fingernail extensions.

▷ Laotian Interpreter

This drawing was taken from a photograph of Alévy, the Laotian interpreter of the Mekong Exploration Commission, 1866–68. He wears a short, boxy silk-satin jacket with metallic trim and an asymmetrical, shaped extension over an ankle-length silk phasin (hipwrapper), and a headscarf tied at the nape of his neck.

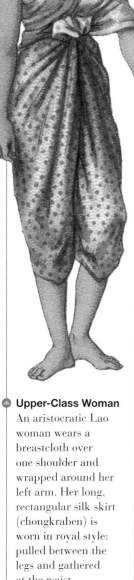

△ Upper-Class Woman

An aristocratic Lao woman wears a breastcloth over one shoulder and wrapped around her left arm. Her long, rectangular silk skirt (chongkraben) is worn in royal style: pulled between the legs and gathered at the waist.

Wife of King Rama IV ◁ of Thailand

From a photograph taken in 1862, the queen wears a gold-brocaded shouldercloth, a belt held with an elaborate buckle, and a silk hipwrapper of *mat mii* (weft threads resist-dyed before weaving), incorrectly painted in the plate. The close-cropped hair on the crown of her shaven head was a mid-19th-century court fashion.

197

South Asia

South Asia comprises the modern countries of India, Pakistan, Bangladesh, Sri Lanka, Nepal, and Bhutan. Racinet and Hottenroth focused primarily on the costumes and cultures of India, Pakistan, Bangladesh (collectively called the Indian Subcontinent but known then as "Hindustan"), and Sri Lanka ("Ceylon"), as these regions were under the dominion of European powers. During the 18th and 19th centuries these regions were the subject of research and reports by numerous scientific and military expeditions (primary preoccupations of colonial overlords at that time), and were visited by many soldiers of fortune.

As evidenced by the wealth of sculpture and painting from ancient sites in this region, many costume elements still in use find their origins in the unstitched and draped textiles of South Asian antiquity. One of the earliest and most famous examples is a steatite fragment that was excavated at the city of Mohenjo-Daro (2600–1900 BC) in Pakistan, depicting the torso and the head of a priest or king wearing a trefoil-decorated cloak draped over his left shoulder. Techniques of textile manufacture and embellishment have also been in use for hundreds of years. For instance, on the walls of the famous 5th-century AD cave complex at Ajanta in Maharastra, India, elegant women are depicted wearing garments made of ikat-dyed fabric. Vibrant ikat textiles are still produced in India in the states of Gujarat, Andhra Pradesh, and Orissa. Adding to this rich indigenous legacy were innovations brought in over the centuries by various groups seeking refuge or riches in this vast region. Among these were the Sakas (Scythians), nomadic horsemen who entered the Subcontinent c. 88 BC, who introduced tailored and stitched garments in the form of tunics and baggy pants.

Many elements of attire worn in South Asia share a common design source. However, the terminology that is used to describe the garment, its cut, material and decorative embellishments can vary according to the region, the community, and the socioeconomic status of the individual wearing it.

South Asia, *16th–18th Century*

Royal Attire

In the 12th century, Central Asian modes of dress were introduced to the Indian Subcontinent by Turkic and Afghan sultans. Under the Mughals, the use of tailored elements became more widespread. Emulating the ruling Mughal élite, this attire was adopted (and adapted) by many Rajput princes, Deccan sultans, and their retinues. During the 16th century the Mughals' economic resources, cultural wealth, and courtly grandeur surpassed that of their contemporary rivals, the Safavids and Ottomans. The Mughal royal family wore elegant attire produced by the most skilled dyers, weavers, gold and silver embroiderers, and tailors.

Prince Murad Baksh

Shah Jahan's son is shown wearing the *patka*, an unstitched, long band of the finest cotton or silk that was wrapped around the waist. The patka was folded or knotted in front, allowing for decorative end pieces to be displayed. These sumptuously embellished textiles were often given as a gift of honor by the ruler to court nobles.

See also
India, 16th–19th Century, *pages 202–03*

Emperor Akbar (r. 1556–1605)

The *jama* was a cotton or silk long-sleeved outer garment worn in the Mughal, Rajput, and Deccan courts. Consisting of a snug-fitting upper portion attached to a waisted, gathered fabric, it fell knee-length or longer. The front consisted of two panels crossed one over the other and fastened near the armpits. The outer tie cords often took the form of elongated decorative fabric strips.

Emperor Jahandar Shah (r. 1712–13)

Jahandar Shah holds a turban ornament (*sarpech*) and wears another tucked into the folds of his turban. An indispensable symbol of royalty, the sarpech was a stemmed, featherlike gold plume that was embellished with pearls and gemstones. The European aigrette was influenced by the sarpech.

Headwear
• turban

Hairstyles

Dress
• elegant, elaborately woven and embroidered layers

Upper Garments
• long-sleeved outer garment (jama)
• shirt (nima or kurta)

Lower Garments
• drawstring pants (pyjama)

Accessories
• aigrette (kalgi)
• sash (patka)
• turban ornament (sarpech)

Footwear

Emperor Jahangir (r. 1605–27)

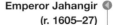

Jahangir wears a nearly transparent fine cotton shirt, or *nima*. Eventually the *kurta*, a variation of this garment, became more popular. A slightly loose-fitting shirt with a round or narrow collar, the kurta is worn above or below the knee.

Sultan Muhammad Adil Shah of Bijapur (r. 1627–56)

Here a decorative aigrette (*kalgi*) made from the black occipital feathers of a male gray heron (*Ardea cinerea*) is worn. To accentuate the backward-curving profile of these plumes, pearls were often attached to their ends, serving as elegant weights.

Emperor Humayun (r. 1530–56)

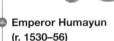

This distinctive turban was initiated by the emperor and was worn only during his reign. Similar to the felt-brimmed hats still worn in parts of Central Asia, Humayun's turban comprised a tall cap with vertical gores and a wide upturned brim with pointed segments. A narrow length of fabric was wrapped around the brim, then crossed and tied near the crown.

Emperor Shah Jahan (r. 1628–58)

Revealed under the emperor's diaphanous jama is the *pyjama*. Pyjama is a generic term for cotton or silk pants that are gathered and fastened at the waist with a drawstring. They are cut in varying styles and worn by both men and women.

India, *16th–19th Century*

Women's Dress

The tradition of *purdah*, the seclusion of women from public gaze, was practiced at the Mughal, Deccan, and many Rajput courts. Within the confines of the palace, the only men who were allowed to visit a woman were her husband and direct blood relatives. Because of this, portraits of royal women were idealized, as court artists typically were not given access to these subjects. However idealized their facial features may be, South Asian women depicted in paintings still provide evidence of the costume elements and accessories that they wore. Racinet's illustrations give us indications of the abundant use of ornaments worn. Their materials and styles varied according to socio-economic status and regional or ethnic origin.

Shawl Washer

Worn by both men and women, the most famous shawls were woven in Kashmir. The most precious of these were made of tapestry-woven fine wool, often embellished with fine needlework. As Kashmiri shawls were coveted by fashionable French and English women, imitations were produced in Europe. By 1870, use of the Jacquard loom caused the collapse of the traditional Kashmiri shawl industry.

See also
South Asia, 16th–18th Century, *pages 200–01*

Mahratta Woman of South India

This upper-class woman's ensemble is enhanced by ornaments. Her gold and gem-set jewelry includes a three-part head ornament, circular and semicircular plaques representing the sun and moon respectively, and earrings with pendant, dome-shaped elements. On her nose is a septum ring and a nose ring.

Mughal Woman

A favored pendant worn around the neck by Muslim men and women is the *ta'wiz*, an amulet made of a thin slab of gold, silver, or stone. Considered by many to have an apotropaic function, ta'wiz were typically inscribed with verses from the Qur'an. The *haldili* was a specific type of jade ta'wiz often inlaid on both sides with gemstones set in gold.

Mughal Woman

A Mughal woman stands holding a wine bottle and a diminutive jade cup. She wears a *farji*, a sleeveless or short-sleeved coat worn by men and women. As depicted here, the collar was often trimmed or lined with fur. Her fan- or crownlike hat (influenced by Persian headgear) was worn by women and small children of the court.

Mughal Woman

In the Subcontinent many women wear a veil cloth that drapes over the head and falls over the upper body. The materials used to produce them are varied, from gossamer silk and cotton, to wool. One distinct type, the *chunri*, is a red bridal veil that is dyed, printed and heavily embellished with silver and gold embroidery.

Woman from the Court of Gingy in Karnataka

In antiquity, South Asian women did not wear upper garments, but instead draped a length of cloth over their breasts. Versions of the *choli*, a midriff-baring blouse, appear in the early centuries AD, probably influenced by foreign costume fashion. In the 19th century Christian missionaries persuaded South Indian women to wear cholis.

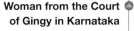

North, West, and Central India, *19th Century*

Men's and Women's Dress

As the illustrations for this group are from Hottenroth's publication, the costume colors cannot necessarily be trusted. For example, the image of the Maharaja of Dholpur was originally a black-and-white engraving published in a Dutch travelogue of 1874, and so we must imagine what the color of the maharaja's sumptuous *choga* (a loose, sleeved, outer garment of Turkic origin, made of soft wool, silk, or velvet and richly embellished with embroidery) really was. The composition is also problematic as the retainer's turban does not match the style in use at the Udaipur court; its exaggerated curved profile is reminiscent of contemporary Maratha fashion at the Gwalior court.

Banjara of Western India

The Banjara are nomads descended from the original gypsies of antiquity. The man wears an *angarki* (a short version of the *angaraka*) and a typical loosely bound turban comprising rolled and wound cloth. The woman wears a necklace (*mala*) of large silver disks (*jhalara*).

Maharana of Udaipur and Retainer

Both men wear the same outer dress (angaraka), but the design and material are of differing quality, appropriate to their status. Wrapped around the retainer's waist is a *kamarband*, a broad sash that protected the lumbar region and provided the inspiration for the Western formal-wear element, the cummerbund.

Woman of Western India

This Gujarati or Rajasthani woman wears a *bandhani* skirt and head covering. Bandhani, meaning "to tie," refers both to the technique (pinching up, tying and resist dyeing) and to the finished cloth. Bandhani work is used to embellish many articles of cotton and silk clothing in India.

Storekeeper from Northern India

This man wears a simple cotton angaraka, a long-sleeved overgarment closely related to the jama but with a fairly high waist and a distinct central oval opening. An inner flap provides a covering for the chest opening. The finest cotton and silk angaraka were embroidered or brocaded with delicate decorative motifs.

Parsi Man, Rajput Woman, and the Maharaja of Dholpur

The Parsis are adherents of the ancient Persian Zoroastrian faith who, in the 8th century, took refuge in India to avoid persecution. Until the 20th century, Parsi men wore the distinctive *phenta* hat, made of glazed, printed cotton on a wicker substructure. Although the origin of the phenta's tall shape is unknown, the lower portion was probably based on the wound-cloth turban.

See also
South Asia, 16th–18th Century, *pages 200–01*

Headwear
• turban
• wicker and cotton hat (phenta)

Hairstyles

Dress

Upper Garments
• long robe (angaraka)
• loose, sleeved robe (choga)
• short robe (angarki)

Lower Garments
• skirt (bandhani)

Accessories
• necklace (mala)
• sash (kamarband)

Footwear

South India, *19th Century*

Men, and Women's Dress

Archeological finds at the Fustat graves in Egypt include numerous South Asian cotton fragments attributable to the 15th century. Embellished with hand-drawn, painted, stamped, and resist-dyed decoration, they are nearly identical to fabrics still worn in Sindh in Pakistan, and in Rajasthan, Gujarat, and Tamil Nadu in India. The Tamil women depicted here wear saris embellished with a stamped, wax-resist, dyed design in imitation of tie-dyed cloth. Racinet's source for some of these illustrations was a group of watercolor paintings, *c.* 1800–25, by an unknown artist in Pondicherry. Paintings by local Indian artists of emperors, rajas, and members of various ethnic, social, and occupational groups were commissioned by Europeans and assembled in presentation albums, providing documentary research or a memento of their visit to the Subcontinent.

See also
India, 19th Century,
pages 208–09

Astrologer and Brahmin Priest of Tamil Nadu with their Wives

One of the traditional forms of dress in India is the *dhoti*, a length of unstitched cloth that is wrapped around the hips, pulled up between the legs and tucked into the waist. Dhoti styles vary according to region and community. In Tamil Nadu the garment is called *veshti* and is made of a length of cloth approximately 15 ft (4.5 meters) long.

Headwear

Hairstyles

Dress
• draped and
wrapped garments

Upper Garments
• coat
• draped whole body
garment (sari)

Lower Garments
• draped, tucked lower
garment (dhoti, veshti)
• narrow, skirt-like
garment (lungi, sarem)

Accessories
• long, shawl-like
wrap (angavastram)

Footwear

Rajas of Karnataka and Tamil Nadu

Two rajas wear elegant coats of brocaded cloth. One of the most heavy and sumptuous brocades is *kinkhab*, produced in Varanasi and other Indian centers, including Ahmedabad and Hyderabad. Kinkhab cloth is made of fine, flattened gold or silver wound around a core of strong silk fiber (*mukta*). To enhance the metal's color, gold is wound over yellow silk, and silver over white silk.

Jewel Merchant

The *angavastram* is a long scarf or shawl-like wrap that can be worn many ways. Angavastram are made of fine wool or silk embellished with decorative end panels, of white cotton with a simple border for Brahmin priests, or unadorned for farmers and manual laborers, who wear them over the shoulder as a sweat towel.

Laborer from Pondicherry

The *lungi* is an unstitched length of cotton (or silk for festive occasions) draped around the waist and falling like a narrow skirt. For manual labor, lungi are usually pulled up and tucked into the waistband. In Tamil Nadu, the garment is called *sarem* and is worn only by men.

207

India, *19th Century*

Women's Dress

One of the quintessential garments associated with South Asian women is the sari. Lengths of unstitched cloth are wrapped around the lower half of the body, then draped over the torso or head. The longest saris measure approximately 26 ft (8 meters). Before the Industrial Revolution, all saris were woven by hand. In the 18th century, the finest and most expensive muslin saris included the *jamdanis* of Dacca (in Bangladesh) and the *shallu* of Chanderi (Madhya Pradesh, India). Famous centers for the production of silk saris have traditionally been Benares (modern Varanasi), a center of fine textile weaving for at least 2000 years and famous for figured, kinkhab-brocaded silks; and Kanchipuram, where wide-bordered Kornard saris were produced. The goldsmith's wife depicted here wears a sari bearing the "temple" motif—a border of triangular or serrated forms.

Bharatanatyam Dancer

This dancer wears a distinctly South Indian silk ensemble. The skirt's *pallu* (the patterned end) is folded in one or more fishtail-shaped and pleated gathers (*thalliappu*). A folded textile (*thavani*) covers her blouse and is tucked in at the waist. Around the dancer's waist is a beautiful gold belt (*oddiyanam*). Her accompanist wears a typical Tanjore turban and plays a pair of finger cymbals (*natuvanga*).

Jewish Woman from Cochin

Based on a mid-19th-century photograph, this woman wears a long-sleeved chemise under an open-front *entari*, similar to contemporary Ottoman-influenced attire or that in North Africa and the Middle East. As depicted here, Jewish (also Muslim and Christian) women in this region adopted the Hindu custom of wearing *tali* or *mangalsutra*, a necklace signifying married status.

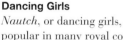

Goldsmith's Wife

A jeweler's wife holds a tube displaying bangles available for purchase, and wears a curved upper armlet (*vanki*). South Asian bangles have been made of diverse materials, including shell, and ivory. Colorful glass bangles are worn by all classes of women and traditionally represent *suhagan*, or happily married women with healthy children.

Dancing Girls

Nautch, or dancing girls, popular in many royal courts of India, often wore *churidar* ("banglelike"), a type of narrow pyjama gathered above the ankles. Their upper garment was the *peshwaz*, an open-fronted, full-skirted, high-waisted gown. Peshwaz were made of superior-quality muslins so diaphanous that they were given poetic names including "white of the jasmine flower" and "cloth of the morning dew."

See also
South India, 19th Century, *pages 206–07*

Banjara Woman

Banjara were known as grain and goods transporters. This woman wears a full skirt or *ghagra* made of straight or pointed, gored fabric that falls to the mid-calf or ankle. Her ghagra is embellished with resist-dyed or woven stripes and a border of stitched red cloth. Banjara women often adorn the ends of the ghagra drawstring and of their headcloths with cotton or wool tassels, and cowrie-shell and coin pendants.

Headwear
• turban

Hairstyles

Dress
• draped and pleated garments

Upper Garments
• chemise
• folded overwrap (thavani)
• open-fronted gown (peshwaz, entari)
• sari (jamdanis, shallu)

Lower Garments
• full skirt (ghagra)
• narrow pyjama pants (churidar)

Accessories
• bangles
• gold belt (oddiyanam)
• necklace (tali or mangalsutra)

Footwear

Sri Lanka, *19th Century*

Women's and Men's Dress

Until the 16th century, when the Portuguese established control of Ceylon (modern-day Sri Lanka), its inhabitants wore draped, unstitched garments similar to those worn in India. A typical ensemble for both sexes included a wrapped white lungi or *comboy*, a veil cloth (*tiraya*) and sometimes a belt or sash (*pattiya*). Aside from the tiraya, women did not wear upper garments or a blouse. The patterned clothes depicted here may represent textiles of Indian origin, or alternatively, the less expensive British reproductions of Indian fabrics available during the 19th century.

Mudaliyar

Mudaliyars were village headmen whose high rank was either hereditary or conferred by the governor. On state occasions, Mudaliyars wore a dark, knee-length, European-style frock coat with gold buttons and gold-worked buttonholes over the traditional comboy. A wide embroidered sash was worn over one shoulder with an ornamented short sword tucked into the lower end.

> See also
> **South India, 19th Century,** *pages 206–07*

Kandyan Noble

Kandyan kings wore large pillow- or saucer-shaped hats with ends that turned up slightly. Emulating this fashion, upper-class Kandyan men wore a large, circular, slightly more shallow version of this hat, in black or white. As depicted here, Kandyan noblemen often wore the comboy in a more traditional manner, without a shirt or jacket.

Novice Buddhist Monk

Sri Lankan Buddhists adhere to the Theravada ("School of Elders") tradition that emphasizes monastic life as the ideal for spiritual achievement. Novices and fully ordained monks wear the same attire as the Buddha: three unstitched pieces of draped cloth (*tricivara*). During the rainy season, the umbrella was no doubt of importance.

Sailor

For centuries, Sri Lanka played host to merchants, sailors, and others who took advantage of the island's strategic position and hospitality. Among these were Arabs and Malaysians who wore their own distinctive costume. In the 19th century, Arab men often wore the fez, a high, brimless felt hat, while Malay men wore a loosely wound cotton turban.

Buddhist Monk

The three prescribed Buddhist monastic garments are the *antaravasaka*, an inner cloth worn almost down to the feet; the *uttarasanga*, a long upper garment that covers the antaravasaka; and the *sanghati*, a shawl worn in cool weather. Ideally, the monk's modest ensemble would be made of discarded cloth or rags; however, simple plain cotton fabric is also appropriate.

Sinhalese Woman

During the 19th and early 20th century, many Sri Lankan women wore a hybrid European and Sinhalese costume in preference to the traditional sarilike *osaria*. The long-sleeved, midriff-covering blouse (*canezou*) worn by this middle-class woman includes Dutch-influenced lace collars and cuffs. Her lower garment could be a skirt or a comboy.

Sinhalese Man from the Coastal Region

Another hybrid costume type brings together a short, white, European jacket and a round-collared shirt tucked into a comboy. The comboy is a traditional garment worn by Sri Lankan men and women, made from a long piece of cotton or silk cloth that is wrapped around the waist and hangs down to the ankles. Typically, this fabric was imported from India.

Headwear
• high felt hat (fez)
• saucer-shaped hat
• turban

Hairstyles

Dress
• mixture of traditional styles, with European influence

Upper Garments
• draped, whole-body garment (osaria)
• frock coat, jacket
• long-sleeved blouse
• monk's attire (tricivara)
• shirt

Lower Garments
• wrapped skirt (comboy)

Accessories
• belt or sash (pattiya)

Footwear

Anatolia, Persia, and Central Asia

Anatolia was the homeland of the Ottomans (r. *c.* 1280–1924), whose territories at their greatest extent included the Balkans, the Levant, Hijaz, and North Africa. Their neighbors and sometimes enemies were the Persian rulers of the Safavid (r. 1501–1732), Afsharid (r. 1736–95), Zand (r. 1750–94) and Qajar (r. 1779–1924) Dynasties. Bordering the Persians to the north were the independent kingdoms of Central Asia. The attire worn by men and women in these regions share common features that ultimately originated in Central Asian prototypes: a shift or a shirt over baggy pants, a series of short or long robes, and lengths of cloth worn as a sash and a head covering. With European contact, members of the court added western clothing (frock coats, pants, collared shirts, and so on) to their wardrobe. These fashions were emulated by the middle class, who often combined European clothing with traditional dress.

Paintings by contemporary court artists provide a rich resource for the study of dress in these regions. Beginning in the 17th century, the accounts of European travelers to the Ottoman, Persian, and Central Asian courts were published. Although these are also important resources worthy of study, as they contain descriptions and engravings of local costume, the narrative sometimes reflects the authors' prejudice if they perceived their host country to be populated by the curious or strange. Additionally, the illustrations are not always wholly reliable, as some costume elements were misunderstood.

Because access to upper-class or royal women was typically prohibited (as in the Mughal court), their portraits were not authentic. Unable to find Muslim women willing to model, European artists and photographers visiting Istanbul employed female residents of the European quarters (Galatea and Pera) to pose for them in Ottoman clothing. In the Persian court, the first accurate representations of royal women and their costume are found in photographs taken by the Qajar ruler Nasir al-Din Shah (r. 1848–96), an enthusiast of the art form and the only man with total access to the harem.

213

Anatolia, *16th–18th Century*

The Ottoman Court

Under Ottoman rule, turbans and ceremonial headgear provided a way of distinguishing court hierarchy according to a person's rank and status. Compared with the elaborate headgear and opulent textiles worn by Ottoman sultans, their personal ornaments were more modest, consisting primarily of turban ornaments (*sorguç*) with the plumes of rare birds, and belts made of linked ivory or mother-of-pearl plaques inlaid with gold and encrusted with turquoises and cabochon rubies. Among the sources for Racinet's images of Ottoman court dress was a portrait of Sultan Süleyman I ("The Magnificent") by Melchior Lorichs. Lorichs accompanied the Habsburg embassy on a visit to Istanbul in the late 1550s and may have observed the sultan at close hand. "Woman in the Home" was based on a Louis Daret illustration published in Nicolas de Nicolay's mid-16th-century travel account.

Woman in the Home

Women of the Ottoman court wore a loose chemise fastened at the neck (*gömlek*) and pants (*şalvar*) under a fitted gown with short sleeves (*yelek*). Always included in a bride's trousseau were high wooden shoes (*kub kob*) with silver and mother-of-pearl embellishments that were worn in the bathhouse.

Janissary (Elite Military Corps) Leader

Robes of honor (*khil'at*) were given by the sultan to high-ranking members of the Ottoman court when they achieved special merit or were promoted. A particular ceremonial robe (*merasim kaftanı*) featured slits at the shoulders through which the arms would pass, and floor-length sleeves that hung ornamentally at the back. As depicted here, one of the favored textile designs was an ogival lattice.

Headwear
• high felt hat (keçe)
• mesh face cover
• tall cap
• veil (yaşmak)
• women's cap (hotoz)

Hairstyles

Dress
• elaborate and hierarchical

Upper Garments
• ceremonial robe (merasim kaftanı)
• chemise (gomlek)
• cloak (feridje)
• kaftan
• robe of honor (khil'at)

Lower Garments
• pants (salvar)

Accessories
• belt
• turban ornament (sorguç)

Footwear
• high wooden shoes (kub kob)

Janissary and General

On the left is a janissary wearing a high felt hat (*keçe*) with a long, rigid pendant cloth. The central ornamental element was most commonly crafted from gold-plated copper (*tombak*) and included a design of granulated gold and gold wire. When more mobility was needed, the janissary could pull the corners of his kaftan up and tuck them into his waistband.

Sultan Süleyman I (r. 1520–66)

The sultan's kaftan may have been made from *seraser*. The most opulent and prestigious of all Ottoman silks, seraser fabric was almost entirely covered with gilt-metal or silver threads. The finest grade was called *has ul-has* or "purest of the pure." Only the sultan and those he permitted were allowed to wear it.

See also
Anatolia, 19th Century, *pages 216–17*

Woman Outside the Home

Worn with the *feridje* was a veil (*yaşmak*) draped over a tall cap (*hotoz*) and a horsehair mesh face cover. Influenced by European fashion in the 18th century, Ottoman women began to wear brightly colored feridje with large collars. Because these styles were considered inappropriate for Muslim women, imperial edicts soon forbade them for Ottoman women.

Anatolia, *19th Century*

Istanbul, Bursa, Yozgat, and Manisa

Racinet's source for illustrations of Anatolian peoples and those of the greater Ottoman Empire was the 1873 publication *Les Costumes populaires de la Turquie*, featuring the photographs of J. Pascal Sébah. Costume details and colors were derived from "les modèles en nature" displayed at the Musée du Costume, Paris, in 1874. Bursa was one of the most important centers of weaving in Anatolia, providing textiles for the clothing and furnishings of the Ottoman court. Syria, for centuries a major center of cotton and silk weaving, also provided textiles for the garments and headdresses of Anatolia. The most prized textiles were the striped, floral, and ikat silk textiles of Aleppo that were exported to other parts of the Ottoman Empire.

See also
Anatolia, 16th–18th Century, *pages 214–15*

Woman of Istanbul (Constantinople) Attired for the Home
Istanbul and Anatolian women wore şalvar, loose, voluminous pants gathered at the ankles. Another indispensable item of clothing worn by both sexes was a sash (*kusak*) made of silk or wool. Also worn here are *pabuş*, slippers of velvet or soft goatskin that were often embellished with embroidery.

Armenian Bride
She wears a diadem of white flowers, a flowing veil and a gold-thread face cover. Anatolian bridal ornament varied according to the community, region, and economic status of the wearer. Real or faux flowers often adorned the bridal headdress and are still worn by some married women.

Middle-Class Man of Istanbul
Racinet notes that this man's costume is devoid of European elements. He wears a long, loose outer garment, the *djubbe* (also known as the *gallibiya*, *dishdash*, according to region), worn by men from North Africa to South Asia. In keeping with this traditional attire, he wears a wound-cloth turban over a short felt cap.

Headwear
• conical felt hat (fez or tarbuş)
• felt cap
• thread face cover
• turban
• veil

Hairstyles

Dress
• accessorized, layered robes

Upper Garments
• chemise
• fitted gown (entari)
• high-necked robe (qumbaz)
• long robe (djubbe, gallibiya or dishdash)
• shirt, short jacket (mintan, salta)

Lower Garments
• loose pants (salvar)

Accessories
• belt
• diadem
• sash (kuşak)

Footwear
• ankle boots (mest)
• high boots (basmak)
• slippers (cedik or pabuş)

Turkish Bride from Bursa

Many women (and men) in Anatolia and Ottoman-controlled regions wore the entari, a front-opening fitted gown worn over a chemise or shift. This bride's floral and striped brocade entari and şalvar reflect French influence. Her sleeved short jacket (*mintan*) is embellished with embroidered metallic-thread motifs.

Kurdish Woman from Yozgat

Although a prototype for this enormous headdress was not found, it reflects the widespread use of a felt fez (or "tarbuş") worn as a base for myriad wrapped and draped textiles. Her belt fastener, a cast or repoussé plaque of silver or silver gilt with a central boss and pendant chains, reflects those worn by Kurdish women in Anatolia and Syria during the 19th century.

Kurdish Man from Yozgat

The cut of this man's garment looks similar to the *qumbaz*, a high-necked, long-sleeved garment popular in 19th-century Syria and other parts of the Levant. Under the robe, men wore salvar tucked into the tops of *basmak* (high boots) or gathered at the ankle when wearing *mest* (light, thin-soled ankle boots) or *cedik* (slippers).

Man from Manisa

In the 1830s, Ottoman civil servants were required to wear the fez. Subsequently, European costume elements were incorporated into their attire and later adopted by the general populace. Here, a hybrid costume is worn: Turkish şalvar, kuşak and fez; a European-inspired collared shirt and a short jacket (*salta*).

Persia, *18th–19th Century*

Men's Dress

The traditional costume for men included pants, a long shirt bound about the waist with a sash, a sleeved overcloak, and a hat or turban of cloth, felt, or lambskin. Undergarments were usually made of cotton; however, silk could be worn by the wealthy. Lower undergarments consisted of *libas* and *zir shalvar*, and over the torso, the *pirahan*, a long undershirt. Of importance were *khalat*, robes of honor given by the shah (often from his own wardrobe) to meritorious persons or honored visitors.

Periodic attempts to modernize and compete with the West were represented by European fashions introduced during Qajar rule. This is first apparent in the new style of military uniforms influenced by French and subsequently British military advisors that were engaged to organize and train Qajar forces in the first half of the 19th century. During Nasir al-Din Shah's reign (1848–96), western-style clothing, such as double-breasted overcoats and pants was introduced.

Mullah
A Muslim religious scholar and member of the orthodoxy sits reading a holy text. His large overcloak is the *aba*, or *abayeh*, a baggy, sleeveless cape-like mantle, originally the attire of Arab Bedouins. In cold weather, handwoven heavy wool aba are worn, with lighter materials used in the summer. His black turban indicates that he is a *sayyid*, a descendant of the Prophet Muhammad.

Two Dervishes
The seated figure may represent Nur 'Ali Shah (d. 1797), leader of the Ni'matallahi Sufi order. His high cap is made of triangular fabric segments that are quilted and embroidered. The dervish standing barefoot wears a woolen *qaba* (robe) and carries a *kashgul*, or begging bowl. His head is partially shaved, as was the style for many men during the Qajar period.

See also
Persia, 18th–19th Century, *pages 220–21*

Headwear
• hat or turban
• kulah

Hairstyles
• full beard and mustache sometimes worn partly shaved

Dress
• mixture of native and European styles

Upper Garments
• coat (farji)
• double-breasted overcoat
• long undershirt
• outer robe, fur lined (katibi)
• robe (qaba), of honor (khalat)
• sleeveless mantle (aba or abayeh)

Lower Garments
• pants (salvar)

Accessories
• sash

Footwear

Man Smoking a Water Pipe (Qalyan)

A tall *kulah* of black lambskin was the favored Qajar hat up to about the mid-19th century. Robes, or qaba, were fastened by decorative froggings and later by buttons. Qaba that cross over the chest and fasten on the side (as depicted here) were also worn during the Safavid period. Noblemen often wore robes made of *tirmeh*, a sumptuous brocade with *butah* (paisley) motifs, a speciality of Kirman.

Persian Noble

This noble's robe includes a long, full fur collar (made of sable, ermine, or marten) that drapes over both shoulders. His headwear evokes the white turban with floral trim over a domed felt base worn during the Zand period (1750–90). The full beard was also popular during this time, culminating in the extremely long beard worn by Fath 'Ali Shah Qajar (r. 1798–1834).

Musician

Although robes might be cut in a similar fashion, their material was appropriate to the social status and financial means of the wearer. *Katibi* were a type of fur-lined outer robe. Knee-length versions of this gathered robe were worn over pants by attendants at Nasir al-Din Shah's court.

Persia, *18th–19th Century*

Women's Dress

Although not originally a Persian custom, during many periods in history purdah, the seclusion of women from public gaze, was observed. Women's clothing was defined primarily by whether it was to be worn in the home or outside. Further differentiation was made according to status or ethnicity. Reflecting varied ranks and duties, members of the royal household often wore distinctive colors, costume, and headgear. The dress and ornaments of immigrant and tribal populations also reflected great diversity. Women of the Safavid and Qajar courts often wore layers of solid-colored textile or a heavily patterned brocaded short robe (*ziri qaba*) under their outer robe (*ruyi qaba*).

See also
Anatolia, 19th Century,
pages 216–17

Young Ilyates Woman from Veramine

Women often wore a short jacket lined with cotton *qalamqar* textiles or woolen shawl pieces. It had a tailored waist, a peplumlike flare over the hip, and long sleeves that extended over the hand in a point. It was worn over a collarless diaphanous blouse.

Woman in a Chador

Outside the house, women wore the *chador*, a large cloth that covered the body from head to foot. The fabric chosen for the chador depended upon the woman's social status. During the Qajar period, upper-class women wore black satin chadors. As depicted here, the separate long, lightweight linen or cotton face veil (*rubandeh*) could be gathered up and folded back or on top of the head.

Woman from Trebizond

This woman wears a short jacket with braided decoration similar to those worn in Anatolia and the Balkans. During the Qajar period, women wore a short jacket (*yal*) in the home. Around her hips is a large wool or cotton scarf with repeated rows of a woven or printed butah motif.

Young Ilyates Woman from Veramine

In the late 18th and 19th centuries, women wore long skirts or wide pants. *Naqsh* (Persian for embroidery) was used to refer to pants made of a heavily embroidered fabric. Woven textiles with floral motifs within diagonal stripes have also been identified as pants fabric due to their similarity to naqsh designs. This woman may be wearing a *qalamkar* cotton cloth to cover her coiffure.

Woman Smoking a Water Pipe (*Qalyan*)

This woman wears a fur-trimmed *kurdi*, a short-sleeved version of the ruyi qaba coat that was often made of silk brocade. As shown here, henna was a popular type of cosmetic embellishment for the skin. Typically, henna was applied to the hands on the palms and fingers (and sometimes up to the wrists), and to the soles of the feet and the toes.

Armenian Woman from Julfa

Typically women's ruyi qaba were designed with a straight front opening. This robe may have been made of a rich velvet edged with brocaded silk and lace. Under her qaba, this woman may have worn *shalvar*, loose-fitting pants that narrowed at the ankles. Women's slippers were worn flat or with a short heel or wedge, and often featured pointed, upturned toes.

Headwear
• veil (rubandeh)

Hairstyles

Dress
• a mixture of fitted and draped garments

Upper Garments
• collarless blouse
• draped whole-body garment (chador)
• outer robe (ruyi qaba)
• short jacket (yal)
• short robe (ziri qaba)
• short-sleeved robe (kurdi)

Lower Garments
• embroidered pants (naqsh)
• skirt
• pants (shalvar)

Accessories

Footwear
• slippers

Central Asia, *18th–19th Century*

Buryats, Kirghiz, and Kalmucks

Central Asia has been the home of many nomadic, seminomadic, and sedentary Eurasian peoples, and was strategically located along many of the Silk Road trade routes. For the study of textiles, Central Asia can be very generally grouped into two areas, with ethnocultural relations to either the Turkic or Mongol peoples. Turkic peoples included the Kirghiz, Uzbek, Turkomen, and Kazakhs. Among the Mongolic peoples were the Buryats and Kalmucks. Many of these peoples shared basic costume types and cuts: the use of wide-legged pants tucked into felt or leather boots, a blouselike undergarment, belted upper garments (the *khalat* or *kaftan*), and a headdress. Certain centers or peoples were known for their specialized textile production. Ikat, made in Samarkhand and Bukhara, was renowned, while the Kirghiz and Kazakhs were known for their felted lambswool cloth.

Buryat Women

Buryat outer robes (*del*) were worn with the upper side folded over the front and fastened under the sleeve. The cut of a Buryat woman's robe consisted of sleeves gathered at the shoulder and a flared skirt attached to the bodice. A sleeveless long or short jacket was often worn over the robe. Buryat belts were made of leather in the western region and of silk in the east.

Kirghiz Women

Kirghiz women wore a shirt (*beldemchi*) of plain or patterned velvet, ikat, or striped fabric, often embellished with a fur trim. Another distinctive costume element was a fine, netlike veil made of colorful woven threads, worn over the headdress of brides, or on special occasions. After the birth of a second or third child, the veil was no longer worn and was packed away.

Kirghiz People

Taar is the Kirghiz word for handwoven textiles made from camel, sheep, or goat wool. The most prized taar were produced from wool shorn from a camel's neck and humps. Khalat made of camel hair were worn as part of the groom's wedding costume. Camel hair was also mixed with silk thread to produce *agar*, a particularly fine textile.

See also
Anatolia, 16th–18th Century, *pages 214–15*

Kalmuck Man

A Kalmuck man turns aside the edge of his khalat to reveal an ikat cloth lining. Ikat textiles were also used for the face of Central Asian khalats and other costume elements. In the 19th century, many Central Asian ikats were weft-faced tabby weaves. Velvet ikats were also worn; one of the finest of these types was woven in Bukhara with a limited production from about 1850 to 1910.

Headwear
• veil

Hairstyles

Dress
• rich layers

Upper Garments
• long robe (kaftan, khalat)
• outer robe (del)
• shirt (beldemchi)
• sleeveless jacket

Lower Garments
• wide-legged pants

Accessories
• belt

Footwear
• felt or leather boots

European Regional Dress

At the time when Racinet and Hottenroth produced their books, the traditional dress of Europe was fast disappearing as rural populations shrank and urban ones grew, and the Industrial Revolution made inexpensive cloth and information about fashion widely available. Traditional dress is antithetical to the restless, changing, individualized expression of fashion; it seeks rather, through markers of cut, color, fabric, embellishment, and the use of specific garments, to pinpoint a wearer's station within a community.

Traditional dress tended to be local rather than national, serving to locate its wearer within a specific community and generally making use of local materials that could be easily made or procured. It also clearly marked and reinforced the divisions of groups within society— one's dress indicated whether one was a matron or a maiden, a young man or an old one. It was special-occasion dress, worn only on Sundays and feast-days, or for important community rituals such as marriages. Girls often made the garments they would wear as adults as parts of their trousseaux; such clothes were treated with great care, and were generally worn until they were worn out.

Although traditional dress was never completely static, change was generally quite slow. Some of its components, like the basic tunic (that is, the shirt or chemise) had been essential components of European dress since ancient times, but many others derived from clothing that was fashionable at one time and was retained by communities when fashion moved on.

In general, the earlier in time that a particular garment appeared in European dress, the closer it is worn to the skin, as newer garments tended simply to be layered on top of what already existed. Traditional dress was also sometimes shaped by earlier sumptuary legislation that had restricted the wearing of certain materials, colors, or garments to certain classes: in Poland, for example, peasants were forbidden to wear red until the early 19th century, but as those laws relaxed red appeared in traditional dress, beginning as a narrow stripe that gradually grew wider and wider until whole garments were made of the formerly prohibited color.

Scandinavia

Sweden

Regional dress in the Scandinavian countries represents a fusing of old and new styles. The plates chosen by Racinet to illustrate the distinctive regional dress of these countries were primarily drawn from studies made in the 19th century. The fashionable dress of this period has a noticeable influence upon these costumes, but certain features can be traced back to the 15th, 16th, and 18th centuries. Features of all these periods can be found in each piece of the regional dress of Sweden. In addition to its historical ties, Swedish regional dress also reflects that of its neighboring countries, in particular the styles found in Norway.

Dalarna Clockmaker
This man's costume features Sweden's distinctive knitted footless stockings. His bare feet would have been wrapped with straw and cloth to keep out the cold. The regional dress of Dalarna may be the most conservative in Sweden: his belted doublet-style jacket and loose breeches echo the 17th century.

Peasant Woman from Dalarna
This woman from the Dalarna region wears the peasant costume of central Sweden. Her jacket has a thick, warm wool trim and the bodice and skirt of her dress are attached slightly above the waist. Her apron, unlike those worn for more ceremonial occasions, is simply trimmed with ribbon.

Married Couple
Similar to Norwegian *bunads* (folk costumes), the gentleman wears high-waisted pants with leather trim and a short jacket. The woman's scarf head-dress, or *kulla*, is made of a large square of starched cotton, folded into a triangle and tied carefully around the head to create a distinctly angular style.

Headwear
• felt cap (picklehua)
• various headdresses (flickhuchkal, klut, kulla)

Hairstyles

Dress

Upper Garments
• double-style jacket
• short jacket
• vest

Lower Garments
• apron
• footless stockings
• loose breeches
• skirt
• pants
• wide-bottomed stockings

Accessories
• sash

Footwear
• cloth and straw foot wrappings

Engaged Couple from Skane

Here the gentleman wears a short jacket, matching vest and breeches, and a shirt with a high starched collar. He clutches a felt cap, possibly the *picklehua* or cap constructed of four pie-shaped pieces. His companion wears the *flickhuchkal* (headdress). In many Scandinavian cultures, headdress signifies a woman's marital status—the one worn here was for unmarried women.

Couple Exchanging Marriage Gifts

Demonstrating another distinctive tradition in Swedish knitting, the lady's stockings are knitted wide at the bottom. This unusual design creates a kind of slouchy fold at the ankle and, contrary to its unfashionable appearance, was considered a sign of wealth and prestige.

See also
Scandinavia,
pages 228–29

Married Woman from Dalarna

The distinctive *klut* headdress signifies that this woman is married. It is constructed of white starched linen over a lightweight framework. Her sash and jewelry bear religious symbols, marking this ensemble as one reserved for ceremonial occasions and feast-days.

Scandinavia

Iceland and Norway

The regional costumes of Iceland and Norway owes much to revivals of national romanticism. In Iceland, the Viking roots of regional dress can be seen in the embroidered motifs worked in rich metal threads that ornament the bridal costume. The cloth seen in the traditional dress of Iceland is almost universally constructed from homespun wool, and black predominates due to the lack of dyeing resources. The late 19th century in Norway saw the widespread adoption of the dress of the Hardanger region as the "national" costume. The distinctive differences in dress throughout the country were later documented and preserved by the National Council for Folk Costumes.

Icelandic Headdress

The curved headdress worn by this Icelandic woman is built on a cloth turban and constructed of white linen stiffened with pins. For bridal costumes, it is decorated with precious-metal thread embroidery featuring Viking, and sometimes Celtic, motifs. Around her neck she wears an embroidered velvet ruff, which is fastened with metal clasps at the front.

Bridal Costume of Norway

The bride (*right*) wears a high, ornate crown and gilded jewelry. The tradition of wearing gilded silver jewelry during important rites of passage is closely linked to Norway's folkloric tradition. Worn to ward off underworld creatures (*huldrefolk*), silver and gilded silver jewelry is an important part of baptismal, matrimonial, and other ceremonies in Norway. Additional gilded silver ornaments can be seen on the streamers hanging from the bride's belt.

Traditional Woman's Dress of Finnmark, Norway

This woman wears the traditional high cap of the Sámi people, many of whom live in Finnmark, in northeast Norway. The crestlike shape is supported by a hollow wooden frame. Her ornate belt and embroidered collar are worn with an animal-skin coat, most likely made of reindeer.

Costume of the Hardanger Region

This Hardanger woman has a sleeveless bodice over a linen or cotton blouse. A piece of beaded and embroidered cloth is inserted between the bodice and blouse. The padded *fedla* (headdress) signifies that she is married. The man's costume (leather breeches, embroidered vest, and homespun greatcoat) is more closely related to the style of the 18th century.

Traditional Man's Dress of Finnmark, Norway

This Sámi man is also wearing a large coat of animal skin. His red cloth cap, trimmed with fur for warmth, is a familiar item of Sámi regional dress.

See also
Scandinavia,
pages 226–27

The Netherlands

From Zuid-Holland to Friesland

In villages and remote areas, where fashion news spreads more slowly, fashionable dress of years past may be worn well after it has become outdated in the more sophisticated urban areas of a country. Often, only the details of the trend that are deemed attractive or important are copied. In countries such as the Netherlands, where sudden surges of immigration occurred, the regional dress is also affected by a melding of cultures and traditions. Echoes of the regional dress of Austria and Scandinavia can be seen in the examples chosen by Racinet to illustrate the dress of the Netherlands. And, like other western European countries, the Netherlands owes the preservation of its regional dress to the national romanticism so popularly embraced in the 19th century.

Couple from the Province of Zuid-Holland

This 19th-century couple from the city of Gouda in Zuid-Holland (South Holland) demonstrates the influence of the 18th century upon the regional dress of the Netherlands. The lady wears a round, flat-brimmed hat called a *bergère* over her *hul*, the traditional white cap worn throughout most of the southern provinces in this country.

Women from North and South Holland

On the left, a native of Katwijk is dressed in the fashionable style of the time, her *bellen*, or small metal ornaments that are attached to a metal cap underneath her headdress, are the only visible sign of regional influence. The woman from Volendam (*right*) wears a skirt constructed in two contrasting fabrics, a style that is still seen in regional dress of the Netherlands today.

Zeeland

Men's regional dress in Zeeland, one of the southernmost provinces of the Netherlands, can be readily identified by the use of two large metal buttons, or *stikken*, to fasten the front flap of their breeches. The young woman wears a fitted bodice over a printed cotton blouse and full skirt. She wears the *oorijzer*, or metal cap, from which the bellen and other metal ornaments are suspended, under her close-fitting cap and straw hat.

See also
Scandinavia,
pages 228–29
Germany and Austria,
pages 234–35

Noord-Holland and Friesland

The bodice of this bride from Marken in Noord-Holland (*far left*) is laced up the front and would have been embellished by seven embroidered roses on the back as a symbol of fertility. Her costume shares much in common with the bridal costume of the women of Voss in Norway. A couple from Friesland are shown on the right. The enduring influence of 18th-century fashionable dress can be seen in the woman's full, wide skirt that echoes the silhouette of the panniered robe à la française.

Headwear
• embellished metal cap (oorijzer)
• round hat (bergère)
• white cap (hul)

Hairstyles

Dress
• 18th-century influence

Upper Garments
• blouse
• bodice

Lower Garments
• stikken- (button-) fastened breeches
• wide skirt

Accessories

Footwear

Scotland

Evolution of Regional Dress

The earliest accounts of Scottish regional dress date to the 16th century, describing a cloak made from a long length of particolored or striped wool. The "plaid," as this would come to be known, would change in shape and use throughout the next few centuries. The color and design of the fabric would develop into tartans unique to each clan of the Highlands, unifying their members through cloth. Practical accessories such as the sporran, or pouch, were added to the costume. The tartan was then pleated and controlled by belts and stitches. Today's regional dress of Scotland represents the evolution of this simple garment into an ensemble with ties to family, rebellion, and, above all, national identity.

Sinclair and Colquhoun
This woman of the Sinclair clan wears a scarf or length of plaid of about 3 yards over her head and gown, a style that was adopted in the early 17th century. To her right, a member of the Colquhoun clan is dressed in trews, or closely fitting pants, constructed from a single piece of tartan.

Ogilvie
The breeches worn by this member of the Ogilvie clan represent a fashionable alteration to the trews brought about in 1745, when Prince Charles Edward Stuart led the Jacobite rebellion against England.

See also
Post Roman Empire,
pages 42–43

Headwear

Hairstyles

Dress

Upper Garments
• belted, draped plaid (filleadh mór)
• bodice
• doublet
• large, draped mantle (arisaid)
• long cloak or shawl (plaid)

Lower Garments
• breeches
• close-fitting pants (trewa)
• skirt

Accessories
• belt
• pouch (sporran)

Footwear

MacIntosh

Following the Battle of Culloden in 1746, many of the rebel clansmen and chiefs found refuge in the court of their supporter in the Jacobite Rising, King Louis XV of France. This member of the MacIntosh clan demonstrates the melding of fashionable and regional dress brought on by this exile.

Robertson

Dressed to attend the French royal court where King George II's proscription of Highland dress could not affect him, an exiled chief of the Robertson clan shows his loyalty to his clan through his tartan. The influence of court fashion can be seen in his red-heeled shoes and short beribboned doublet.

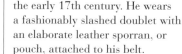

Skene

The *filleadh mór*, or belted plaid, is shown here on a chieftain of the Skene clan dressed in the style of the early 17th century. He wears a fashionably slashed doublet with an elaborate leather sporran, or pouch, attached to his belt.

Arisaid

The earliest form of women's dress in Scotland was the *arisaid*, a large, unsewn length of fabric that extended to the heels. Made of undyed wool with stripes, it secured around the waist with a long belt, often adorned with silver. This woman displays the predominant dress before the 17th century, wearing a skirt of striped wool and a sleeved bodice.

Germany and Austria

Baden-Württemberg, Bavaria, Sachsen, and Tyrol

The dress traditions of Germany and Austria have much in common. From the materials used in their construction, such as leather and felted wool, to the language used to describe the regional dress of these countries, their similarities are apparent. This interchange of cultural traditions is not merely due to their geographical proximity, but owes a great deal to the shifting political borders that affected both these countries. In Germany, especially, changes in the shape of the country can be seen from the time of the Roman Empire through to the late 20th century. The influence of eastern European dress traditions as well as those of Italy and Scandinavia can all be seen in the regional dress of Germany and Austria.

▶ Southern Tyrol

Now part of Italy, the area known as Sarnthal or Sarntal was once part of the larger Tyrolian region. Shown here is a man dressed in *lederhosen*, or leather breeches, with green damask suspenders. His jacket, or *joppe*, and *brustfleck* (stomacher) are both of red wool.

▶ Bavaria

The woman on the right is dressed in everyday costume with a red cotton fichu, or *einstecktüchl*, printed with flowers. Her *mieder*, or bodice, is laced up the front. In later years, this ribbon lacing would be replaced with *geschnür*, or chain lacing, affixed with decorative hooks. Her companions are dressed more formally, having exchanged their colorful einstecktüchl for white ones trimmed with lace and embroidery.

Northern Tyrol

In the valley of Ziller, located in the northern Tyrolian region of Austria, pants made of leather, or loden, a feltlike woolen fabric, are found. Shown here wearing a vest without suspenders, this man sports a black felt hat with a *scheibenbart*, or bunch of feathers, affixed at the crown. The woman on his right is from Auhertz, which is now part of the Czech Republic. She wears a pleated skirt that is supported by padded petticoats.

Sachsen

On the left, a woman from Altenburg in Saxony wears traditional dress dating back to the early 18th century. On her right, we find the more fashion-conscious dress of a woman of Leipzig. She wears the fashionable silhouette of the 19th century with a more traditional headdress of black, stiffened lace.

Baden-Württemberg

Although the *bollenhut*, with its flat brim and collection of large black or red pom-poms on the top, may be the most familiar of women's hats in the Baden-Württemberg region, it is only worn in select areas of the Black Forest. Shown here is a woman wearing a large black silk bonnet over her carefully braided hair.

Switzerland

Women's Festival Dress

The costumes most often seen as reflecting the spirit or taste of a nation are those that are reserved for feast-days and religious celebrations. This is the case in Switzerland, where regional dress has grown out of the practical necessities of the peasant class as well as the desire for ostentatious display embraced by the wealthier urban classes. Witness the ceremonial role of regional dress in Appenzell Innerrhoden, where the *schlappe*, or fan-shaped bonnet, was worn by married women on specific religious holidays or on special occasions such as the weddings of their children. Today, the regional costumes of Switzerland are worn on Trachtentag, a day dedicated to the preservation of Swiss traditional costumes.

Lucerne

The regional dress of Lucerne is rich in accessories with religious symbolism. This woman from Lucerne wears a *deli* around her neck—a pendant of worked silver featuring a miniature of a religious subject. The small bonnet at the back of her head is the *capudüshli* and, with a nod to fashionable dress of the 18th century, she carries a bergère in her hand.

Saint-Gall

Women's dress in the canton of Saint-Gall remains fairly consistent throughout the region. It comprises a full skirt and apron, a fitted overbodice or corselet, and a full-sleeved blouse. The primary differences between the three regions of this canton can be seen in the amount of embroidered work on the bodice and the type of headdress worn. Shown here is a woman from the Toggenbourg region, whose small, winged headdress is reminiscent of the schlappe worn in Appenzell.

Zurich

Interest in the regional dress of Switzerland grew during the late 18th century as the romanticism of an escape to the Alps drew more visitors. Small books featuring images of dress from each region, such as this woman's dress from Zurich, became popular souvenirs.

Headwear
• bergère hat
• bonnets of various
types (capudüshli,
schlappe)

Hairstyles

Dress
• fitted bodices and
full skirts

Upper Garments
• blouse
• bodice insert (plastron)
• corselet
• long-sleeved jacket
(schlotte)
• overbodice

Lower Garments
• apron
• skirt

Accessories
• pendant (deli)

Footwear

▶ Neighborly Influences

Aspects of regional dress in many countries may reflect that of their geographical neighbors. Illustrating this, the influences of the regional dress traditions of Italy can be seen in this woman's ensemble from one of the southern cantons of Switzerland.

See also
Italy, *pages 238–39*

▲ Zug

A pleated collar of wool lace adorns the blouse of this woman from the canton of Zug. Her bodice is laced over a black silk plastron, or bodice insert, which is heavily embroidered. Underneath her apron, the top of her skirt features horizontal stripes of blue and yellow, a color combination consistent throughout the region.

Appenzell ◀ Innerrhoden

The smallest canton in Switzerland, Appenzell Inner-rhoden is also distinctive for the ceremonial headdress worn by married women, the schlappe. Her long-sleeved jacket, called the *schlotte*, is also a feature unique to the region.

Italy

Regional Dress from Rome to Milan

The origins of Italian regional dress can be traced to the time of the Renaissance, when Italy was at the center of the fashionable world. The dress in courts throughout Europe reflected an Italian influence, and artists such as Albrecht Dürer painted themselves wearing the fashions of Italy, using their clothing to identify their art with that of the revolutionary Italian artists. From the fashionable silhouette to details such as embroidery and tailoring techniques, Italian fashions were mirrored everywhere. In Italian regional dress of modern times, design details such as bodices and doublets with separate, laced sleeves worn over full shirts recall the style of Renaissance Europe.

**See also
Italy, 1450–1500,**
pages 106–07

Rome
Wearing close-fitting breeches and a matching jacket, this gentleman of Rome displays a calculatedly casual air. His overlarge shoe buckles and use of sumptuous materials, such as silk and velvet, betray a close attention to the details of dressing.

Rome
Part of the same tableau as the figure far left, these gentlemen provide an excellent view of the silk netting they wear at the back of their heads. Worn underneath the large brimmed, sugarloaf-style hat, these nets encase their long hair, leaving only a single curled lock visible over one ear.

Venice
This peasant woman wears a pleated lace-trimmed shawl, similar in style to the Spanish mantilla. Her dress is simple, made of wool and trimmed with ribbon at the hem.

Padua

A bodice is worn over the *camisa*, or full white shirt with large, voluminous sleeves. Her skirt may be part of this oversized garment. The ornaments that hold her hair are similar to those that would fix the *tovaglia*, or folded linen headdress, in place.

Loreto

The long cap, or *gorro*, is worn with a suit of matching vest and jacket.

Loreto

A simple kerchief is folded into an impressive headdress. The *fascelete*, or neckerchief, is draped over the shoulders and might be fixed with a brooch at the waist.

Umbria and Milan

On the left, a woman from Umbria wears a headdress of layered starched linen. Over her camisa she wears detachable sleeves, a sleeveless dress, and an embroidered apron. The woman to her right, from Milan, has sleeves attached with ribbons and her tabbed bodice is fitted by lacing in the back.

Rome

Costume in Rome, the Eternal City, draws inspiration not only from the Renaissance but from its earlier history as well. The sashes and neckcloths of these two men recall the draped togas of the Roman Empire. They are worn with single- or double-breasted jackets and breeches.

Headwear
- folded headdress (tovaglia)
- hairnet
- long cap (gorro)
- sugarloaf hat

Hairstyles

Dress
- neat, fitted clothing

Upper Garments
- bodice
- doublet
- jacket
- pleated shawl
- skirt (camisa)
- sleeveless dress
- vest

Lower Garments
- apron
- breeches

Accessories
- brooch
- neckcloth
- neckerchief (fascelete)

Footwear
- buckled shoes

Spain

Aragon, Castilla y León, Catalunya

The themes of color and surface design play important roles in shaping the traditional dress of the Spanish people. The colors most commonly observed change from region to region. In one region, such as Catalunya, blue may dominate both men's and women's costume while in others red is more likely to be seen. The use of embroidery and appliqué also differs throughout the regions. In the following examples from Aragon and Catalunya, there is little use made of these types of surface decoration. In Ávila, however, the use of appliqué in women's skirts is an important element of their design. The use of metal-thread embroidery features prominently in the dress of Salamancan women.

Aragon

The woman's traditional headcovering of a white scarf is worn pulled down to her shoulders in this example of regional dress in Aragon. She wears a full woolen skirt and fitted velvet bodice, with an embroidered scarf wrapped around her shoulders and fixed at her waist with a brooch or pin.

Catalunya

The short jacket, called a *marsille*, is paired with matching velvet breeches in this man's ensemble from Catalunya. He also wears *alparagatas*, or shoes laced around the ankle and up the leg, over his white stockings. A pair of buttoned leather gaiters is worn over these.

Castilla y León

In Salamanca, women wear the *dengue*, a scarflike cape that is elaborately embroidered front and back. Adding to this splendid display of needlework is a velvet apron embroidered with gold thread and with a wide silk band at the hem. The skirt is embroidered in a similar fashion with metal-wrapped thread.

Aragon

Dressed for his wedding, the man in this plate illustrates the black cape traditionally worn by grooms in the Spanish region of Aragon. His laced shoes are worn over blue stockings, and under his broad, round-brimmed hat his hair is kept in place by a tightly tied red scarf.

Castilla y León

Women's dress in Ávila is among the most distinctive in Spain. Their skirts, or *manteos*, are always made of either yellow or red baize, a type of fulled woolen cloth, similar in texture to felt. The black velvet appliqué treatment around the hem of their skirts is called the *tirana*. A triangular-folded scarf rests, untied, under their black straw hats decorated with flowers, ribbons, and glass ornaments.

Aragon

Wide bands of appliquéd velvet trim this man's pants. He wears a beret on his head and carries a short jacket over his shoulders. His bright-red sash is an accessory seen throughout Spain's regional dress.

See also
Spain, *pages 242–43*

Headwear
- beret
- headscarf
- straw hat

Hairstyles

Dress

Upper Garments
- bodice
- scarf-like cape (dengue)
- short jacket (marsille)

Lower Garments
- apron
- breeches
- gaiters
- skirts (manteos)
- stockings
- pants

Accessories
- brooch or pin
- sash
- scarf

Footwear
- ankle-laced shoes (alparagatas)

Spain

Balearic Islands, Galicia

Located near the eastern coast of the Iberian Peninsula are the Balearic Islands. The most familiar of these autonomous islands of Spain are Majorca and Ibiza. Before they became the popular tourist destinations they are today, they were the frequent conquest of groups such as the Moors and pirates from the Barbary Coast of Africa. The influence of these invaders can be seen in elements of their traditional dress, particularly that of the men of Majorca. On the opposite side of the Iberian Peninsula, the small province of Galicia traces its roots and its name to the Celtic tribe that once resided there. Although the dress of this region does not overtly reflect this heritage, traces of the Celtic tradition in music and spirituality can still be found.

▶ Galicia
Dancing with his castanets in hand, this young man from Galicia wears the traditional *montera*, a pointed cap decorated with black silk pom-poms. His loose breeches are worn with a white shirt and red vest with contrasting revers. He also wears leather gaiters over his shoes, and around his waist is a red sash, or *faja*.

▶ Balearic Islands
Reflecting an Arabian influence, the traditional costume of men in Majorca consists of loose pants, sometimes gathered at the ankle or knee with decorated bands. Here a long robe is shown, loosely belted at the waist, over which is worn a large cape and brimmed hat.

Balearic Islands ◀
The dress typical of Majorcan peasants in the 19th century is shown here. A short dress similar in silhouette to the panniered gowns of the 18th century is worn with a fitted bodice. A *rebozilla*, the traditional headcovering of women in the Balearic Islands, is worn loosely tied under her chin, perhaps indicating that she is unmarried. In one hand she carries a fan, an accessory commonly seen throughout most of Spain.

Headwear
- brimmed cap
- draped shawl (mantilla)
- head scarf (rebozilla)
- pointed cap (montera)

Hairstyles

Dress
- fitted tops with full skirt and loose breeches

Upper Garments
- bodice
- cape
- long robe
- shirt
- short dress
- stomacher
- vest

Lower Garments
- apron
- breeches
- skirt
- pants

Accessories
- fan
- sash (faja)

Footwear
- gaiters over shoes

Balearic Islands

Wearing a more modest version of the rebozilla, a hood or headcovering constructed of two pieces, this woman of Majorca wears a more fashionable gown than the peasant shown on the page opposite. Over her rebozilla she wears a mantilla.

Balearic Islands

With a boned, pointed stomacher attached to her bodice, this woman wears a less concealing headcovering attached at the back of her head.

See also
Spain, *pages 240–41*

Balearic Islands

Fashionably dressed, this wealthy Majorcan merchant's wife wears a white rebozilla under her black mantilla. With one piece of the rebozilla tied under the chin and the other draped over the shoulders, only her face is seen when wearing this distinctive headcovering.

Balearic Islands

This woman of the Balearic Islands wears a fitted bodice with lace *engageantes* draping from her elbows. A sheer cotton apron covers her full, ankle-length skirt.

France

Women's Regional Dress

In France, the regional costume for women is typically made up of a sleeved bodice, a full skirt, and an apron. This silhouette remains fairly consistent throughout the country, with accessories such as fichus, or lace-trimmed scarves, being added. One sees minor regional differences in the length and fullness of skirts. Regional differences are also observed in the types and colors of textiles used as well as the level of ornament or embroidery. Women's headwear in France, however, differs greatly from region to region, from the tall bonnets of Aquitaine and Normandy to the close-fitting coifs of Alsace and the distinctive "chimney" hats of the Alpine regions.

◗ Upper Normandy

This woman of Le Pollet, a port city near Dieppe, is dressed in festive attire. Her embroidered silk bodice is laced up the front with silk ribbons. It is in the style of the 18th-century *caraco*. Her festive costume is finished with a cotton bonnet and embroidered stockings.

Aquitaine ◗
The organdy headdress tops a formal regional costume from the city of Bordeaux. Pleated into a fan shape at the back, her headdress is complemented by a fitted bodice of silk and a lace-trimmed fichu.

Aquitaine ◗
Another woman from the port city of Bordeaux, this figure wears an ensemble more suitable for daily wear. The fan-shaped headdress is maintained but a simpler fichu and apron are employed. Her detached pocket can also be seen at her side underneath the apron.

See also
France, *pages 246–47*

Bourg-en-Bresse

The costumes of the Rhône-Alpes region of France betray a Dutch influence, including this distinctive headdress called the *houppe* or *huiken*. These influences can be traced back to the Franco–Dutch war of the 17th century. This costume is an example of the more formal, festival dress of the region.

Bourg-en-Bresse

A scaled-down version of the houppe, a chimneylike hat of black silk, is still worn by women in the Rhône-Alpes region of France as part of the region's characteristic costume. It is trimmed with a gold metal chain and black lace or net.

Alsace

Two girls from the Alsace region are shown here, on the right a representative of Strasbourg and on the left, Colmar. The modest bow tied around the embroidered bonnet of the Strasbourg girl reaches greater proportions in other areas of the region, such as Mietesheim, where it can be around 18 in. (45 cm) wide.

France

Normandy and Brittany

The northern regions of Brittany and Normandy offer a striking example of the diversity of regional dress that may be seen in geographically close areas. The dress traditions of Brittany reflect the influence of this region's early inhabitants. The Celtic motifs found on the embroidery of both men's and women's dress are indicative of this. In Normandy, the dress traditions are more closely linked to those of the rest of France, as evidenced in the high headdresses, which are successors to the 15th-century *hennin*, or conical headdress.

▶ Brittany

A woman wearing festival or Sunday dress from Quimperlé is shown here. Her woolen dress is trimmed with an embroidered plastron, and she wears a cotton bonnet decorated with flowers and a silk apron. Unlike the woman from Quimperlé shown below, she does not wear the *tavanger*, or apron in silk with floral embroidery.

▶ Brittany

From left to right, representatives of Faouet, Quimper, Quimperlé, and Pont-l'Abbé are dressed in the typical costume of their villages. The men each have a black felt hat with a rolled brim, trimmed with a length of ribbon secured at the back with a silver buckle. The loose breeches worn by the man from Faouet are a less voluminous version of the *bragou-braz*, the traditional breeches of the region. Like the man from Quimper to his right, he wears a short wool jacket and vest. Their leather belts are trimmed with metal plaques and embroidery. The woman from Pont-l'Abbé wears the *mitre bas*, or short, miter-shaped lace headdress typically found in this area.

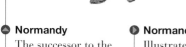

Normandy
Wearing a neck ruff with her fashionable silk gown, this woman from Normandy is dressed for a festival day or other special occasion. Atop her bonnet sits a pleated bunch of lace.

See also
France, *pages 244–45*

Normandy
The successor to the 15th-century hennin, or conical headdress, is worn by the woman on the left. Both women are dressed in the style of the early 19th century, wearing high-waisted dresses and flat-soled slippers. A beaded or embroidered reticule dangles from the wrist of the standing figure, a very fashionable accessory of that period.

Normandy
Illustrated here is the conical bonnet worn for everyday occasions in some parts of Normandy. On festival days or special occasions, this bonnet might be topped with pleated lace or a tuft of feathers.

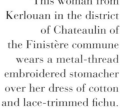

Brittany
This woman from Kerlouan in the district of Chateaulin of the Finistère commune wears a metal-thread embroidered stomacher over her dress of cotton and lace-trimmed fichu.

Headwear
• conical headdress (hennin)
• miter-shaped headdress (mitre bas)
• rolled-brim hat

Hairstyles

Dress
• neat clothes with strongly regional detailing

Upper Garments
• dress
• short jacket
• stomacher
• vest

Lower Garments
• apron
• apron in embroidered silk (tavanger)
• loose breeches (bragou-braz)

Accessories
• belt
• reticule
• ruff

Footwear
• flat slippers

Russia

Boyars and Russians

Imperial Russia from the 17th to 19th centuries encompassed a wide range of dress styles. Varied climatic and geographic conditions, hundreds of ethnicities. and differing histories all contributed to variations in costume. In particular, interactions with the Mongols in the 13th century and the Ottoman Turks from the 15th century left their imprint: the kaftan for men and women, frog fastenings, metallic embroidery and braid, and long narrow sleeves with slits for the arms. For the wealthy, garments were of imported brocades and velvets. By the 1680s Russia was producing silks, but it was not until the 1730s that elaborate metal-thread brocades were being made domestically. From the mid-18th century the upper classes began to emulate French fashionable dress, largely abandoning Russian styles.

A Boyar Man

The highest rank of the Russian feudal aristocracy, the Boyars were distinguished in the 17th century by their tall fox or sable hats and soft red leather boots. He wears a Russian form of kaftan (*ferezja*) with two frog closures on the chest and a stand collar. One sleeve is extended, showing how long and narrow it is. The ferezja is of silk brocade.

Russian Boyar

Based on a print reputed to be of Boris Godunov, czar of Russia from 1598 to 1605. In the original he wears a collarless robe with frog fastenings at the neck, over which he has a mid-calf-length, short-sleeved kaftan of gold-ground Turkish brocade, with a sash at the waist.

Woman in Summer Dress

From Torzhok in the Tver region northwest of Moscow, she wears the tall headdress of a married woman covered with a silk-gauze veil that has been embroidered in gold thread and falls in points to the hem of her sleeveless, high-waisted dress (*sarafan*) beneath. Both veil and sarafan are trimmed in gold braid.

Headwear
• 'cock's comb' headdress (kokoshnik)
• half-moon headdress
• round caps
• tall fur hat
• veil

Hairstyles

Dress
• layered, full and long

Upper Garments
• blouse
• collarless robe
• long dress (sarafan)
• Polish kaftan (kontuz)
• Russian kaftan (ferezja)
• sleeveless jacket

Lower Garments
• apron
• stockings

Accessories
• carrings
• frog fastenings
• sash

Footwear
• flat shoes and boots

Khanty Woman

From an engraving published by Braun and Schneider between 1861 and 1890. The Khanty are a dwindling ethnic group in northern Siberia. She wears a fringed scarf wrapped around a small cap. Her coat is trimmed with glass beads. A cape with stand collar is trimmed with beads and shells. Long earrings of cowrie shells blend with the shells and metal bells down the front of her coat.

Two Girls From Tver

They wear the sarafan, a dress either cut on the bias or gored to give fullness at the hem, open down the front, and trimmed with lace, ribbon, or gold braid. The younger girl wears an embroidered apron and a short sleeveless jacket, gored and gathered at the back. Both wear white linen blouses with full sleeves. The older girl wears the *kokoshnik* ("cock's comb") headdress of central Russia.

Peter the Great

The czar wears a Polish kaftan (*kontusz*) in an engraving of *c*. 1689. This garment survives in the Kremlin Armory and has multicolored braid trim, frog fastenings, and full upper sleeves narrowing from the elbow to the wrist. Characteristic of the kontuz at this time is a narrow center-back panel flanked by wedge-shaped gussets inserted at the waist.

Khanty Man

Wearing a wool cloth over his head and tied under the chin, this man holds a knitted tobacco pouch and wears white knitted stockings. He wears flat leather shoes; strips of sinew secure them to his feet. His leather coat has two rows of purely decorative buttons, suggesting a fashionable late 18th-century man's greatcoat as its inspiration.

Poland and the Ukraine

Nobles, Jews and Cossacks

Culturally, and often politically, united, Poland, Lithuania, the Ukraine, and Russia shared a fascination for elements of Ottoman Turkish and Central Asian dress. For example, "national dress" of Polish noblemen in the 17th century—the *kontusz*, *żupan*, and *pas kontuszowy*—were all derived from Ottoman styles. In the 18th century, French fashions become popular, but with uniquely Polish touches. By that time Jews were no longer required to wear special clothing; however, they continued to wear their own dress styles well into the 19th century. The Cossacks were free men from around the region who migrated to the Ukrainian Steppes (a kind of "Wild West") in the 16th century, seeking opportunities.

Polish–Jewish Woman and Child

Both are from 1817 engravings. She wears a lace-trimmed cap under a scarf tied at the back of her head; a ribbon-trimmed plastron (*brüsttück*) identifying her as Jewish; an embroidered apron; white stockings; and mid-18th-century-style shoes. The boy wears a *kaftan* girdled at the waist and the *streimel*, a circular hat with a flat fur brim, one of several styles of hat worn only by Jews.

Lady from Cracow

This aristocratic woman wears the fashionable European Neoclassical silhouette of the late 18th to early 19th century: a gown with a train; high waist, belted under the bust; a thin silk or linen underdress; and turban. However, her outer robe is specifically Polish: a fur-trimmed fashionable version of the kontusz worn by noblemen. The cockade in her turban is also a Polish touch.

Polish Nobleman

"Roman Sanguszko, from a 16th-century portrait" according to Racinet, wearing a sable-lined kontusz worn only by the nobility at the time; an outer garment also worn unlined; long hanging sleeves; and front button, or frog (*pelticami*) closure. His kontusz appears to be of shot silk (different-colored warps and wefts), popular in Poland at the time. Beneath he wears a silk *żupan* with high neck and pelticami.

Jewish Man of Poland

From an 1817 engraving, he wears a dark żupan (often referred to as a "kaftan") with stand collar, pelticami, and a soft, wide sash. Originally only for nobility, by the 19th century żupan were worn by all classes as "Polish national dress." Over his shoulders is a "Sabbath cloak" and on his head, a softly peaked fur-trimmed hat (*spodic*). He also wears white stockings and buckled leather shoes.

See also
Anatolia, 16th–18th Century, *pages 214–15*
Central Asia, 18th–19th Century, *pages 222–23*

Ukrainian Cossack

He wears a soft, elongated cloth cap. His full, Turkish-style pants with galloon trim are tucked into soft leather boots; the long sleeves of his tunic are tied behind his back (ready for action); a leather pouch for ammunition hangs across one shoulder; and he holds a long Turkish pipe.

Polish King

Stefan Batory, 1576, wears a żupan of silk brocade under a red, sable-lined kontusz, high fashion from the 16th to mid-17th century, fastened with ball buttons, vertical slash pockets at the waist, and vestigial sleeves hanging to the hem. A sable hat with a feather cockade and leather-heeled shoes complete the outfit.

A Cracow "Lawyer"

An 18th-century gentleman identified as a nobleman by the following: a kontusz (hanging sleeves tied off); the *pas kontuszowy*, a long narrow sash with metallic fringe; and a long sword. In the 16th century, pas were imported from India, Iran, or Turkey, and by the 17th century they were being woven in Poland.

Headwear
• cap
• circular hat with a flat fur brim (streimel)
• peaked, fur-trimmed hat (spodic)
• turban

Hairstyles

Dress
• Ottoman-inspired styles

Upper Garments
• caftan (żupan)
• high-waisted gown with train
• long-sleeved tunic
• sable-lined kontusz

Lower Garments
• apron
• stockings
• Turkish-style pants with galloon trim

Accessories
• feather cockade
• leather pouch
• sash

Footwear
• buckled leather shoes
• leather boots

Central Europe

Romania, Croatia, and Hungary

Central Europe has a rich and varied history of traditional dress. The popular long-fringed apron or string skirt can be traced back to the Balkan Paleolithic period. Romania traditionally held pride of place for its beautiful and elaborate embroidery, and the Saxons of Romania are known for their extensive use of leather, velvet, lace and metal ornaments. Costumes of the contending Habsburg and Ottoman Empires also influenced the region. The proportions and fabric types of garments (especially those worn by the wealthy) evolved over time to keep in step with the fashionable European silhouette. Some costume elements, including the Turkish boot, transcended gender or economic status and found widespread popularity in Hungary, the Balkans and other regions.

Romanian Woman
Shown here, single or paired aprons were worn over a beautifully embroidered under-garment consisting of either an ankle-length smock or a chemise with petticoat. This woman also wears peasant sandals (*opinci*) over white stockings.

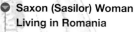

Saxon (Sasilor) Woman Living in Romania
From a minority community living in the Bistritza Nasaud Valley, this woman wears a wedding ensemble that includes an embroidered sheepskin overcoat. Sheepskin overcoats and jerkins with silk-embroidered floral designs, trimmed with fox and ferret fur, were worn by both sexes. Her distinctive hat (*borten*) was made of black velvet and decorated at the top and back with jeweled ornaments and long trailing ribbons.

Croatian Man
This man wears an embellished bag worn in many Balkan communities as a wallet or holdall. He does not, however, wear a *hrvat*, the traditional Croatian neckwear that became a popular European necktie or cravat.

See also
Anatolia, 16th–18th Century, *pages 214–15*

Woman from the Banat Village of Timişoara

Fringed skirts and apron styles varied according to community. Banat Romanian women wore *opreg*, a distinctive apron of woven wool, silk, or cotton cloth embellished with metallic threads and an extremely long, colored wool fringe. As depicted here, it was worn over a cotton chemise.

Hungarian Noblewoman

This woman wears the Hungarian woman's national folk costume, dating from about 1800. Influenced by German and Spanish Renaissance styles, this attire consisted of a ruffled blouse and laced bodice, a floor-length skirt (sometimes with a train), and a lace-edged apron. She wears a fur-lined pelisselike cape in dark red with gold embellishment.

Hungarian Kaposvar Magyar Man

Magyar men wore a simple collared shirt and a woolen scarf thrown around the neck. The shirt was either tucked into tight pants inserted into high black boots as shown here, or into white linen divided, skirtlike pants. Also characteristic was the braid embellishment applied to the pants, which varied in color and design according to the social status and region of the wearer.

Hungarian Nobleman

The *mente* was worn as an outer coat in the 16th and 17th centuries, with the finest examples featuring a fur trim and even silver or gold buttons encrusted with precious stones. Worn underneath the *mente* was a kaftanlike short coat (*dolman*) with Ottoman-inspired braid and frogging. The velvet and sable hat (*cuşma*) was often adorned with a silver aigrette and a feather.

Headwear
- brimless hat (cuşma)
- tall hat (borten)

Hairstyles

Dress
- wide variety of regional detailing

Upper Garments
- blouse
- bodice
- cape (dolman)
- outer coat (mente)
- shirt
- short coat

Lower Garments
- fringed apron (opreg)
- skirt
- tight pants
- wide skirt-like pants

Accessories
- aigrette
- embellished bag
- neckerchief (hrvat)
- scarf

Footwear
- high boots
- sandals (opinci)

Central Europe

Albania and Bulgaria

Related to the Roman tunic and Byzantine *dalmatic*, the chemise is one of the oldest garments worn by the Slavic peoples. Another traditional Slavic garment worn in Bulgaria, Romania, and the Ukraine is the double apron. Both Albania and Bulgaria were under Ottoman rule for hundreds of years and so it is not surprising that Ottoman attire and decorative embellishment were influential. Although many of the same Slavic and Ottoman garment types were worn throughout central Europe, they were given names according to the local language.

See also
Anatolia, 16th–18th Century, *pages 214–15*

● Albanian Woman from Scutari

This woman, a farmer's wife, wears a long-sleeved, loose-fitting, embroidered linen chemise. Subsequent layers include a felted wool sleeveless vest and skirt (loose pants were also worn), an apron and a silver belt. Typical headwear for Albanian women consisted of a short fez or, as shown here, an embroidered brimless hat.

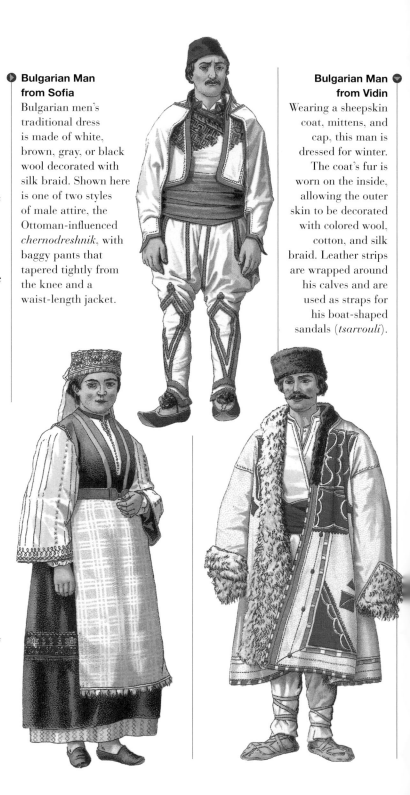

● Bulgarian Man from Sofia

Bulgarian men's traditional dress is made of white, brown, gray, or black wool decorated with silk braid. Shown here is one of two styles of male attire, the Ottoman-influenced *chernodreshnik*, with baggy pants that tapered tightly from the knee and a waist-length jacket.

Bulgarian Man from Vidin ●

Wearing a sheepskin coat, mittens, and cap, this man is dressed for winter. The coat's fur is worn on the inside, allowing the outer skin to be decorated with colored wool, cotton, and silk braid. Leather strips are wrapped around his calves and are used as straps for his boat-shaped sandals (*tsarvouli*).

Bulgarian Woman

Bulgarian peasant costume was traditionally cut, sewn, and embellished by women in the family. If affordable, metallic ornaments made by town artisans and locally produced silk were obtained for use on festive costume. This shy woman wears a pair of billowing salvarlike pants and striped socks under her embroidered chemise of homespun and woven hemp, linen, or cotton.

Middle-class Albanian Man from Janina

Originating in southern Albania, the *fustanella* is a full white skirt like those worn in Greece and Macedonia but longer and less full. A white shirt and *tchepken* (short coat) were worn on the upper body. Tight wool stockings and elegant pointed shoes with silk pom-poms (*tcharik*) complete the ensemble.

Albanian Man and Woman from Janina

Ottoman fashion is evident in this woman's entari and sleeveless coat, both made of wool or silk velvet richly decorated with silver cord and heavy gold braiding, and her fez with a full silken tassel. Her companion wears an embroidered *sihlahlik*, a belt with multiple compartments, and in place of stockings, he wears wool gaiters.

Headwear
• brimless hat
• cap
• fez

Hairstyles

Dress
• wide variety of regional detailing

Upper Garments
• chemise
• coat
• gown (entari)
• jacket
• long-sleeved vest (tchepken)
• shirt
• sleeveless overgown
• sleeveless vest

Lower Garments
• double apron
• full skirt (fustanella)
• loose pants (salyar)
• skirt
• stockings
• tapering pants

Accessories
• belt
• belt with compartments (sihlahlik)
• mittens

Footwear
• pointed shoes with silk pom-poms (tcharik)
• sandals (tsarvouli)

Africa, Oceania, and the Americas

Much of the world was still relatively unknown to the majority of Europeans in the late 19th century. News traveled by boat and the printed page, and was slow in reaching its audience. Travel accounts were popular forms of literature, often emphasizing the strange, dangerous, and exotic. Racinet, as a compiler of other people's observations, was passing on second- and third-hand knowledge. Many of his illustrations are composites. His description and depiction of foreign peoples and their dress was not often accurate. The supposedly "savage" and "uncivilized" nature of these people was highlighted by Racinet's fascination with weapons. The depiction of bare-breasted women also emphasized their "primitive" state, as did body tattoos, a habit picked up by whalers from islanders in the southern Pacific Ocean.

Although Europeans had known since antiquity that sub-Saharan Africa existed, their knowledge was very superficial until the mid-1800s. Explorers and merchant ships touched the coast from the 15th century but seldom ventured inland. Because of this, coastal peoples are over represented by Racinet. Explorers and colonial administrators left their accounts, but serious research on the dress and textiles of Africa, Oceania, and the Americas only commenced in the mid-20th century.

Indigenous natural materials, an essential component of dress, varied widely. Cotton grew in West Africa and South America but not in South Africa or the islands of Oceania. Imported fibers such as silk from China and wool from northern Europe, acquired through trade, provided variety. Metals such as gold and copper from Africa and South America were made into jewelry. Plants and minerals were used for dye and pigments, and everywhere bones, shells, and feathers were used to adorn the body. In Africa and the Americas, wildlife supplied skins for leather and hide garments. The pelts of small mammals were used to make ruffs and headgear, and were attached to garments for decoration.

Although changing fashions, as understood in Europe and North America, were neither quick nor noticeable to outsiders, they did occur. New materials were adopted, new styles created, and differences between social classes and ethnic groups were delineated through dress.

Algeria and Tunisia

Arabs, Berbers, and Jews

In North Africa there are two distinctions that affect our understanding of dress in the region. The first is geographic: the cities, particularly along the coast—urbanized for almost 2500 years—and the countryside, mountains, and fringes of the Sahara. The second is stylistic: draped clothing (originating in classical Greek dress) versus cut-and-sewn garments, either made of folded and sewn lengths of cloth, or tailored clothing such as Turkish-inspired jackets. Geography and dress converge, however. Along the urbanized coast, influenced by the region's long history of invasion, migration, and trade around the Mediterranean and other regions of Africa, cut-and-sewn clothing was introduced and worn; while the inhabitants of the interior, particularly the Berbers, maintained the tradition of draped clothing styles. By the 19th century, however, there were many examples of the mixing of the two styles.

Arab Man
This man from the Algerian Arab community is wearing a simple version of the jacket and vest, open in the front showing a short, sleeveless undershirt and a wide sash. His loose-fitting white cotton pants, gathered at the waist with a knitted cord, are widely worn by North African men.

Two Berber Women
Two of the many ways of wearing the North African *haik* (large cloak): on the left, draped and held by fibulae (brooches) at the shoulders and a girdle at the waist, forming a deep fold at the back; on the right, worn over the head, open in the front, and tied into a knot at the hem.

Tunisian Men
The man on the left is wearing the ubiquitous North African garment, a hooded *djellabah* of black-and-white-striped wool, accented with pom-poms; his arms extend from slits in the sleeve seam. The man on the right, identified in the original as a wealthy *qadi* (judge) of Tunis, wears a *burnous* (capelike outer garment) over an open kaftan lined with printed cotton.

Two Algerian Women
The woman on the left, dressed for town, wears a scarf around her neck to wrap around her face below the eyes when outdoors. Dressed for home, the woman on the right wears a tiny vest fitting snugly around the bust and decorated with metallic braid, over a sheer blouse held with a multifolded brocade belt with long fringe.

See also
Algeria, *pages 260–61*

Algerian Zouave
A member of the native regiment wears a turban over a fez, the long tassel behind his head; a short fitted jacket and matching vest; a wide, long striped sash and voluminous pants. He carries a hooded burnous over his shoulder.

Algerian Jews
The woman on the left wears a robe of gold brocade over a sleeved vest, the sleeves tied behind. Her fringed headdress and long, beribboned braids indicate that she is unmarried. The second woman is married, as shown by her tall conical headdress draped with a sheer cloth. The man wears the dark-blue cap, blue stockings, and long hair required of Jewish men.

Headwear
• cap
• fez
• headdress (fringed or conical)
• turban

Hairstyles

Dress
• many variations on drapery and robes

Upper Garments
• cape-like robe (burnous)
• cloak (haik)
• hooded robe (djellabah)
• jacket
• kaftan
• sheer blouse
• undershirt
• vest

Lower Garments
• loose pants
• stockings

Accessories
• belt
• brooch
• girdle
• sash
• scarf

Footwear

Algeria

Arab, Berber, and Jewish Women

Algerian women's dress in the 19th century
reflected the cultural mix of the country: Arabs,
Berbers, Turks, sub-Saharan Africans, Spanish
Muslims, and Jews. Each community had its distinctive
dress, although many elements of costume were also
shared, the large cloak (haik) in particular. Women's
dress modes were governed by a basic distinction:
streetwear (in public) or at-home wear (in private).
In her home, a woman's dress allowed more freedom
of movement as it usually consisted of a sheer chemise,
tiny vest (*frimla*), and baggy pants. All of this was
covered by a kaftan or haik when going out. The
Algerian love of decoration, especially metal
embroidery, was seen on all types of dress, but
was particularly elaborate for festive dress, as it
still is today.

◗ Woman in Outdoor Dress

An Algerian Arab
woman from Bône
is dressed for town,
wearing a veil over her
head, coin necklaces,
and a kaftan, under
which she wears two
additional gowns of thin
cotton or linen. Both
men and women of the
Arab communities in
North Africa wear the
kaftan, a simple
tailored garment
originating in
Mesopotamia (Iraq).

◗ Kabyle Berber Woman

This woman from Algeria is
wearing coral earrings hung
from a hook around her ear
and a pair of triangular fibulae
holding her haik, set with
coral and joined by a chain.
The haik, widely worn by
both sexes in North Africa,
is a rectangular cloth
approximately 3 ft
(1 meter) wide by
20 ft (6 meters)
long, usually
striped, and is
wrapped and draped
around the body
in various ways.

◗ Woman with Oud

Identified by Racinet
as a Jewish woman
from Constantine,
she wears a short vest
(frimla) and wide-
sleeved gown, both
heavily decorated
with metal-thread
embroidery, an
embroidered apron,
and a pointed cap.
She leans on the
traditional stringed
instrument, the *oud*.
Her outdoor shoes
have a wide leather
band over the instep
and a flat sole.

See also
Algeria and Tunisia,
pages 258–59

Berber Leader's Wife

This is the high-status wife of the leader of the Kabyle Berber community. Like many Berber women, her mother tattooed her face, hands, and feet when she reached puberty for protection, to enhance her beauty, and to announce her eligibility for marriage. Her earrings and necklace are coral, a material considered to have protective properties.

Kabyle Berber Women

The woman on the left wears festive dress with a silver diadem, braids looped and tied on her head, coin necklaces and fibulae holding her narrow-edged haik. In the center the woman wears a flat headdress for carrying a water jug on her head, and silver, enamel, and coral jewelry. On the right a snugly fitted frimla is worn.

Headwear
• pointed cap
• veil

Hairstyles

Dress
• loose robes

Upper Garments
• chemise
• cloak (haik)
• gown
• kaftan
• vest (frimla)

Lower Garments
• apron
• loose pants

Accessories
• coral, silver and enamel jewelry of various sorts

Footwear
• flat, slip-on shoes

Guinea Coast to South Africa

African Trade

Trade was a long-established activity of Africans when Portuguese mariners arrived along the coast from Senegal to South Africa in the 15th century. They brought cotton cloth woven in India, woolens from northern Europe, and glass beads, and metal implements to trade for gold, ivory, and slaves. Africans, like all people, treasured exotic items and immediately incorporated these new materials into their clothing. While Europeans saw only "naked savages," Africans, in societies where kings and chiefs prevailed, recognized a hierarchy based on wealth and prestige reflected in dress. In egalitarian societies, differences in dress were based more on personal esthetics and skill in making clothing and jewelry.

See also
Nubia and Senegal,
pages 264–65
South Africa, Zimbabwe and Botswana,
pages 266–67

Galla

The Galla people, now known as Oromo, live in Ethiopia, Kenya, and Somalia. Some were farmers, others nomadic herders. This is a warrior chief (identified by the leopard headband) carrying his weapons. The number of ivory bracelets is said to equate to the number of foes he has vanquished. His hair is dressed with butter, his forehead tattooed.

Gabon

This woman is said to belong to the M'Pongwe ethnic group in eastern Gabon. She wears cotton pants held around her waist by a sash, and a cotton cape over her shoulders. The cloth would have been traded as Gabon is tropical rainforest. Leg bands, bracelets, and earrings of locally mined copper and beaded necklaces complete her outfit.

Gabon

The second M'Pongwe woman wears a wrapper, not pants. Fitted or wrapped upper garments were not worn until the 20th century. Both women are married, as shown by their high-braided hairstyle. Hairstyles and headgear were often indicative of social status in Africa, as in most other parts of the world.

Zulu, South Africa

The Zulus became a military force in the early 19th century under Shaka. This warrior chief is dressed for battle. His garments and jewelry demonstrate his prowess in battle and at hunting; the leopard skin, a plastron of animal tails on his chest, and arm and leg ornaments made of leather and fur are all trophies.

Guinea Coast

Europeans knew coastal West Africa as the Guinea Coast. The figure of this hunter shows aspects of dress from many different places along the coast, some anomalous. His hat seems to be made of raffia and red wool, both available on the coast. His loincloth is leather. The blue leather pouch is typically Tuareg from the Sahara Desert.

Gabon

Called Pahouin by Racinet, this man would today be called Fang, an ethnic group in northwest Gabon. He wears a black monkey pelt as a loincloth, carries a monkey-pelt bag and a coconut-fiber bag, and wears a palm-leaf hat. His long dagger is sheathed in snakeskin. They are all materials of the tropical rainforest.

Headwear
- headband
- palm-leaf hat
- raffia and wool hat

Hairstyles
- high-braided

Dress

Upper Garments
- breastpiece (plastron)
- cape

Lower Garments
- loincloth
- pants
- wrapper

Accessories
- bags (variety)
- copper and bead jewelry
- sash
- tattoos

Footwear

Nubia and Senegal

Cotton in Africa

Nubia was an ancient kingdom along the Upper Nile River, in the south of present-day Egypt. It formed a corridor for trade between tropical Africa and Egypt, facilitating the movement of gold, incense, ivory, and ebony from south to north. Senegal, on the other side of the continent, has a primarily savannah-type climate: dry, with a short rainy season. Both these places were home to cotton species that provided fiber for clothing. Both were also very attractive to European powers who, among other things, needed cotton to feed their textile industries developed during the Industrial Revolution.

Nubia

The ancient kingdom of Nubia, along the Upper Nile River, was divided between Egypt and Sudan after the First World War. The two men illustrated wear white cotton cloth draped around the waist, over short pants. One man wears red leather shoes typical of the Middle East. They both carry spears and hippo-hide shields.

Senegal

Senegal has very little tropical rainforest, and has a good climate for growing cotton. It was also the first French possession in West Africa and an important trading center. This man is wearing a hand-woven strip of cloth as a wrapper and an imported cloth called *guinée* as his *boubou*, or overrobe. Guinée, a coarse blue cotton woven in India, was very important in the slave trade.

Senegal

Wearing a wrapper, a blouse, and a shoulder wrap called a *ferdah* of locally woven cotton, this Muslim woman from Senegal is modestly dressed. Her braided hair is covered with another type of hand-woven cloth, and she wears earrings and a necklace. The ferdah is gracefully draped over one shoulder and held with a pin.

264

Liberia and Sierra Leone

Racinet calls this man a hunter from Côte des Graines (coastal Sierra Leone and Liberia; *graine* meaning a type of pepper grown there). The man has a cotton loincloth, a wool turban and a leopardskin sash that forms a pouch where the two ends meet. His neckpiece, or *hausse-col*, is leather and cloth.

Senegal

In agricultural societies, hunting is often a specialized occupation indicated by particular items of dress. This man wears a white cotton cap tied under his chin. He also wears a white undergarment covered by a boubou with wide sleeves that are folded to give him free movement. A red leather belt with a pouch, sash, powder horn, and leather sandals complete his outfit.

Liberia and Sierra Leone

This West African man wears similar garments to the figure on the left, although his loincloth is made of leaves, a very ancient material used by forest dwellers. He wears a similar sash, a neckpiece of simpler construction, having only one strip of cloth instead of two, and a cotton cloth on his head.

See also
Guinea Coast to South Africa, *pages 262–63*
South Africa, Zimbabwe and Botswana, *pages 266–67*

Headwear
• cap
• turban

Hairstyles
• braided

Dress
• simple wrapped and draped clothes

Upper Garments
• blouse
• neckpiece (hausse-col)
• overrobe (boubou)
• shoulder wrap (ferdah)
• underrobe

Lower Garments
• loincloth
• short pants
• wrapper

Accessories
• belt
• jewelry
• pouch
• sash

Footwear
• leather shoes
• sandals

South Africa, Zimbabwe and Botswana

Natural and Imported Materials

The main elements used for dress in the southern part of Africa before Europeans arrived were natural materials such as animal skins, feathers, and shells. Glass beads first appeared in the 16th century, introduced by Portuguese traders, and were quickly adopted as a colorful novelty, becoming a profoundly important part of the dress tradition. Ethnic groups such as the Zulu, Ndebele, and Xhosa developed distinctive styles of beadwork that reflected ethnic identity and esthetics. The use of imported materials such as beads implied wealth and prestige, as they could only be obtained through trade.

Botswana

With his feather parasol, leopardskin hat, and cloak, this man certainly has the air of a chief. The beaded leather sash he wears holds up a leather loincloth. Beaded leather bands are wrapped around his ankles and wrists. All his garments graphically illustrate the importance of these two materials in southern Africa.

Sarah Bartmann

Sarah Bartmann was a Khoikhoi woman who was taken from her home in South Africa to Paris, France, in 1815 and displayed as the "Hottentot Venus." Although she was exhibited naked, this portrait shows her wearing a white figure-hugging garment, a beaded apron over a leather apron, beaded necklaces and bracelets, and an animal pelt over her shoulders. Pink shoes were a concession to the weather in France.

Matabhele

This Matabhele woman from Zimbabwe is shown wearing a leather skirt and beads. A beaded band is draped over her head, indicating that she is a married woman. Shell anklets and necklaces, and bracelets of leather, complete her outfit. The Matabhele are related to the Ndebele of South Africa. They moved north to Botswana in the 18th century.

Headwear
• headband
• leopardskin hat

Hairstyles

Dress
• simple shapes,
often heavily beaded
and ornamented

Upper Garments
• animal skins
• cloak
• two-sided leather
cape (krosse)

Lower Garments
• beaded apron
• leather apron
• loincloth
• pants

Accessories
• bead, feather and
coral ornaments
and jewelry
• feather parasol
• garters
• sash

Footwear

Khoikhoi

Southern Africa is known today as a land of big game and dangerous predators. The warrior/hunter wears a panther-skin garment that uses the natural shape of the skin to hold it together. The feathers on his head are held by a leather band. He wears bone earrings and carries a spear.

Khoikhoi

A wealthy Khoikhoi woman of Namibia wears a two-sided leather cape called a *krosse*. One side is painted leather, while the other is panther skin. She is shown wearing a feather in her hair, waist beads, a glass bead and coral bracelet, and leather garters around her knees. Glass and coral beads were imported and were used as status symbols.

Khoikhoi

Khoikhoi are cattle herders who live on the edge of the Kalahari Desert in Namibia. Cattle are an important source of leather for their clothing. This man's krosse is a simple one, while his necklace is made from seeds and metal. The pants he wears are modeled on the garment introduced by European colonizers and missionaries.

See also
Guinea Coast to South Africa, *pages 262–63*
Nubia and Senegal, *pages 264–65*

New Guinea, Melanesia, and Polynesia

Tapa Cloth

The islands in the South Pacific present a seemingly idyllic climate, especially suited to human habitation. Food is readily available from the ocean and from trees on land. What is missing is any cultivated textile fiber for weaving. Instead, islanders have used tree bark for centuries to make *tapa* cloth. Sections of tree bark are stripped, beaten, and then painted in intricate designs to make garments. Tapa cloth can be as fine and pliable as silk or as coarse and stiff as burlap. Other natural materials such as plant fiber, feathers, shells, and bones are used creatively to make jewelry and headdresses.

See also
Malaysia and Polynesia,
pages 270–71

New Guinea

This man, dressed as a warrior, comes from New Guinea and wears a wooden comb topped with feathers in his hair. His *péda* (all-purpose knife) is under his chin. Around his neck is a pendant shaped like a human figure, carved of bone. He wears a piece of tapa, or bark, cloth decorated with geometric patterns around his hips.

Marquesa Islands

Marquesan islanders also made and wore tapa cloth, as shown by this chief's cloak. Europeans were fascinated and repelled by the idea of head-hunting. This man, with a few heads 'under his belt', is wearing some of them on his belt, bracelets, and anklets. Tattoos wrap his body in protective images and identify his status and gender.

Papua New Guinea

Papua New Guineans treasured feathers of the cassowary, using them to decorate the body as well as their spears. The bones of the bird were used as daggers and are seen on this man's headdress, enhanced with a band of shells. His necklace has whale teeth and shells, and his bracelet is a human jawbone, no doubt a prize of war.

Solomon Islands

In the Solomon Islands warriors were celebrated because enemy heads were needed to inaugurate canoes and canoe houses, that in turn were used in head-hunting. This warrior carries a deadly club and wears a shell pectoral, shell nose ornament, and a necklace of human teeth. His headdress is made from plant fiber and feathers. A small bag for his personal goods hangs at his waist.

New Hebrides

In preparation for war this Vanuatu man is wearing a carved wooden mask with plant-fiber hair and beard, a tooth necklace over a white tapa-cloth fringe, and a loincloth. His spear has bone points, while the sword he carries has shark teeth embedded in the edge. Pacific Islanders had virtually no access to metals and thus used wood, stone, and bone for weapons.

Headwear
- comb with feathers
- feather and bone headdress
- wooden mask

Hairstyles

Dress
- abundant use of feather, bone and shell as ornament

Upper Garments
- cloak

Lower Garments
- loincloth

Accessories
- bag
- bone and feather ornaments
- pendants
- tattoos

Footwear

Malaysia and Polynesia

War and Prestige

The islanders of Oceania and Southeast Asia were often engaged in war with each other. Head-hunting was essential to ritual life on Borneo and in New Guinea, while warfare for territorial expansion and self-protection was practiced in other parts of the region. Iban Dayak women of Borneo wove elaborately patterned ikat cloths whose production paralleled the taking of heads for men. Tattooing the male body was usually associated with virility, strength, and prowess in war. Some designs were universal, while others were strictly associated with a particular place, such as the unique designs of the Marquesas and of the New Zealand Maoris.

Philippines

This short blouse is an idealization of a garment worn by ethnic groups in the mountains of Luzon Island. The red, blue, and white color scheme is common to many groups. Her wrapped skirt appears to be made of tapa, a material widespread in the area. Her torque is probably brass with beads.

Sino-Malay

Chinese merchants migrated to all parts of Southeast Asia and married local women. This woman is dressed in garments that reflect the blending of the cultures—a sarong, or wrapped skirt, worn in Malaysia and the islands, and a long tunic called a *baju panjang* that originated in Fukien Province, China. The small cap would be worn when going out.

Borneo

Dayak warriors of Borneo wore a bark breastplate arranged in a fish-scale pattern as protection during war. Other pieces of bark cover his sides, held in place by a cotton belt. His cotton loincloth would have identified his group by its length, design, and manner of wrapping. His necklace is of honey-bear teeth, cowries, and glass beads.

Borneo

A Dayak woman wears commercial cotton cloth garments. Hand-woven patterned skirts called *bidang* were worn every day, while upper garments such as shoulder cloths, jackets, and blankets worn around the shoulders were reserved for ceremonial occasions. The blouse is a concession to a "civilized" sensibility. Her carrying basket has woven patterns and she wears silver earrings.

Borneo

A tattooed Dayak man is dressed for hunting or war. He carries a sword in a carved wooden sheath along with other weapons. He has a tapa loincloth and a plaited plant-fiber belt. The tattoo designs on his back are generic. Tattoos serve the same purpose as in the South Pacific, conferring honor and identity on the wearer.

See also
New Guinea, Melanesia and Polynesia, *pages 268–69*

Hawaii

This royal Hawaiian shows his status by wearing the feather cape, or *ahu'ula*, and a helmet that mimics the shape of the feathered war god, Ku. Feathered garments were made from hundreds of thousands of tiny red and yellow tuft feathers plucked from forest birds. Cloaks were believed to protect the wearer in battle. His loincloth is made from tapa.

Headwear
• cap
• helmet

Hairstyles

Dress
• a mixture of indigenous and imported materials

Upper Garments
• bark breastplate
• blouse
• feather cape (ahu'ula)
• jacket
• long tunic (baju panjang)
• shoulder cloth

Lower Garments
• loincloth
• patterned skirt (bidang)
• wrapped skirt (sarong)

Accessories
• belt
• carrying basket
• earrings
• necklace
• tattoos
• torque

Footwear

South and Central America

Chile and Mexico

Indigenous peoples of Latin America were fine weavers long before the Spanish arrived in the 15th century. Cotton grew widely and wool-bearing llamas, alpacas, and vicuñas inhabited the slopes of the Andes. Animal skins were used for clothing as well. In Chile, the peoples who inhabited the western slopes of the Andes to the Pacific were called Mapuche. They resisted Spanish domination until the 19th century and retained their local dress styles longer than other Chileans. Where the Spanish had more influence men's dress changed rapidly, incorporating foreign materials and styles. Women tended to be less open to changing their traditional dress.

See also
North America,
pages 274–75

Mapuche

These three women are wearing the older form of dress that was influenced by the Incas. Their large llama-wool mantles are fastened with silver *tupus*, while their dresses are held together with leather or finely patterned woven wool belts. The central figure is wearing a turban of wrapped cloth strips. They all have beaded necklaces.

Lipan Apache

The Lipan people are Apaches who were pushed south into Texas and then moved into Mexico in the 1860s. Although Racinet calls this an illustration of a Lipan warrior, he is actually wearing generic Plains Indian dress made from deerskin decorated with metal jingles, eagle feathers, and trade cloth. Apaches are not considered Plains, but are related to the Navajo people of the Southwest.

Headwear
• brimless hat
• sombrero
• turban

Hairstyles

Dress

Upper Garments
• mantle
• poncho

Lower Garments
• leather pants (calzoneras)
• leggings
• underpants (calzonchillas)
• wide pants

Accessories
• bead necklace
• belt
• pin disc ornament (tupu)

Footwear

Chile

This *huaso* wears a typical striped red wool poncho, pants protected by leather leggings, boots, and spurs, all necessary cowboy gear. His leggings are held up with narrow woven bands. His brimless hat, typical of the 19th century, was later modified with a brim to become the shape now worn by Chilean cowboys—a flat-topped crown with stiff brim.

Rural Chile

This man wears transitional styles with elements of Mapuche and Spanish costume combined. The poncho is an indigenous garment, but when horses arrived with the Spanish and riding became an art among the Indians, the poncho grew longer. This long wool poncho shows a modified Mapuche design, while the wide pants are similar to those worn by the Argentine cowboys called gauchos.

Mexico

The long poncho, finely woven and decorated with gold at the neck, probably comes from the market in Saltillo, Mexico. In the mid-19th century cowboys wore leather pants open to the knee and decorated with silver buttons, called *calzoneras*. *Calzonchillas*, ruffled white underpants, were allowed to show. Both were worn very long. The large sombrero protected his head and shoulders from the sun.

North America

Native Americans

At the time of European contact, the native peoples of North America brought enormous regional and individual variation to a fairly limited range of garments that were worn throughout most of the present United States. The breechclout apron and leggings, along with a robe for winter, were typical dress for men regardless of climate, while an apron or skirt, and later a dress made from animal hides, was standard for women. Plant materials were used for baskets, hats, footwear, and garments, and animal products such as feathers, furs, and hides for decorative purposes as well as for warmth. Inhabitants of the Southwest grew cotton to weave for garments and blankets.

South-west Oregon

The round basketry cap and the double-apron skirt that this woman wears make it likely she lived in southwest Oregon. South of the Columbia River along the coastal river valleys, Native Americans dressed more like the California groups than like the Northwest Indians. In an earlier time her skirt would be made from bark instead of cloth. Strings of glass trade beads are worn around her neck.

Unidentified

Called a "red skin type of New Mexico" by Racinet, this man may be dressed in a blend of Taos Pueblo and Teton Sioux styles. Taos people were hunters and famous for the quality of their tanned hides. Side-fringed and painted leggings were common among the Sioux. The buffalo robe was ubiquitous on the Plains and as far south as Taos.

See also
South and Central America, *pages 272–73*

Sauk

The Sauk, also known as Sac, of Kansas originally lived in Michigan. They incorporated trade goods, such as the wool cloth used for his mantle and the cotton cloth for his headband and garters, into their dress. The feathers in his hair and in the fan he carries, bear-tooth necklace, and deerskin shirt and leggings embellished with quills were all local products.

Fox

The Fox share many Sauk characteristics, including clothing style. The shaved head, deer-hair roach, single feather, and bear-tooth necklace identify this man as a warrior. Cotton pants, shirt, and a mantle of English wool cloth were all popular in the mid-19th century. Men and women wore earrings.

Ute

Cloth pants, painted deerskin shirt, red cloth apron, and leather chaps are mid-19th century style. Earlier, a larger apron (breechclout) adorned with porcupine quills was the main garment. The war shirt with beaded shoulder panels was adapted from the Plains style.

Generic Plains

Possibly a depiction of a Plains Native American, this man wears his hair wrapped in fur—a common Plains style. The long fringes on his poncho, or cape, were also characteristic of the Plains peoples. His cloth mantle, shown around his lower body, replaced the lighter-weight robes made from deer and antelope hides. Feathers were worn in the hair everywhere.

Ponca

This man, whom Racinet called Ponca, wears a mix of styles typical of the late 19th century. The feather war bonnet, originated by the Sioux, was worn all over the American interior. A bead or shell choker was typical of many groups. Leggings, later pants, had a decorative band down the leg.

Headwear
• basketry cap
• feathers and fur hair ornaments
• war bonnet

Hairstyles
• shaved head

Dress

Upper Garments
• buffalo robe
• cape
• dress
• mantle
• shirt

Lower Garments
• apron skirt
• chaps
• large apron (breechclout)
• leggings
• pants

Accessories
• earrings
• fan
• garters
• glass beads
• necklace

Footwear

THE ELEMENTS
OF COSTUME

Clothing Through the Ages

Each era in history can be defined by the clothes people wore. The first section of this book attempted to chart a relatively linear progression through the evolution of fashionable dress in the West from ancient times to the mid-19th century, while also glancing at dress in non-Western cultures and recording the traditions of European folk dress that were swiftly vanishing in the Victorian era. "Clothing Through the Ages" focuses attention on individual elements of Western dress, such as bodices and skirts or doublets and breeches, beginning in the 14th century, which is the era when fashion in the West can be said to have become firmly established. Unfortunately, space constraints, as well as the limitations imposed by the source material, have not allowed for anything like a comprehensive treatment of this very complex subject. Instead, noteworthy styles from a span of decades and centuries have been singled out to help convey the flavor of various eras.

The evolution of fashion has often been likened to a pendulum's swing, as individual elements travel to their logical developmental extremes before changing direction. Clothes not only conceal the body, they distort its natural shape through extension and constriction, and this is perhaps most clearly evident in the study of a costume's separate parts. For instance, skirts swell in all possible directions with the aid of pads, rolls, hoops, and trains before shrinking again. Bodices and jackets, long and short, may be stiff with bone, closely tailored, or loosely draped; doublets emerge as an outer garment from beneath the gown, only to contract until they disappear completely; and endless changes are rung on the display and concealment of layers. What makes the parade of styles consistently interesting is that every time a specific element of dress reappears it invariably does so in a slightly different guise from before.

What characterizes each successive era is its unique combinations of recurring elements. The pages that follow examine women's and men's dress separately, looking at it closely from above and below the waist, and spotlighting changes in elements such as sleeves, collars, aprons, and outerwear.

Women's Dress, *1300–1600*

Above the Waist

Throughout the 14th, 15th, and 16th centuries a number of countries could lay claim to being the center of fashionable dress. In the 14th century, France reigned supreme over all matters of sartorial taste, that Flanders presided over the court of fashion during most of the 15th century. It is Italy, however, which seems to have had the greatest influence on fashion in the Renaissance period. From the overall silhouette and color scheme to the construction details of individual garments, the courts of Europe looked to Italy throughout most of the 16th century for guidance in all fashion matters. This shifting of fashion influence is only one aspect of change discernible over this period. Construction techniques also radically changed throughout the course of three hundred years.

France, 1450–1500
Women's dress of the 15th century consisted of two parts: an underdress, or chemise, and an overdress. In the latter half of the 15th century, the neckline of the overdress was cut lower, either in a V-shape or square, as shown here.

See also
Women's Dress, 1300–1600
pages 282–83

Italy, 16th Century
This noblewoman from Naples wears a shortened tunic with open, hanging sleeves over her full gown of rich cut and uncut velvet. At her neck and wrists, pleated ruffs of stiffened lace appear, defining the snug fit of her undersleeves.

France, 14th Century
This group demonstrates the changing fashions of the 14th century. The figure on the left wears a surcoat, or fitted overdress, with long, open sleeves, scalloped or dagged at the edges. The pleated gowns of the middle figures resemble houppelandes, a type of loose man's garment adopted by women in the late 14th century.

France, 15th Century

This image of Bathsheba at her bath demonstrates the early Renaissance use of lacing to achieve a more perfect fit. Bathsheba's chemise peeks out from under an overdress with slightly bell-shaped sleeves. The gown is laced over a blue plastron at the center front.

Italy, 15th Century

Over a fine chemise, or camisia, of sheer muslin embroidered with red, the short bodice of this figure is constructed from velvet. Its slashed sleeves are a calculated measure to allow the fabric of the chemise to show through. Her hair is held by a pleated snood of black silk or linen.

Flanders, 15th Century

The gowns of these two Flemish women appear to be constructed in two parts, with a separate bodice attached to the skirt. Although the chemises of neither are visible under their overdresses, or surcoats, a pair of sleeves of contrasting material can be seen on the figure on the left.

France, 15th Century

This image of a servant depicts the V-shaped neckline that was popular in the last decades of the 15th century. A triangular insert can be seen at the bust, and the higher waistline is emphasized by a wide belt.

France, 15th Century

Here a *surcote ouverte*, or open-sided gown, trimmed with fur is worn over a chemise of linen with tubular-shaped sleeves. A set of tight-fitting oversleeves cover the arms from above the elbows to the wrist.

France, 15th Century

The fur used to trim the bodice of this young woman might indicate her prominent place in society. It emulates the style of a surcote ouverte, although it does not appear to be a completely separate garment.

Headwear
• pleated snood

Hairstyles

Dress

Upper Garments
• bodice
• chemise (camisia)
• full gown (houppelande)
• open-sided gown (surcote ouverte)
• overdress • tunic

Lower Garments
• skirt

Accessories
• belt
• ruff

Footwear

Women's Dress, *1300–1600*

Below the Waist

The role of dress in visually defining rank and status is clearly demonstrated from the 14th to the 16th century. Through sumptuary laws, which limited the use of fur, silk, and rare dyes by all but the highest echelon of society, monarchs throughout Europe attempted to keep a tight grip on the way fashionable dress could be used to demonstrate wealth, class, and rank. Although these sumptuary laws often failed to stem the growing tide of conspicuous consumption by the merchant classes, the social rank of women can still be interpreted by examining the cut and construction of the garments they wore. In a time when daily life amounted to hours of hard physical labor for many, only the wealthiest women could bear the inconvenience of fashion.

See also
Women's Dress, 1300–1600, *pages 280–81*
Women's Dress, 1600–1800, *pages 286–87*

Circa 1540
The deflated silhouette of this skirt is a clue to its date. Although the construction of the skirt is similar to those of the mid-16th century, it is worn without the farthingale, creating a gently pleated effect.

14th Century
The tunic or dress of this Italian woman of high social rank reaches below her ankles and pools on the floor when seated. It is fitted to the hips, where it would have swelled slightly to attain a moderate fullness.

14th Century
Unlike the dress of wealthier women, this French peasant's attire reflects more practical concerns. Her fitted tunic is lifted up to reveal the chemise underneath, a measure taken to aid her work as a gardener.

Circa 1545
The bell-shaped silhouette of the skirt is achieved by a supportive undergarment, the verdugale. This stiffened petticoat would have hung from the lowest part of the corset to create a conelike silhouette from the waist down.

Mid-15th Century

The use of fur to trim bodice and skirt, as seen on this French example, was reserved for those who could afford it. Its use could serve multiple purposes, from warming the body to conveying importance and wealth.

Circa 1560

The Spanish farthingale (also known as the verdugale) was constructed of a series of concentric hoops, radiating from below the hips to above the hem. In this later example, the skirt has been gathered to create a fuller, less conical silhouette.

Circa 1590

Toward the end of the 16th century, the shifting silhouette of skirts culminates in the wheel-shaped farthingale seen here. Extending straight out from the waist, the wheel farthingale supported the skirt in a perfectly cylindrical shape.

Circa 1590–95

At the end of the 16th century, the farthingale evolved into a fuller shape. Referred to as the French farthingale, the full skirt it supported was paired with a pointed bodice, with the volume of the skirt pleated over the hips.

Circa 1590–95

This middle-class woman from the late 16th century wears a less voluminous version of the French farthingale silhouette than that seen at court. Her pointed bodice extends to her hips, ending in scalloped tabs.

Circa 1595

At the very end of the 16th century, the wheel farthingale was paired with a very pointed bodice. With the fullness of the skirt pleated into the waist beneath this bodice, the illusion of a small waist was even more exaggerated.

Women's Dress, *1600–1800*

Above the Waist

The extremes to which the natural silhouette of the human form was altered by fashion were achieved through often painful means. By the 17th century the use of whalebone to rein in the woman's torso was commonplace. In the form of a stiffened bodice, commonly referred to as a "pair of bodies" in historical documents, fashion was used to manipulate the waistline and even the posture. Through the insertion of a busk, made of carved whalebone or stiffened leather, at the center front of the bodice, the woman's bust was flattened and the shoulders and torso pushed backward to create a tilted posture. The distortion of the body through costume continued into the mid-18th century.

France, c. 1675–80
This dancer at the court of Louis XIV wears a stiffened bodice trimmed with a rosette at the bust. The graceful pose belies a truth about the fashion of the late 17th century—her controlled movements were due as much to the constriction caused by her costume as to her training.

See also
**Women's
Dress
1300–1600,**
pages 280–83

France, c. 1635–40
Like the boned bodice and busk, the off-the-shoulder neckline of the 17th century was successful in restricting natural movement. Here, the sleeves are built in two pieces, revealing the sleeves of the chemise underneath.

England, c. 1641
A linen collar trimmed with delicate lace is worn over a pair of bodies or boned bodice. It is tabbed to allow for a smoother fit at the hips.

England, c. 1641
The period from the 1620s to the 1640s saw a change in the construction of women's clothing. The bodice and skirt were now made separately, creating a less constrictive style than that seen at the beginning of the century.

Headwear

Hairstyles

Dress

Upper Garments
• bodice
• chemise
• cotton gown
• jacket
• overbodice (casaquin)

Lower Garments
• apron
• skirt

Accessories
• fichu
• lace-trimmed cuffs
• rosette

Footwear

Holland, *c.* 1660

The simplicity of the satin bodice and plain linen fichu is due in large part to the location of its wearer. Due to proscriptions on the use of lace and trim, trends in dress in the Netherlands lagged behind those of France.

France, Early 1700s

Although aprons were at once fashionable and functional garments, the one worn by this peasant lacks the embroidery and lace trim that would mark her as a lady of rank. Still, her robe is artfully trimmed with ribbon bows and lace trim on the sleeves.

France, *c.* 1730s

The casaquin, or loose-fitting overbodice, came to be known by a number of names during the 18th century. As the *pet-en-l'air*, or caraco, it could be worn belted at the waist as in this example, or loose from the shoulders.

France, *c.* 1780

The fitted bodice of this robe is laced up the center front over an inserted panel of embroidery or a cotton chemise. At her wrists, cuffs trimmed with lace would have been inserted and removed for washing after each wearing.

France, *c.* 1785

When Elisabeth Vigée-Lebrun painted Marie Antoinette in a simple cotton muslin gown in 1783, a fashion revolution was begun. The *chemise de la reine* introduced lightweight cotton gowns as acceptable daywear.

France, *c.* 1789

The late 18th century saw the introduction of a number of jackets for women. Meant as casual daywear, this Pierrot jacket features long fitted sleeves and was worn with a lightweight cotton or linen fichu.

Women's Dress, *1600–1800*

Below the Waist

By the end of the 16th century, women's skirts had reached great circumferences. Through the use of the French farthingale, also called a bum roll or *cul postiche*, the silhouette below the waist had become wide and columnar in shape. Before the dawn of the 17th century, the wheel farthingale further exaggerated the shape of skirts, and it continued to be worn into the early 17th century. However, it soon fell out of fashion as a less structured silhouette became favored after the 1620s. By the 18th century, however, a distortion of the body below the waist had returned in the form of panniers. Extending the hips to the sides, the silhouette became wide and flat from the waist down.

France, c. 1727
The bell-shaped pannier is worn with the mantua, a style that was introduced at the end of the 17th century. It would evolve into the robe à l'anglaise of the mid-18th century.

See also
**Women's Dress,
1300–1600,**
pages 282–83

France, c. 1765
The pannier, or hoop petticoat, was first seen in England around 1710, but quickly entered the fashionable French wardrobe as well. At first a rounded dome shape, the silhouette had compressed into a broad flat shape before the 1740s.

England, 1619
In this illustration, with the woman's skirt pulled to the back, the extremely pointed bodice that was typical of the early 17th century is clearly visible over the plain petticoat below.

England, 1643
Here the skirt is pulled up at the back, revealing the petticoat at the front. It is held in place with a simple pin or decorative clasp, which leaves the woman's hands free to be engulfed by the large fur muff on her left arm.

Headwear

Hairstyles

Dress

Upper Garments
- bodice
- loose robe (robe battante)
- mantua
- overbodice (casaquin)

Lower Garments
- apron
- bustle
- hoop petticoat (pannier)
- petticoat
- skirt

Accessories
- decorative clasp or pin
- fur muff
- ornamental trimmings (passementerie)

Footwear

Early 1700s
In a practical measure, the overskirt of this peasant woman is bundled up to the waist, front and back, revealing a striped petticoat. Over both, she wears a long white linen apron.

France, *c.* 1725
A loose *robe battante* is worn over a petticoat and a less voluminous hoop petticoat in this illustration. The robe battante hangs loosely in pleats from the shoulders, front and back.

France, *c.* 1727
The full petticoat can be seen here, worn with a casaquin. The silhouette would have been supported by the bell-shaped hoop petticoat.

France, *c.* 1727
A belted casaquin or pet-en-l'air is worn over a full petticoat supported by bell-shaped hoops, trimmed with gold metal *passementerie* (ornamental trimmings) at the hem.

France, *c.* 1760s
A jacket is worn with a lace-trimmed petticoat, revealing the moderately wide, rectangular structure of the panniers during this time. The panniers have been reduced to smaller cane structures resting on either side of the hips.

France, *c.* 1775
The robe à l'anglaise is worn over a matching petticoat; the panniers have been replaced with a new understructure—the bustle. The bustle draws the bulk of the skirt to the back, reducing the width but maintaining the volume.

Women's Dress, *1520–1785*

Sleeves

Throughout the history of dress, sleeves often provide visual balance to the silhouette. They may become full when the skirt is full, helping to highlight a diminished waistline or elongated torso. Sleeves are also seen to shrink and narrow as the focus shifts from the bodice in women's dress to the skirt. As the art of dressmaking and tailoring became more sophisticated in the 17th and 18th centuries, so women's sleeves became more complex components of fashionable dress. From the trunk sleeves of the late 1500s through to the tightly fitted sleeve of the 18th-century robe, sleeves provide essential information in the dating of costume.

See also
Women's Dress, 1600–1800, *pages 284–85*

Circa 1595–1605
In the style of men's trunk hose, these sleeves have been slashed in an evenly spaced design to reveal the white chemise underneath. Balancing the width of the wheel farthingale, these sleeves may also have been supported by padded inserts.

Circa 1530
Suspended from the shoulder, the oversleeve is gathered into two sections and lined with fur. These sleeves are worn over an undersleeve executed in a contrasting fabric, culminating in lace at the wrist.

Circa 1540
Reflecting a slimmer silhouette, here the oversleeve is fitted to the upper arm, angling out toward the wide turned-back cuff. The undersleeve is cut in two pieces and tied together over the chemise sleeve.

Circa 1545
Ruffled epaulets are applied at the shoulders in this illustration of a wide fur oversleeve. In this instance it is worn over a sleeve split to reveal the full chemise sleeve underneath.

Headwear

Hairstyles

Dress

Upper Garments
• chemise
• oversleeve
• undersleeve
• slashed sleeves

Lower Garments
• wheel or French
petticoat
(farthingale)

Accessories
• epaulets
• fastening buttons/
pins

Footwear

Circa 1560

As the 16th century progressed, a less full sleeve accompanied the rounded shape of the French farthingale. Here it is trimmed with metal-thread embroidery and large epaulets at the dropped shoulders.

Circa 1590–95

A more modest sleeve size is worn by the middle-class woman depicted in this illustration. Reflecting the need for more ease of movement, they are paired with a French farthingale, or bum roll, to create a narrow silhouette.

Circa 1595

The width of the wheel farthingale is offset by the fullness of trunk sleeves in this illustration. Constructed with pinked edges, the black fabric of the sleeves provides a striking contrast against the white stripes.

Circa 1595

Large epaulets at the shoulders are slashed to reveal contrasting fabric underneath. The theme of contrast is continued onto the rest of the split sleeve, which fastens over a green undersleeve with buttons or pins.

Circa 1614–15

The fashion for blackwork embroidery on sleeves and bodices was introduced to the English court through relations with the Spanish in the 15th century. Its popularity declined only in the late 17th century.

Early 1700s

For activities such as riding, women would don costumes reflecting a masculine style. This riding ensemble features the same large turned-back cuffs trimmed with jeweled buttons that were seen on men's coats of the time.

Women's Dress, *16th–17th Century*

Aprons

The apron, as a fashionable accessory, was introduced in the late 17th century. Worn with the mantua or one-piece gown of the period, it offered the wearer additional opportunities for the display of wealth through its material and decoration. But aprons had been worn well before this time, primarily for their practicality. Easily removed and cleaned, these accessories would protect more precious garments from becoming damaged or dirty while women went about their daily tasks. For the peasant and growing middle classes, the apron was an essential accessory. In regional dress, this necessity was translated into a valued piece of traditional costume.

Norway

The drawn threadwork of this Norwegian *bunad* is referred to as *hardangersøm* in modern sources, tracing its origins back to the Hardanger region of Norway. Used to decorate the linen items of traditional dress such as cuffs, collars, and aprons, it is a form of embroidery in which threads are removed from the fabric to create an open weave.

See also
Women's Dress, 1300–1600, *pages 282–83*

Circa 1570

In this illustration a shepherdess from the Loire Valley wears a utilitarian apron over her petticoat. The material of the apron falls in pleats, mimicking the silhouette created by her French farthingale.

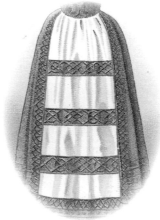

Circa 1592

In a state of undress, this sheer lace apron is worn with a petticoat and bodice at the end of the 16th century. The rest of her costume consists of a *peignoir*, or combing drape, worn while the hair was being dressed for the day.

Circa 1690

A decorative apron of silk, embroidered with silk and metal threads, was worn with the mantua. More practical aprons of cotton or linen were also worn to protect the skirts of the mantua and petticoat.

Berne, Switzerland

The apron of this woman from Berne is constructed of less humble material than its practical cousin. Made of taffeta, the apron is trimmed with lace and a contrasting material at the hem.

Bavaria, Germany

Racinet identifies this costume as that of a citizen of Upper Franconia, located in the Bavarian region of Germany. The apron is comparable to those found in fashionable dress of the late 18th century.

Zuid-Holland, the Netherlands

Here, the full striped skirt is almost completely covered by a checkered apron. In many parts of the Netherlands, aprons were constructed of two parts: a top panel, which might be adorned with embroidery or woven designs, and a long and gathered skirt that was attached to it.

Sissek, Croatia

This illustration shows two aprons worn together as part of the regional dress of this Croatian woman. On top, a short apron with long fringe is worn, while underneath it is an apron with red embroidered designs.

Asturias, Spain

In northern Spain, the regional dress for women of Asturias consists of a small apron worn over a skirt of contrasting material. A mantilla is wrapped over the bodice and tied at the back of the waist.

Scania, Sweden

Aprons of embroidered and pulled threadwork are layered in this ceremonial costume. A belt with two large decorated tablets is worn over both the shorter apron trimmed with tassels, and the longer apron, almost to the hem.

Headwear

Hairstyles

Dress

Upper Garments
- bodice
- combing drape (peignoir)
- loose robe (mantua)
- shawl (mantilla)

Lower Garments
- apron
- petticoat
- skirt
- stiffened petticoat (French farthingale)

Accessories
- belt

Footwear

Men's Dress, *1300–1600*

Gowns and Surcoats

Men's dress at the start of the 14th century largely reflected that of the century before, but became more sophisticated as the tailor's mastery of cloth was refined. The tunic, with its T-shaped sleeves, worn with a cape, was the primary silhouette for the first decades of the 14th century. However, in the third decade, the shape of the outer tunic, or surcoat, began to change. The sleeve became more fitted to the lower arm through the use of buttons along the side of the sleeve, sometimes up to the elbow. Around the middle of the century, there was another radical change as the hems of men's surcoats were raised to above knee-level. A short fitted silhouette continued in popularity until the turn of the 15th century, when the gown would reach its greatest popularity.

15th Century
By the 15th century, long gowns were worn only by professional men. Here, the central figure, possibly a representative of the clergy, stands out in his long gown. The other men are wearing shortened, fitted surcoats, except for the king on his throne, whose garb is most certainly ceremonial.

Late 14th Century
This surcoat has open or hanging sleeves. The slits from below the shoulder to just above the wrist are lined with fur and the shoulders are padded.

13th–14th Century
Here we see men's dress from the period, flanked by examples of the preceding century. The three figures in the middle show the styles available to men, from the supershort *paltok* of the 1360s at the back, through to the long gown in the center and the relatively short surcoat of the 1320s in the foreground.

Headwear

Hairstyles

Dress

Upper Garments
• fitted sleeves
• full gown
  (houppelande)
• paltok surcoat
• surcoat
• tunic

Lower Garments
• skirt

Accessories
• buttons

Footwear

Mid-14th Century
As the surcoat became more fitted through the chest in men's dress, the silhouette was balanced by a flaring of the skirt. With this additional yardage, the fashion for creating scalloped hems or dagged edges arose, as seen here.

Circa 1440
Although Racinet indicates that this figure dates to the reign of Charles V (1364–80), the gown has more in common with those of the mid-15th century. Identified as an outdoor costume, it is trimmed with fur and worn over a surcoat, the collar of which can be seen above the neckline of the gown.

Early 15th Century
Worn over a suit of armor, this surcoat with hanging sleeves is unbelted. It was most certainly part of a ceremonial costume that would not have been worn on the field of battle.

Early 15th Century
Fitting tightly through the torso by the use of a center front button fastening and featuring fitted sleeves, the skirt of this houppelande is quite full, with the yardage pleated into the body at the waist.

See also
Men's Dress, 1300–1600, *pages 294–97*

Men's Dress, *1300–1600*

Doublets

The doublet, in many ways, can be seen as the grandfather of today's three-piece suit. Worn with breeches or hose and a cape, these three garments made up the wardrobe of most men from the 14th to the 17th century. Called by varying names throughout the centuries and featuring a variety of silhouettes that emphasized different parts of the body, its construction remained relatively unchanged. Typically, it consisted of two front pieces and two back pieces, buttoned or laced up the front. Sleeves were considered separate and, when worn, they were tied onto the doublet at the shoulders.

Early 16th Century

This Italian figure wears a doublet that has been slashed to reveal his undershirt of silk. The doublet sleeves are attached at the shoulders with eglets or ribbons, and the entire garment is made of contrasting materials in the miparti style.

See also

Men's Dress, 1300–1600, *pages 292–93*

Men's Dress, 1300–1600, *pages 296–97*

Mid-16th Century

The low-waisted doublet of the mid-16th century was fastened to the trunk hose by a series of ties. This example has been stitched into panels, each panel decorated with diagonal slashes cut into the fabric.

Circa 1470

The doublet was laced to the breeches by ties or eglets. When the strain of bending at the waist proved too much, these ties would break, allowing the long shirt underneath to become untucked, as it has done here.

Late 15th Century

Doublets are often referred to as *pourpoints* in the 14th and 15th centuries. During this time, they are almost invisible underneath the full surcoat or houppelande. In this case, only the standing collar and sleeves can be seen.

Headwear

Hairstyles

Dress

16th Century

The large belly shown in this French or Flemish infantry uniform is formed by padding (*panseron*). The "peacod belly" silhouette is amplified by the doublet, which could be belted to fit over the panseron.

Circa 1620

The pointed doublet of the early 17th century retained a bit of the peascod-belly silhouette of the previous century. Here the panseron might have been replaced by two separate panels of padding, attached on either side of the center front of the doublet, which is less slashed than before.

Circa 1635

Here the doublet is belted slightly above the waist. Once again, the body and sleeves have been slashed to reveal the shirt worn underneath. A separate lace collar was now worn instead of the full ruff.

Upper Garments
- cape
- doublet (pourpoint)
- fitted sleeves
- loose gown (houppelande)
- undershirt

Lower Garments
- breeches
- hose
- trunk hose

Accessories
- lace collar
- ribbon ties
- ruff

Footwear

Circa 1640

The peascod belly was eventually replaced by a silhouette more true to the human form. Here, the waist of this leather doublet is placed at the natural waistline. The sleeves are sewn in panels to reveal a contrasting silk.

Circa 1660

The sleeves of this short doublet are attached with ribbon ties. The plain linen collar distinguishes this Dutch figure from members of the French court, whose costume would have been lavishly trimmed with lace and ribbons.

Circa 1660

The fashion for denying human anatomy returned in the later decades of the 17th century. This short doublet shows how fullness could be taken to the extreme. It is worn with a large shirt belted at the waist to create a bloused effect.

Men's Dress, *1300–1600*

Hose and Trunk Hose

Hose or stocks were initially constructed in two pieces, one for each leg. Typically, these leg coverings were made from woven wool, cut and sewn on the bias to achieve a more fitted appearance. Ultimately, the stocks were joined up the center back with a seam, becoming hose. As the hem of the doublet rose, the codpiece was introduced to provide protection for the genitals. At first it was a small triangular scrap of fabric tied to the hose, but it would take on grander proportions as the 16th century progressed. Just as advances in tailoring affected the silhouette of men's upper garments, so men's hose reflected a growing consciousness and then a rejection of the natural form.

Circa 1595–1600

The points or ties that attach the padded trunk hose to the hose are highly visible here. The fashion for wearing a large padded codpiece had faded by this time.

See also
Men's Dress, 1300–1600, *pages 292–95*

Cannions

The wearing of cannions—a length of fabric connecting the trunk hose and the nether hose—came into fashion in the 1570s. This fabric followed the line of the leg from the trunk hose above the knee to the hose just below it.

Late 15th Century

Wearing hose in a miparti style, where one leg is of a contrasting fabric, this Italian figure illustrates the distinctive style of men's dress during the Italian Renaissance. The shortened doublet displays most of the hose.

Circa 1370

The miparti hose worn in this illustration would have been sewn together at the back, with a small codpiece tied in place over the genitals. The hose covered the entire leg and foot, extending into a pointed toe at the end. Leather soles protected the bottom of the foot.

Circa 1570

Here the trunk hose are not worn with cannions. Instead, the nether hose and the trunk hose are tied with points (ties that are attached to an undergarment). Although it is not visible in this illustration, a padded codpiece must have been worn with this ensemble.

Circa 1578

Paned trunk hose were made of lengths of material, often satin or velvet, through which the shirt tails might be pulled. The exaggerated puffing seen on this illustration of a German figure is in line with the prevalent fashion of the Northern Renaissance.

Circa 1605

Although also wearing paned trunk hose, this figure from the start of the 17th century illustrates the refinement of this matured style. These short trunk hose would have been worn with cannions, reaching below the knee and attaching to the nether hose.

Late 15th Century

The small codpieces of the period can be clearly seen here. The figure on the left illustrates the manner in which they were tied on three sides.

Late 16th Century

Long and slashed paned trunk hose almost resemble breeches in this illustration. The distinction is in the length. Breeches of the period extended beyond the knee, while trunk hose were typically only as long as the mid-thigh.

Headwear

Hairstyles

Dress

Upper Garments
- doublet
- shirt

Lower Garments
- breeches
- cannions
- codpiece
- hose or stocks
- nether hose
- trunk hose

Accessories
- points
- ties

Footwear
- leather sole-pieces attached to hose

Men's Dress, *1550–1670*

Cloaks

By 1540, fashions from the French court were influencing the rest of Europe. The cloak was worn at its longest length by professionals, while the shorter length became an important part of civilian and military dress. By the 17th century it had evolved into a shape more recognizable as a coat, with sleeves and a buttoned center front. This *casaque*, or *mandilion*, can be seen as the predecessor to the riding coat of the succeeding centuries, in this way influencing both men's and women's costume.

Circa 1578
A cloak with a wide, turned-back collar is worn by this man from Germany. Worn over the shoulder and held in place by the hand, it acts as both a protective and a fashionable garment.

> See also
> **Men's Dress, 1670–1840,** *pages 300–01*

Early 17th Century
The fashion for ruffs in the Netherlands continued well into the 17th century. Here, a cloak with what might be referred to as a falling-band collar is worn with the standing ruff most popular in the preceding century.

Circa 1565
This illustration features the hooded cape, or *cape à capuchon*. The name refers specifically to the pointed shape of the hood, which might resemble the capuchon, or pointed cap, when pulled onto the head.

Circa 1570
Made of a wide, lined fabric, the collar of this short cape wraps around the body. Going over one shoulder, it is turned back to reveal the doublet underneath. It is trimmed with echoing lines of applied braid.

Headwear

Hairstyles

Dress

Upper Garments
- cape
- cloak
- doublet
- hooded cape
(cape à capuchon)
- paneled cape (casaque)

Lower Garments
- breeches

Accessories

Footwear

Late 16th Century

The cape or cloak, as seen on this German figure, was worn with the doublet and breeches for military and civilian dress. It was cut to accommodate the physical needs of the period, such as riding and the carrying of swords.

16th Century

As part of military dress, the cloak could serve an additional purpose—that of identifying the wearer as a member of a specific rank and loyalty. The cloak might also feature the fashionable slashing that adorns the doublet and breeches in this illustration.

Circa 1600

Worn here with the falling-band collar of the early 17th century, the cloak extends below the trunk hose. A notched collar can be seen at the neck on one shoulder, while the bulk of the garment drapes down the back.

Circa 1640

An alternative to the casaque, the short cape or cloak might be worn when not engaged in riding. Draped across one shoulder and under the arm of the other, the notched collar of the cape was allowed to drape across the back.

Mid-17th Century

At this time the casaque might replace the circular cape for riding. It had separate front, back, and side panels. The front and back might be buttoned together to create a coatlike garment, with the side panels hanging like sleeves.

Circa 1654

By this time the casaque had become rather more formalized, although it was still slit center back and sides to allow for easy wear while riding. Here it is also trimmed with gold thread embroidery or braid.

Men's Dress, *1670–1840*

Coats and Vests

As the tight-fitting and often padded doublet fell out of fashion in the 1660s, a new style arose in menswear. The coat, cut in four pieces as the doublet had been, now also featured sleeves eased into the armscye (armhole). This feat of fabric manipulation was a milestone in the art of tailoring. A matching vest and pair of breeches would eventually be added to the silhouette, setting the stage for the three-piece suit that would become a staple in men's dress of the 19th and 20th centuries.

Circa 1685

As the 17th century wore on, coats became more sophisticated, with sleeves tightening and lengthening, the cuffs becoming fuller and more ornate. Here the coat is worn with a contrasting vest.

Circa 1837

The 19th century saw an innovation in the materials used in the production of men's coats, namely woolen cloth. With this more malleable material, close attention could be paid to the fit of the garment, as seen here.

Circa 1664

The fashion for trimming the coat with ribbons at the shoulders and sleeves caused one contemporary observer to remark in 1663 that it was "a strange effeminate age when men strive to imitate women in their apparel bedecked with ribbons of all colors."

See also
**Men's Dress,
1300–1600,**
pages 292–93

Circa 1667

The rejection of the doublet silhouette in the 17th century is clearly illustrated here. Depicting a member of the bourgeoisie, this figure wears a long coat with short full sleeves, modestly trimmed with ribbons and embroidery.

Circa 1675–80

Illustrating the more exaggerated silhouette adopted for ceremonial dances, the length and excess of trim on this coat from the last quarter of the 17th century represent the exuberance of the court of Louis XIV of France.

Headwear

Hairstyles

Dress

Upper Garments
• coat
• double-breasted coat
• doublet
• vest

Lower Garments
• breeches

Accessories
• cravat
• ribbon and embroidered trimmings

Footwear

Circa 1685

Coats of the 17th century were collarless, allowing the cravat to be seen. The sleeves of the vest were also seen under those of the coat. As the period progressed, these would be turned back over the sleeves of the coat.

Circa 1720

Men's dress now consisted of a coat and vest, cut of the same fabric, with matching breeches. Both the vest and coat featured wide skirts, although the vest was not cut as full as the coat.

Circa 1729

Echoing the wide, panniered skirts of his dancing companions, the full skirts of this man's coat would have been achieved through the careful cutting of a single piece of fabric. The purely decorative buttonholes down the center back of the skirt were embroidered with gold thread.

Circa 1729

This illustration shows the way in which the shape of the vest shadowed that of the coat. With his coat buttoned only at the waist, a double row of buttons and buttonholes rises up the center front of the garment layers.

Early 18th Century

Trimmed with braid at the shoulders, cuffs, pockets, and down the center front, the collarless silhouette of the coat can be seen here. It was not until the final quarter of the century that the collar would reappear.

Circa 1786

The style of men's military dress often reflects the fashions of previous decades, but in this uniform of the Royal Marines the double-breasted coat is in the style of the period in which the gentleman served.

Accessories Through the Ages

This chapter looks at neckwear, bags, belts, footwear, and headgear. It is, perhaps, as notable for what is missing as for what is included, with women's shoes foremost on the list. Women's shoes are rarely visible in works of art until skirts shortened for good to above ankle length during the early 20th century. So, although women's footwear evolved at the same rate as men's shoes, as surviving examples attest, the evidence does not exist in pictorial sources. Also missing are items such as fans, which were a must-have for upper-class women from the end of the 16th century to the beginning of the 20th, and parasols, which women used to shield their complexions from the sun during the late 18th and 19th centuries. Other omissions include jewelry, which is a vast subject in itself, and men's swords, which served as accessories and weapons alike. Gloves, worn for centuries by both men and women, and frequently employed by artists as a component of proper deportment in portraiture, are also not examined, since their stylistic changes over the centuries are not well represented in the available illustrations.

Hats and hairstyles are among the most sensitive indicators of date, so therefore they occupy the largest portion of this section. Here the coverage stretches right back to ancient times and expands to include non-Western images. For much of Western history neither men nor women went bareheaded in public, and both Racinet and Hottenroth provide ample evidence of the multiplicity of ways people covered their heads. Moreover, the dressing of the hair beneath the hat or hood is also of paramount importance and has been as varied over time as any garment. No other aspect of dress conveys societal norms of age and sex as clearly as hair, and this is true of all human societies. As Mary Jo Arnoldi noted in *Crowning Achievements* (a study of traditional and modern African headgear), "Hats and hair styles… need to be understood as one of the technologies that people use to construct social identities and to produce, reproduce and transform their relationships and situations through time."

Neckwear

Men and Women, 1550–1650

During the mid-16th century it was common to see the squared-off edge of the shirt collar in men's dress displayed beneath that of the doublet. The neckline of the shirt was eventually raised, however, and what began as a small ruffled collar attached to the shirt became a garment in itself—the ruff. Made of starched linen or lace, the proportions of the ruff fluctuated from the 16th through to the early 17th century, until at last it was replaced by the equally monumental standing collar. Also constructed of stiffened lace, the largest of each of these styles required additional support in the form of a frame, sometimes referred to as the "supportasse."

Circa 1570
In this illustration the influence of fashionable dress on military uniforms is visible. Not only is the small pleated ruff worn in the fashionable style of the day, but the uniform shown here also features other items of fashionable dress such as trunk hose and a codpiece.

See also
Neckwear,
pages 306–09

Circa 1555
In the early stages of the development of the ruff, it was little more than an extension of the collar of the shirt. This illustration shows the ruff rising above the high collar in soft narrow pleats.

Early 1560s
A narrow ruff, or perhaps the extended collar of the chemise, protrudes from the high collar of the robe in this portrait of Elisabeth de Valois.

Circa 1570
The neckline of this squared bodice is filled in with a partlet of sheer material. Its collar is gathered to the neck and extends to the ears, with a ruffled edge. This style is most often associated with the Spanish court.

Headwear

Hairstyles

Dress

Circa 1590

Although ruffs continued to be worn during the same period, the standing collar shown here would gain in popularity, reaching similarly grand proportions. Also referred to as the "open ruff," it appears as early as the 1570s in European portraits of royalty.

Circa 1592

In this portrait of Elizabeth I, she wears the open ruff or standing collar supported by a frame. The outlines of the lace-trimmed headrail can be seen behind. This was separate from the ruff, a transparent veil also referred to as the conch, or *conque*.

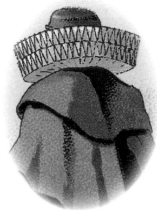

Circa 1618

Although the wide, pleated cartwheel ruff had lost favor among the fashionable élite of the rest of Europe, it was still worn by many in Spain and the Netherlands in the early 17th century.

Upper Garments
• bodice
• chemise
• doublet
• neckpiece (partlet)
• shirt

Lower Garments
• codpiece
• trunk hose

Accessories
• cartwheel ruff
• falling-band collar
• headrail (conch or conque)
• ruff
• standing collar

Footwear

Circa 1622

The fashion for large ruffs in the low countries of Europe continued into the early 17th century, although they had been replaced by the standing collar in most of the fashionable European courts long before.

Circa 1630

The more fashionable falling-band collar can be seen alongside cartwheel ruffs and standing collars in this early 17th-century depiction of the interior of a Dutch residence.

Neckwear

Men, 1620–1800

Around 1620, the voluminous ruffs of the 16th century gave way to a softer style. The collar visible over most garments was once more attached to the shirt underneath. Referred to as the falling band, this length of fabric was composed of several layers of lightly pleated lawn and was often trimmed with lace and embroidery. Simpler styles in band collars emerged around the middle of the century. By 1670, however, a new style in men's dress had appeared: cravats. These scarflike accessories were long and narrow, sometimes extending to the middle of the torso. Made of linen and sometimes trimmed with lace, the cravat was popular throughout the 18th century.

Circa 1660
Here, the falling band is worn unadorned with a waist-length doublet. The lack of lace and embroidered decoration may be due in part to the fact it is a Dutch costume, as the wearing of lace and excessive trim were often considered inappropriate in the Netherlands.

See also
Neckwear,
pages 304–05

Circa 1664
Worn by the King of France, the falling band seen here is constructed of fine lace. It has a fairly stiff appearance, perhaps indicating that it may have been starched or cared for separately from the shirt.

Circa 1690
These figures represent the variety of ways of wearing cravats in the 17th century, about one hundred years before figures such as George Bryan Brummel made the cravat legendary. On the left, the cravat is pulled through a buttonhole of the vest, presaging a similar style that would be known as the *steinkirk*.

Late 17th Century
The small falling band, or *petit collet*, was assigned only to certain members of the clergy in the 17th century. Here it is worn by a French abbot, who also wears a peruque, or wig, and the round hat associated with his vocation.

Headwear

Hairstyles
• short wig
(peruque)

Dress

Upper Garments
• doublet

Lower Garments

Accessories
• cravat
• falling-band collar
• kerchief
• ribbon tie
• ruff

Footwear

Circa 1670

The cravat first appeared around 1665, when the collarless coat made its appearance. The lace ends and ribbon tie of this cravat are probably separate from it.

Circa 1700

The cravat would become abbreviated in the 1720s, wrapped tightly around the neck of fashionable gentlemen of the period. Here the long, loose style of previous decades can be seen.

Circa 1730

Illustrated here is the abbreviated cravat that would remain the fashion for most of the 18th century after its introduction in the 1720s. It was formed in careful folds, fitting tightly to the neck.

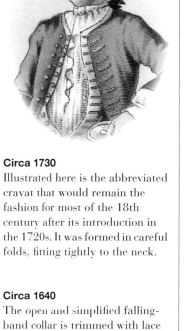

Circa 1640

The open and simplified falling-band collar is trimmed with lace and worn with a long leather doublet with paned sleeves. The decoration at the neck identifies it as military costume.

Circa 1795

The rising collar underneath a voluminous and artfully tied cravat identifies this French man as a member of the Incroyables. His cravat is tied in a style referred to as *cravate à la Laiguadier*.

Circa 1797

The Incroyables did not subscribe to strong political beliefs. However, this French gentleman, who is dressed in the Incroyable style, wears a black collar around his cravat, perhaps in mourning for the fall of the monarchy.

Neckwear

Women, 1600–1800

Neckwear in the 17th and 18th centuries was an essential part of fashionable dress for both men and women. The act of tying a cravat, for example, was sublimated to the point that a man's character might be judged by the practiced perfection of its knot. For women, the addition of kerchiefs and fichus to one's wardrobe provided not just an added layer for display of beautiful embroidery, but a layer of warmth as well. The shape and placement of necklines during the Baroque and Rococo periods was consistently low, sometimes to the point of providing very little protection from the elements.

Holland, Mid-17th Century
This wide kerchief, which is folded and draped around the figure's shoulders, mimics the silhouette of the falling band. Here it is worn modestly arranged to the neck.

See also
Neckwear,
pages 306–07

Circa 1660
The off-the-shoulder silhouettes of the mid-17th century would often be graced by a frill of the chemise, peeking out just above the neckline. For daywear, a folded neckerchief is tucked into the bodice to cover the shoulders.

Circa 1700
When engaging in activities such as riding, it was now the norm for women to don more masculine apparel. This style was complemented by masculine neckwear such as the cravat and bow tied at her neck.

Circa 1725
Here a shawl-like garment called the mantilla is drawn around the shoulders. It crosses over the bodice to wrap around the waist and tie at the back. It was sometimes made of a warm material such as wool.

Headwear

Hairstyles

Dress

Upper Garments
• apron
• bodice
• chemise
• shawl (mantilla)

Lower Garments

Accessories
• buffoon
• cravat
• fichu
• neckerchief

Footwear

Circa 1725
The mantilla is shown from the back, where the knot tied at the center back can be clearly seen. The trailing tails of this wrap would extend to almost the knee or mid-thigh.

Early 18th Century
Here, a kerchief and fichu can be seen layered and tucked into the bodice or apron of this peasant woman. Her apron has then been pinned to her bodice at the sides.

18th Century
This woman's kerchief is folded and wrapped around her body. The kerchief is constructed of a cotton or linen material and is trimmed with lace along the edges.

Circa 1790
The neckline of the bodice depicted in this illustration features a ruffled collar, into which a buffoon or kerchief of lawn is tucked. Lawn is a type of fine, open-weave linen or cotton material.

Circa 1790
It is easy not to confuse the volume of the buffoon with the finer silhouette of the fichu, as illustrated here. Like the buffoon, however, it is draped over the shoulders and tucked into the bodice at the center front.

Circa 1790
The sheer volume of material that made up the buffoon is clearly visible in this illustration. The rows of soft pleats would have been arranged carefully by hand and fixed in place at the center front.

Belts and Bags

Middle Ages to *c.* 1800

Men and women have used small pouches and bags to carry daily necessities with them for many centuries. Most depicted in medieval and Renaissance sources hang from the belt; depending on the bag's use and the status of its owner, it could be made of utilitarian leather or of luxurious materials attached to fancy metal frames. This style went out of fashion in the 17th and 18th centuries; men moved the purse to their coat or breeches pockets and women replaced it with large pockets tied around their waists beneath their skirts. Late in the 18th century women's dresses became so light and slender that pockets could not be used, so purses returned to fashion.

Girdle, Mid-16th Century
Jeweled or chain girdles marking the line of the pointed bodice and extending to long central pendants were popular among European noblewomen in the 16th century. Some terminated in rosaries or small books of hours, others in a larger jewel or a tassel, but they are not the type of belt from which a purse would hang at the waist.

Large Leather Bag, Middle Ages
Large bags like this were often used for documents in the Middle Ages. The names given to them in English eventually transferred to the bags' usual contents—a "budget" was a document bag and a "male" held letters.

Money Bag, 12th or 13th Century
This large, plain bag appears to be set onto a rigid frame and is slung from a wide and sturdy belt. Its size most probably relates to the occupation of its owner: he is a moneylender.

Bag, 15th or 16th Century
Both this and the bag opposite top left are detailed drawings from photographs of 19th-century reproductions of 15th- and 16th-century Italian purses. Racinet assured readers that the reproductions were accurate.

Bag, 15th or 16th Century

Another reproduction of an Italian Renaissance-era bag that was intended to be worn hanging from a belt. It measured 27 cm (10½ in.) in height and appears to be flat or square on the bottom, which was a common shape during this period.

Bag, 1510–40

This bag was drawn from a photograph of a surviving 16th-century bag with a rounded shape that stood 8½ in. (22 cm) high. Bags such as this could be worn by a man or a woman, usually hanging from a belt. They often had compartments inside.

Knotting Bag, 1729

Knotting, a means of producing decorative braid, was a popular pastime for 18th-century women, who carried knotting shuttles and thread in decorative drawstring bags. They developed into reticules at the end of the century.

Handbag, 1799

The cameo painted on the side of this basketlike handbag shows the influence of the Classical revival then in full swing. Women often made their bags themselves at this period, but this one was probably professionally made.

Basket, 1800

The woman carrying this round basket is a well-to-do German from Frankfurt dressed in the French informal style of the 1780s, although the illustration from which she was taken dates to 1800.

"Indispensable," c. 1805

Empire-style dresses were too narrow and lightweight to enable belongings to be kept in pockets, so handbags became necessary. They were known initially as "indispensables" in English and *réticules* in French.

Footwear

Men, 1st Century AD–1700

Shoes are among the most powerful of garments. They affect posture, gait, and demeanor in a way that other garments do not. From earliest times, beautiful shoes made with precious or exotic materials have identified their wearers as people of high status. They have also functioned as ritual and symbolic objects. Prior to the 20th century, women's shoes were only sporadically visible beneath long skirts, although men and moralists have been keenly aware of their power. Indeed, in the 17th century the English Parliament decreed that it would grant a divorce to any man lured unwittingly into marriage by a woman wearing high heels.

Roman Shoes, c. 1st Century AD

We think of Roman shoes as strappy leather sandals, but Romans also wore closed shoes and boots. These are boots and may be a Romanized version of boots worn by the Gauls, which, like the pants that he wears, the Romans adopted from the Gauls around this time. The bright color was intended by Racinet to denote imperial purple.

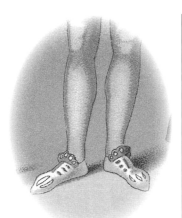

Poulaines, 13th or 14th Century

This man is a cowherd; he wears ankle-high black boots with poulaines—long pointed toes. Poulaines were revived several times during the Middle Ages, and among the leisured classes were often much longer than this.

Slashed Shoes, c. 1570–75

These flat white leather shoes show the narrowed toe of the second half of the 16th century. They are gold-trimmed and slashed to match the clothes King Charles IX of France wears with them.

Boots, 1630s

This Dutch soldier wears his rounded-toe boots with the tops high to the knee, although they are wide enough to have allowed him to fold them down. Bucket-topped boots were another option in the 17th century.

Headwear

Hairstyles

Dress

Upper Garments

Lower Garments

Accessories

Shoe Roses, *c.* 1630

These brown leather shoes are cut quite low at the sides, with a long tongue and narrow latchets that tie across the instep, square toes and a curved heel. The shoes are nearly engulfed by the enormous ribbon rosettes.

Riding Boots, *c.* 1640

These are black leather riding boots worn by a French cavalry officer. The butterfly-shaped leathers across the instep were used to attach the spurs, and they also protected the boot from abrasion by the stirrup.

Bucket-Topped Boots, Mid-17th Century

This was a wildly popular form of boot across Europe in the 17th century. Although the boots look stiff, the tops were supple enough to be folded down at the knee and then up again to form the cup of the "bucket."

Footwear
• ankle, bucket-topped and riding boots
• flat, heeled and slashed shoes
• ornament of bows and rosettes
• sandals

Bows, 1670s

Shoe roses gave way in the 1670s to huge, flat, stiff bows that extended beyond the sides of the shoe. This particular pair is worn by a French courtier whose red heels were de rigueur at the court.

Red Heels, *c.* 1670

Black and brown were the most common colors for men's shoes in this period. These buff leather ones with plain tie closures belong to a member of the French royal household and, characteristically, have red heels.

High Tongues, 1690s

These shiny black leather shoes have a fashionably wide toe and a stiffened tongue so long that it curls back on itself. These are lined in black, but such tongues were often lined with a contrasting color, usually red.

Headwear and Hairstyles

Women, Ancient World to the Middle Ages

Women in ancient Greece and Rome are thought to have expended a tremendous amount of time and effort on dressing their hair, including dyeing it and, when necessary, augmenting or replacing their own with false hair or wigs. Like men, they are often depicted bareheaded, although it is known that Roman women especially were customarily veiled when they went out of doors. Women in the Middle Ages also spent considerable time and money on hairdressing and headdresses that sometimes revealed and sometimes completely concealed the hair. Jeweled caps and coifs, elaborate braids, and veils arranged in an endless array of styles were customary.

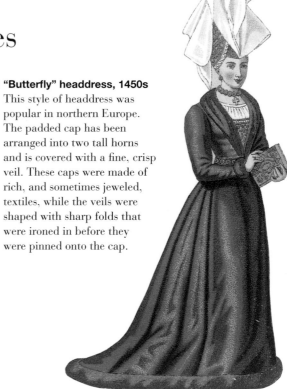

"Butterfly" headdress, 1450s
This style of headdress was popular in northern Europe. The padded cap has been arranged into two tall horns and is covered with a fine, crisp veil. These caps were made of rich, and sometimes jeweled, textiles, while the veils were shaped with sharp folds that were ironed in before they were pinned onto the cap.

See also
Headwear and Hairstyles,
pages 316–19

Greek Hairstyle, *c.* 4th–5th Century BC
This image was taken from an unspecified Greek vase painting. The hair is cut in bangs over the forehead and arranged behind the ears in thick, long, ordered tresses held in place with a bandeau.

Woman, *c.* 1st Century AD
The image source is unknown, but it seems clear that this large confection of curls and braids is augmented either with false hair or, more probably, a wig. Both Roman and Greek women are known to have worn them.

Julia Flavia, Late 1st Century AD
This portrait of Emperor Titus's daughter is engraved on a gemstone. The original shows her hair massed in tight curls over her forehead and separated by a diadem from the braided back tresses pulled into a bun.

Queen Clotilda, 12th Century

Based on a sculpture from Notre Dame de Corbeil, this drawing shows the hair divided into two long tresses bound with latticed ribbon. Other sculptures from the same church also depict women with two long braids.

Agnès de Chaleu, 1370s

Beneath a jeweled tiara, the hair is worn in cornettes—stiff doubled plaits that jut forward to frame the face. Cornettes were a French fashion of the second half of the 14th century that also caught on elsewhere in northern Europe.

White Mourning,15th Century

White has a long history as a mourning color in both Western and non-Western cultures. The long, veiled widow's hood and pleated barb under the chin were distinctive mourning garments for upper-class women from the late 14th century into the 16th century.

Spanish Women, c. 1275–84

These tall white coifs with their upturned, pointed crowns seem to be peculiar to Spain during the 13th century. Interestingly, they also closely resemble the corno that became the distinctive form of headwear of the doge of Venice several centuries later.

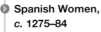

Beatrice d'Este, c. 1495

Beatrice, the fashionable Duchess of Milan, wears her long, smooth hair in a *coazzone*: bound, braid-like, with latticed ribbons, a style that originated in Spain. She also wears a *lenza*, a thin ribbon or braid, tied across her forehead.

Headwear and Hairstyles

Women, 1485–1600

The development of style in women's headdress differed from country to country throughout Europe. In Spain and the Netherlands, styles tended to lag behind those of France and England by decades, while in Italy, styles unlike any other on the continent were being worn. Religious and cultural differences certainly played a role in how the history of headwear would unfold in the 15th and 16th centuries. The practice of completely covering the woman's head was wholeheartedly adopted in countries such as England, while the Italian Renaissance saw women nearly bareheaded, frequently wearing just a hairnet, or caul, to cover their locks.

Circa 1540

The French hood consisted of an undercap of stiffened material, which arched forward over the ears. It was trimmed with braid along the top edge, and at the back a rectangular-shaped drape of velvet hung.

See also
Headwear and Hairstyles,
pages 314–17

Italy, c. 1495

The custom in women's dress for covering most of the hair did not take root in Italy in the 15th century. Instead, metal-thread nets tied around the head, such as the one illustrated here, allowed most of the hair to be seen.

Italy, Late 15th Century

A cap of velvet with a net of braid was also worn by women during the Italian Renaissance. This style, because of its association with the period, would be reborn in the 20th century with the name "Juliet cap."

England, c. 1530

The English hood consisted of a stiff frame, cubelike in shape, with lappets on the side and a drape of velvet fabric at the back. Here the lappets, possibly of cloth of gold, have been pinned up onto the top of the hood.

Circa 1570

Worn over a cap of black trimmed with gold metal-thread braid, the presence of this tall hat might indicate that the subject is dressed for activity outside. A length of fabric is suspended from the back of the hat and allowed to flow freely.

Elizabeth I, *c.* 1592

To achieve such height and form, the hair was arranged on top of a wired support. It is ornamented with pearls and a crown-shaped headdress. The pearl suspended over the forehead is reminiscent of the *ferronnière* of the Italian Renaissance.

Holland, *c.* 1618

Here, the hair has been captured under a high, jewel-encrusted cap. Called the capotain, it first rose to popularity in the late 16th century, although women in countries such as the Netherlands and Spain continued to wear the style until well into the early 17th century.

Germany, Late 16th Century

The highly ornamented headdresses of Germany differed greatly from those of the rest of Europe at this time. Here, instead of the small French hood worn throughout most of the continent, a crown-shaped headdress is worn.

Germany, Late 16th Century

Unlike headdresses in England and France during this period, those in Germany tended not to have a draped back. Where the French or English hood would have a curtain of velvet or other weighty fabric, there is none.

Germany, Late 16th Century

In this style, distinctive to Germany in the 16th century, the hair is coiled on both sides of the head and a piece of cloth is draped over it. Here, a gold metal-embroidered coif is placed over the cloth, securing it in place.

Headwear and Hairstyles

Women, 1680–1804

The 18th century marks the birth of two professions closely related to the dressing of the head and hair. The occupation of hairdresser reaches celebrity status with the rise of Léonard, hairdresser to Marie Antoinette. But Léonard was not the first hairdresser of note. He was preceded by Alphonse Legros, who founded the Academy of Hair in Paris during the 1760s. The 18th century also saw the rise in importance of the milliner. At once saleswoman and designer, the first milliners traded in not only hat trimmings, but also trim for dresses. It was not until the 19th century that the profession would be dedicated solely to the production and decoration of hats and bonnets.

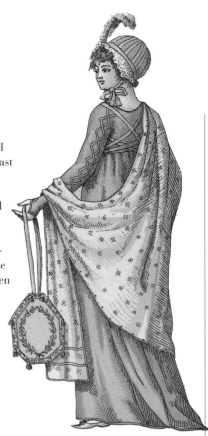

Neoclassicism in Headdress

Inspired by Classical Greece, hair in the last part of the 18th century was softly curled and arranged around the face. This stands in stark contrast to the high-reaching styles of the mid-century and even the *tour*, or high, vertical style of padded hair rolls worn at the end of the 17th century.

See also
Headwear and Hairstyles,
pages 314–17

The Turban

The turban-style cap appeared in the 1760s but continued to be popular throughout the rest of the century. This softly arranged headdress was made from a long length of lightweight material, wrapped around the head.

The Cap

This day cap is in the style of the French *dormeuse*, which was worn in the last quarter of the 18th century. Similar to a mob cap, it was distinguished by a pair of frills that curved over the ears, framing the cheeks.

The Cap

Most caps, whether for day, or evening-wear, were constructed of starched linen. Many, like here, were trimmed with ribbons and lace. Here, the cap accommodates the wide, loose-curl coiffure of the late 18th century.

The Straw Hat

Straw hats were first worn for masquerade balls in the 17th century. They were a product of the romanticizing of the simple life of the "milkmaid" that continued throughout the 18th century. By the 1730s straw hats with wide brims were fashionable day dress for European women.

The Bonnet

The growing taste for straw hats and bonnets spurred on the creation of unique styles such as the Theodore. This bonnet was distinguished by its tall cylindrical crown and sloping brim. Veils, as seen in this illustration, were often attached at the back of the crown or around the brim.

The Bonnet

This silk bonnet, with large brim and gathered crown, is in a style reminiscent of the mob cap. In contrast to the mob cap's informality, this bonnet, *c.* 1800, is trimmed with lace at the brim and with ribbons on the crown. Ties are drawn from the sides and tied at the back of the head.

The Toque

Unlike the bonnet, the woman's toque of the 18th century was brimless. Its cylindrical crown was constructed of silk and ribbon. A toque was often trimmed with feathers, and silk or ribbon tied it under the chin.

The Caul

The soft hairdressing inspired by Neoclassicism at the turn of the 19th century was often paired with a hairnet of gold—wrapped thread or silk called a caul. It would often be lined with silk and trimmed with gemstones.

The Hood

Another expression of the Neoclassical is this fabric hood, fastened with ribbon around the head. Illustrating the fashion in headdress of the last decade of the 18th century, this figure wears a long veil attached to the hood.

Headwear and Hairstyles

Men, Ancient World to the Middle Ages

Men in ancient Greece and Rome are often depicted with their heads uncovered and their hair carefully arranged. In medieval Europe, by contrast, men are frequently shown wearing hoods, hats, and coifs. The 15th century was a time when the headgear of both sexes was often very elaborate. The hood in particular, which men had begun to wear sideways on the head during the previous century, acquired a padded roll around the face opening—equivalent to a hat brim—that gave the hood new possibilities. Men also wore their hair progressively longer as the century advanced, and some are even reported to have dyed it.

Hood, c. 1412–15

This dagged red hood is adorning the head of Louis II of Anjou. The king, in accordance with contemporary fashion, is wearing it like a hat, with its face opening rolled up and pulled over the crown of his head, and its shoulder piece and liripipe wrapped turban-fashion around the whole.

Felt Hats, Mid-15th Century

These two men wear variations on the popular felt "acorn-cup" hats. The hat on the left is unusually tall, mimicking, perhaps, the steeple headdresses worn by women in the same period.

See also
Headwear and Hairstyles,
pages 324–25

Roman Man

This man has a head of long, carefully ordered curls confined with a fillet across his forehead. Although he is taken from a statue found at Herculaneum, his hairstyle seems more Greek than Roman.

Hood, Early Centuries AD

This peasant from Gaul wears the hood typical of the region. Known as a cucullus in Latin, it was a form that Gaul's Roman conquerors also adopted. The cucullus was also sometimes attached to a cloak.

Hood, Middle Ages

Hoods were seemingly more popular than hats all across Europe during much of the Middle Ages, especially for the lower classes. This appears to be a simple one of red cloth without any extraneous embellishment.

Coif, 12th Century

Coifs were close-fitting caps that tied beneath the chin. From the 12th to the 15th centuries they were everyday wear for a broad spectrum of men, alone or under additional headgear. This man is from a 12th-century copy of an earlier manuscript.

Doge's Corno, *c.* 14th or 15th Century

The official headgear of the doge, the ruler of Venice, was the corno, a cap characterized by a large point curving up at the back of the crown. It most likely developed from the fashionable hood of the 13th and 14th centuries.

Charles VII, *c.* 1455

Charles wore this tall-crowned, curly-brimmed hat, a favorite style of his, in a portrait by Jean Fouquet. It is made of shaggy plush trimmed with applied gold braid set in a sawtooth pattern (in Fouquet's portrait it is black).

Italian Hairstyle, Late 15th Century

Fashionable Italian men of the 15th century often paid as much attention to the styling of their hair as women did. Dark hair was in fashion for men, and some dyed theirs to achieve this.

Gondolier's Beretta, Late 15th Century

The beretlike red felt cap is part of the gondolier's official dress. The cap and the flowing hair are similar to caps and hairstyles worn by fashionable young Venetian men at the same time.

Headwear and Hairstyles

Military, Ancient Greece to the Renaissance

Armor, by definition, is clothing intended to protect the body, particularly in combat. Given the importance of shielding the head, helmets are among the most important and earliest armored garments. Not all ancient warriors wore helmets—the Egyptians, for instance, did not—but most seem to have used some kind of cloth, leather, or metal garment to protect their heads, and these were often highly decorated.

The helmet developed a variety of forms in medieval Europe, some based on types used by the Romans, others on helmets worn by invading northerners such as the Vikings. Iron gave way to steel as the metal of choice and was often elaborately embossed and engraved.

Crested Helmet
Greeks first made bronze armor between 1450 and 1350 BC. Bronze armor may have fallen out of favor between about 1100 and 800 BC, but by the beginning of the 8th century BC, it was being made once again. This hoplite, or infantryman, wears a bronze helmet with elaborate earpieces and an eyecatching multicolored horsehair crest.

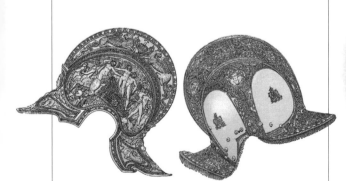

Burgonet-Morions, Second Half 16th Century
Both these elaborately engraved helmets belonged to noble Spaniards and are probably northern Italian work. As the name suggests, the helmet combined the morion's curved brim and comb with the pointed tail and overall shape of the burgonet. Both were worn by light cavalry and infantry.

Gladiator's Helmet
This elaborate, enclosed bronze gladiator's helmet is Thracian, which indicates its style and the style of combat its wearer practiced, not its ethnic origin. It has only two tiny openings for the wearer to see through.

Helmet and Coif, 11th Century
This knight wears a coif of mail under a conical banded helm of a type widely adopted in Europe and used for centuries. This is the style of knightly headgear that is depicted in the Bayeux tapestry.

Helm, Late 12th Century

This flat-topped, painted iron helm has a gold or gilded face guard and is the type worn during the Third and Fourth Crusades. It developed into the heavy, barrel-shaped helm of the 13th and 14th centuries.

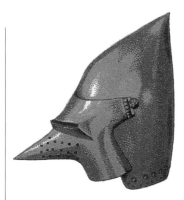

Bascinet, c. 1400

This helmet has a pointed visor, a style that became known in the 19th century as "houndskull" or "pig-faced." The extremely elongated point was intended to deflect an oncoming lance, thereby providing better protection for the face.

Bascinet, Mid-15th Century

The raised visor reveals a helmet with oval eye holes and a short, projecting nasal that create a T-shaped face opening. It is similar to a contemporary visorless helmet called a *barbut*. The visor is of the style known as "frog-mouth."

Bascinet, c. 1450

This helmet is similar to one that was worn by Frederick I, Count Palatine of the Rhine, which was made in Milan. The finest armor of the period came from northern Italy and southern Germany.

Swiss Guard, 1520–34

The Swiss Guard, formed in 1496 to protect the French king, were known for their colorful slashed uniforms and elaborate hats like this red, white and yellow plumed toque. This is parade dress, however, not armor.

Morion, 1559–72

Morions—16th-century helmets with a deeply curved brim extending to points at center front and back, and a comb running along the center of the crown—were worn primarily by light infantrymen.

Headwear and Hairstyles

Men, 1485–1600

In the centuries preceding the Renaissance, the hood had presided over men's fashionable headwear. As it changed in shape to become the chaperon with extended tippets and dagging, it reflected the silhouette of its day. The taste for wrapped headwear continued into the late 15th century, but more formalized styles had now begun to appear. The bonnet, a hat of cloth with either a brimmed or a brimless band, would be the dominant style throughout most of the late 15th and 16th centuries. Blocked hats of fur felt were also seen, the most notable being the sugarloaf. Shaped like the conelike blocks of caked sugar, the sugarloaf was popular amongst most classes.

Brimmed Bonnet, c. 1500
Complementing the squared-off necklines of the late 15th century, square-crowned caps were often seen in this period. The brims were upturned and either segmented or whole. The fabrics reflected the rest of the costume.

See also
Headwear and Hairstyles,
pages 320–21

Chaperon Style, Late 15th Century
In a style that reflects that of the rolled chaperon, this turbanlike style was popular throughout most of the second half of the 15th century, primarily in Italy.

Toque, Late 15th Century
The toque, or flat cap, with a very narrow brim can be seen as a male counterpart of the woman's caul, or hairnet, of the Renaissance. Here, it is worn with a single plume, in a style that was native to Venice, Florence and Milan.

Bonnet, Late 15th Century
In this brimless bonnet of cloth or velvet, the manner in which it was fitted into the band is observed. Large folds of material are eased into the narrow band at the front, providing support for its tall crown.

Feather Trim, Mid-16th Century

The use of trims such as feathers appears first in the late 14th century. This innovation, along with the use of decorative hatbands, would remain in the vocabulary of men's hat fashion for the next six centuries.

Brimmed Bonnet, *c.* 1570

The soft bonnet would remain popular amongst men through to the end of the 16th century. Here, an example of a brimmed bonnet is illustrated. Note that the volume has now been somewhat deflated, with most of the fabric pushed to the back of the crown.

Sugarloaf, Late 16th Century

With its tall, slightly pointed crown, the sugarloaf might be worn with a brim, as here, or without. The shape and stiffness was achieved much as it would be today, by pulling fur felt over a wooden block and using a form of sizing to stiffen the material.

Royal Livery, *c.* 1580

Dressed in the livery of the French royal household, this gentleman wears a flat-crowned hat with a relatively narrow brim. At the back of the crown, a trimming of color-coordinated pompoms appears.

Sugarloaf Variant, *c.* 1595–1600

Similar in silhouette to the sugarloaf, this hat features a small divot or pleat in the top of the crown. A braided hatband and feather trim decorate the crown, while the sloping brim is trimmed to a narrow width.

Felt Hat, *c.* 1600

The 17th century would see the introduction of fur-felt hats with particularly large brims and feather trims. In the last gasp of the 16th century, this style is foreshadowed on a much smaller scale.

Headwear and Hairstyles

Men, 1680–1800

The fashionable use of wigs among men came to prominence in the court of Louis XIV. This style was born out of necessity, as much as a growing trend toward fuller hairstyles for men. Louis XIV, like Louis XIII before him, had grown prematurely bald, and so played a major role in this fashion. In addition to covering bald heads, wigs were much more convenient for men as the complicated hairstyles of the day might require hours of hairdressing to perfect. And just as hairstyles in wigs changed with rapidity, so too did styles in men's hats. By the end of the 18th century, the fashionable gentleman would not be seen outside without a hat in the style of the day.

Circa 1790
A cocked bicorn, most likely of wool felt, is worn with the understated Cadogan or club wig. This style became popular in the 1770s as styles in men's hair tended toward more natural shapes. By the turn of the century, most men would be wearing their own hair, with only the more staid and elderly still wearing wigs of the old style.

Circa 1802
Worn with high-reaching collars and perfectly tied cravats, the *chapeaux-bras* and tall top hats complete the dandified ensemble of these gentlemen strolling through the park.

See also
Headwear and Hairstyles,
pages 324–25

17th Century
The fashion for morning or bathrobes can trace its origins to the courts of Europe. It was not unusual for the king to receive visitors during morning ablutions, therefore necessitating another style of dress.

Circa 1685
The full-bottomed wig is the style first adopted by Louis XIV. Variations, such as the dressing of a high, horn-like toupet shown here, would continue until the discontinuation of this style in the first quarter of the 18th century.

Headwear
- bicorn hat
- night cap
- top hat
- tricorn hat
- toupet
- wigs in various styles

Hairstyles

Dress

Upper Garments
- bathrobe
- fitted morning gown (banyan)

Lower Garments

Accessories
- cockade trimming
- cravat

Footwear

18th Century

Nightcaps with embroidered motifs might be completed as a demonstration of the needle skills of young, eligible women for their future husbands. Worn with the banyan, a fitted style of morning or bathrobe, they continue the tradition of Orientalism in textile design of the period.

Circa 1729

The bag wig is perhaps the best-known wig style of the 18th century. Here the queue, or ponytail, has been inserted into a silk bag at the nape of the neck, which is then tied onto the neck.

Mid-18th Century

Seen from the side, this more formal style of the bag wig should be noted. Here, the single-roll-curl style of the mid-18th century is worn powdered. This style was introduced to fashionable society around 1715.

Circa 1775

A tricorn hat is worn here with an unpowdered wig. The tricorn played an important part in the military dress ensembles of the 18th century, although it was quickly adopted for fashionable dress as well.

Circa 1786

The queue, or braided ponytail, of this man's wig can be seen under this cocked tricorn hat à l'Androsmane with its high, flat back. In addition to the cockade at the front, this hat might also be trimmed with braid.

Late 18th Century

Sometimes referred to as a "natural" wig, this style could have straight hair extended down the back or, as it is here, arranged in loose curls. Short, tight curls cover the top of the wig.

Regional Headwear

Europe

Headdresses are often the most recognizable piece of regional dress in countries throughout Europe. In some countries, it has been said that the style of bonnet or cap worn can be used to identify the exact town or village in which it is worn. Either through its shape or the materials from which it is made, a headdress may signify whether the person wearing it is dressed for a day of work or a festival. Regional styles of headdress for women, in particular, may often be linked to significant religious events or rites of passage. Some of the most ornamental styles are reserved for weddings and funerals.

Poland
Racinet identifies this woman and her child as part of the Jewish population of Poland. The fur-trimmed cap worn by her young son is similar to those worn by members of the Hasidic movement.

See also
Regional Headwear, *pages 330–31*

Finland
This man is a member of the Sami people, the indigenous people of Scandinavia. He is wearing a tall square-crowned hat that is trimmed with embroidery over his shoulder-length hair.

The Netherlands
This man from Friesland wears a tricorn—a round-crowned hat with the sides of its large brim pulled up on three sides. It was fashionable throughout the 18th century and was worn as regional dress into the 19th century.

Spain
The influence of military dress and traditions can often be seen in a country's regional dress. Here the Castilian man's hat reflects the military style of a century before.

Turkey

This peasant woman of Malissor wears the *bashlik*, or large embroidered cloth, draped as a headcovering. Delicate chains of gold cover her forehead, with small spangles of gold that dangle to just below her eyebrows.

Germany

Dressed in the traditional festival costume of Saxony, this woman from Altenburg wears a large headdress constructed of cloth, surmounted by a loop of braided fabric. In early depictions of this style, one finds a smaller scale overall, from a more modest-sized bow to a lower crown.

France

A woman from Dieppe in upper Normandy wears a simple cotton bonnet with a large crown and a wide brim folded back on itself. The sides of this brim could be drawn under the chin and secured there with a pin.

Ukraine

With long braided tresses, this young woman from Ukraine wears a wreath of flowers, straw, and ribbon as part of her festival attire.

Spain

Wearing the traditional Galician red denque (shoulder cape) bordered with black, this woman's hair is covered with a simple square kerchief that is folded in half and tied above the forehead.

Italy

A silk hood, or snood, captures the hair of this woman from the Travestere quarter of Rome. It is attached with ribbon in a large bow at the crown of the head.

Regional Headwear

Europe

Typically the most ornamental part of a regional dress ensemble, headwear also acts as a signifier of social rank and marital status. From the montera of Galicia with its pom-poms, to the carefully arranged cap and bonnet of women in some regions of France, regional headdress betrays an individual's place within his or her society. Regional headwear is equally affected by the fashionable dress of any era. Styles such as the tricorn or the sugarloaf are often seen in the regional dress ensembles of many countries throughout Europe. These styles may also appear as festive headwear, set apart through the use of seasonal decorations such as fresh flowers, grain, or other produce.

Hungary
Dressed for a feast-day in Hungary, this young man wears a wide-brimmed felt hat with a flat crown, decorated with ribbons and flowers.

See also
Regional Headwear,
pages 328–29

Italy
In this tableau depicting a group of young Roman men, the brimmed sugarloaf hat is worn with a silk hairnet of gold on the right.

Poland
Identified as an onion merchant by the garlands of onion worn over his shoulders, this man wears a short cap with no brim that has been trimmed with wool or fur for warmth.

Poland
This gentleman wears the *krakouska*, a flat, beretlike cap trimmed with a feather plume that takes its name from Krakow, one of the oldest cities in Poland.

Italy

The millinery style of Spain can be seen in this Italian man's long stocking cap, or *gorro*. In some regions this cap might also be worn underneath a wide-brimmed felt hat.

Spain

This illustration clearly depicts the Phrygian bonnet-style cap made of red wool. This particular style of cap is commonly worn throughout Catalunya and other regions of Spain.

Turkey, Greece and Bulgaria

The fez originated in ancient Greece and is today part of the traditional dress of regions within Turkey, Greece, and Bulgaria. This truncated cone of felt, most often in red, typically features a tassel or ornament extending from the center of the crown.

Spain

From Galicia comes the spiky montera, a hat with a triangular crown and a double set of visors, one on either side of the crown. The position of the frayed silk pom poms indicates that this man is unmarried.

France

Dressed for a feast-day in the Dieppe region of Normandy, this man has donned a round cap of velvet trimmed with wool. Attached with a knot of silk ribbon at the front is a plume of glass ornaments.

France

In this illustration you can see the back view of the white or powdered wig shown on the left. This style continued in some regions of France long after the fashion for them had died out in the 19th century.

Regional Headwear

Sri Lanka, Siam, China, Central Asia and Japan

The variety of hats, headdresses, and hairstyles in Asia in the 19th century, when our authors were compiling their publications, was the most complex and varied in the world. This is partly because Asia encompasses a vast geographic area and hundreds of cultures and subcultures, but also because the dress of the head served to identify the wearer's geographic origin, communal affiliation, marital status, occupation or social position. Equally varied are the materials—silk, wool, bark, lacquer, shell, and horn, feathers, metal, gemstones, glass, and bamboo—to name a few.

Kirghiz Headdress

Constructed on a hollow bark framework, this headdress (*bocca*) is further heightened by quills or light cane; silk and felt textiles cover the bocca and a network of wool tassels hangs down the back. Her hair is piled inside and the whole is secured with a chinstrap.

Japanese Pilgrim

He is wearing a large flat-topped hat called an *ajirogasa*, made of finely woven bamboo. To make the hat waterproof it could be impregnated with persimmon-tree sap (*kakishibu*), which turned it a dark orange-brown.

Japanese Unmarried Woman

The *tsubashi-shimada* hairstyle requires a professional to mould the hair with cosmetic grease, creating fullness at the sides, and loop the back into a flattened knot held with string and stiffened blue paper. Ornaments may be added.

Chinese Summer Court Hat

Belonging to a member of the gentry, it is made of finely woven bamboo, covered with thin silk and bound with metallic brocade. Twisted red silk cords descend from the finial, the material and color of which indicate rank.

Chinese Winter Court Hat
A Chinese scholar-official wears a winter court hat (*chaoguan*) of quilted silk with an upturned fur brim. The hat knob, or finial, is an indicator of rank, but the peacock-feather ornament is an imperial award of merit.

Han Chinese Silk Headband
Pictured here is the wife of a high official wearing a silk headband, often embellished with embroidery. Married Han Chinese women pulled their hair back in a bun decorated with ornaments or artificial flowers; this eventually led to a receding hairline, which the headband covered.

Thai Classical Dancer
A tall metallic headdress studded with cut-glass "stones" is worn. The shape of the headdress echoes the finials on Thai *chedi* (pagodas). Strings of jasmine flowers hang down the right side of the dancer's face.

Typical Mudaliyar (Sri Lankan Headman) Hairstyle
A bun at the nape of the neck is held with a large, rectangular tortoiseshell or horn comb with a crenellated top; a second, curved comb with a carved top is inserted across the front of the head.

Silk Brocade Turban from Tanjore, Southeast India
Tied around the front is the *sarpatti*, an ornament developed in the late 18th century consisting of hinged segments with a central jeweled pendant, often worn with a white egret feather.

Banjara Woman in Festival Dress
She is wearing a *chundas*, a high headdress. A heavy stick with a knob at the lower end is braided into the hair, then balanced by a weight hanging down the back. The whole is covered with a veil.

Regional Headwear

India and North Africa

Headdress in North Africa in the 19th century was extremely varied for both men and women as it was one of the essential expressions of personal identity: place of origin, ethnic affiliation, and marital status. For example, Jewish women in Algeria wore headdresses reflecting their place of origin: Spain, Majorca, Italy, France, Turkey, and those from the region since the Roman period. The most common headdress for men and women was a turban or cloth wrapped around a felt cap of varying shape. When outdoors, headdresses protected against the harsh climate and on festive occasions were vehicles for the elaborate display of wealth among Berber groups.

Algerian, Jewish and Moslem Women
Çarma, worn by Algerian Moslem and Jewish women, were introduced in the 18th century but went out of fashion by the end of the 19th. Moslem çarma could be silver or gold, but only brass for Jews, who covered theirs with a gold-embroidered veil.

Algerian Jewish Woman
Pictured here is an Algerian Jewish woman, *c.* 1842. She wears a long single braid tied with a ribbon and a fringed scarf (*mharma*), usually of plain cotton, over a cone-shaped felt cap, like the one shown on the right.

Algerian Jewish Woman
A cone-shaped felt cap decorated with silk ribbons was worn by married women. Although many chose to keep their regional dress, by the mid-19th century there were no dress restrictions on Algerian Jews.

Kabyle Berber
Ceremonial headdress: thick false braids over the ears were tied on top of the head. A sheer scarf hangs down her back, held by a stiff band of cloth and leather covered in coins; chains under the chin hold the headddress in place.

Kabyle Berber

The woman pictured here wears a softly pointed felt cap held with ropes of camel hair. A sheer scarf hangs down her back, held by the cap. She has typical Berber tattoos on her forehead and chin.

Mzabite Berber

From southern Algeria, this woman's hair is braided on one side of her head and brought under her chin. A triangular head cloth ties in front and a sheer scarf drapes around her neck and shoulders. She wears gold hoop earrings.

Algerian Zouave

An Algerian Zouave (soldier) wears a large wrapped turban over a felt cap, the long tassel of which hangs behind his head. His luxurious mustache was an essential facial adornment for the Zouave.

Striped Silk Turban

This woman wears a striped silk turban wrapped over a felt cap that peaks toward the forehead (not visible), with a gold brooch set with red and green glass. Her heavy earrings are a cluster of coral drops set with gold and held with a hook over the ear.

Headwear
• Algerian fringed scarf (mharma)
• Algerian metal cone headdress with veil (çarma)
• Berber headdress
• cone-shaped head cloth
• turban

Hairstyles

Dress

Upper Garments

Lower Garments

Accessories
• brooch
• earrings
• tattoos

Footwear

335

Regional Headwear

Africa, Oceania, and the Americas

The head is one of the most visible parts of the body, as well as being metaphorically important. Visibility makes the head a locus of communication: symbolic headwear such as crowns and bishop's mitres are worn only in public. In Africa, Oceania and the Americas, hats and headdresses communicate gender, status, age, personal taste, religion and sometimes ethnic affiliation. Materials may be readily available or acquired through trade or conquest; they are therefore limited in their use and highly valued. A great diversity of engaging shapes and colors enriches daily and ritual life.

Zulu Man
A Zulu warrior and chief wears a hat of small animal pelts and feathers, materials that demonstrate his reliance on and relationship with the natural world.

Galla Man
Dressing the head includes hair ointment and hair styling as well as hats. Coating the hair with grease, as this Galla man has done, or with mud or lime, is a method of keeping the hair clean as well as aiding in styling.

Gabon Man
A pointed palm-leaf hat sheds water efficiently and protects the head from the equatorial sun. Gabon straddles the equator; it is an area of tropical rainforest that provides the materials as well as the need for a hat like this.

Sauk Man
Native Americans wore a variety of headdresses and hairstyles. Men who lived in what is now the American Midwest shaved some or all of their head and wrapped furs around it, leather and later cloth, and attached feathers.

Headwear
- animal-fur hairpiece (roach)
- Apache feather headdress
- Borneo tree-bark helmet
- Botswanan leopardskin hat
- Marquesas feather hat
- Oregon basketry hat
- Sauk wrapped headdress
- Zulu animal-pelt hat

Hairstyles
- head dressings of grease, mud and lime

Dress

Upper Garments

Lower Garments

Accessories

Footwear

Fox Man

Roaches made from moose hair and deerhide were common among people of the eastern United States. They were worn ceremonially in some places, and in others only by accomplished warriors. A roach was either tied to the wearer's own hair or held on by a strap.

Borneo Man

A fish-scale armor helmet made from tree bark protects this Dayak warrior's head. The hornbill feather shows the courage and steadfastness of the wearer.

Lipan Apache

The feather war bonnet of the Plains Indians took a few different forms. This is known as the "halo" style, with erect feathers around the head and a train of feathers at the back. Elaborate headdresses were traditionally limited in use to great leaders and warriors, and were highly symbolic.

Botswana

Hats associated with chieftaincy usually make use of materials that are rare or difficult to acquire. Leopardskin, obtained by killing a dangerous predator, is a prime example. The skin is stretched over a form to make the shape.

Marquesa Islands

Feathers are colorful and showy, thus a favorite material for hats and headwear. This spectacular hat made with feathers, seeds and shells, and worn by a high-ranking man in the Marquesas, is everything a hat should be.

Southern Oregon Woman

Basketry hats were made the length of the west coast of North America, from the Queen Charlotte Islands in Canada to California. Tightly twined roots and bark kept the rain off and provided a canvas for creativity.

Glossary

AEGIS Ceremonial shield or breastplate particularly associated with the Greek deities Zeus and Athena.

AIGRETTE Feathered decoration for headwear.

AJIROGASA Traditional Japanese bamboo hat in a number of styles but always wide and roughly dome-shaped.

AKETON Quilted, padded undertunic worn beneath armor for comfort and extra protection.

ALB Full-length, usually white linen ecclesiastical vestment with long sleeves, gathered at the waist with a cincture (a cord or sash of cloth).

ALPARAGATAS Traditional Catalan shoes that laced around the ankle and up the leg.

AMICE Liturgical vestment made of an oblong piece of cloth, often white linen, worn by the priest about the neck and shoulders and under the alb.

ANGARAKA Men's long outergarment in India and parts of Central Asia, related to the jama. Design and material varied in quality according to the wearer's status.

ANGARKI Shorter version of the angaraka.

ANGAVASTRAM Indian long scarf or shawllike wrap worn in many ways and in many styles according to caste.

ANTARAVASAKA Inner cloth worn by Sri Lankan Buddhist monks, often made of discarded cloth.

APOLLO KNOT Women's hairstyle popular in the late 1820s and 1830s in which the hair is dressed on the top of the crown in a knot topped with vertical loops of stiffened, often plaited hair.

ARISAID Traditional Scottish women's full-length woolen outergarment. It was worn wrapped around the body, belted at the waist, with the rest of the material either pinned at the breast or brought over the head for protection from the elements. Usually undyed and sometimes decorated with precious-metal pins and ornaments.

ARMSCYE Armhole of any garment to which the sleeve is sewn on.

ARQUEBUSIER Operator of an arquebus, an early flintlock rifle.

BAG SLEEVES Bombarde or ducal sleeves gathered at the wrist so creating a "bag" around the arm. Popular in England during the 15th century.

BAG WIG 18th-century man's formal wig with the back hair enclosed in a small, usually black, silk bag.

BALDRICK Belt, often ornamented, worn across the chest to carry a sword or other item.

BALZO Bulbous, back-heavy women's headgear that first appeared in 15th-century Italy, spreading in various forms to other parts of Europe during the century. Height was important, and balzi tended to be highly decorated.

BANYAN 18th-century men's bathrobe worn at home over the shirt and breeches.

BARBE A long linen vertically pleated veil worn beneath the chin. Fashionable during the 14th century and remaining as a component of mourning dress until the late 16th century.

BARBET/BARBETTE In the 13th and first half of the 14th centuries, a linen band worn passing beneath the chin and pinned at the top or sides of the head. Also, the French term for the wimple.

BARDOCUCULLUS Hooded cloak worn in various styles throughout the sphere of Roman influence.

BATISTE Fine, soft, plain-weave fabric made of various fibers; in the 18th century usually linen or cotton.

BECHO Long, narrow strip of fabric worn over one shoulder by Venetian officials. The becho was a vestigial remainder of the long, hanging end of the rolled hood that was popular during the 14th and early 15th centuries.

BELLEN Small metal ornaments used on traditional Dutch costumes.

BERETTA Italian rounded, semiconical cap with turned-up brim or no brim at all.

BERGÈRE Style of women's round hat characterized by a wide, flat brim.

BEVOR Armor protection for the wearer's neck, similar to a gorget.

BEZANTS Thin metal disks used to decorate items of clothing.

BHANDANI A form of tie-dye used to decorate cloth in India.

BICORN HAT 18th-century and early 19th-century hat with its brim folded up along the sides to form two points. Could be worn with the points facing front and back, or side to side.

BIRETTA Cap, originally Italian, with three or more ridges on top, often worn by clergymen but also by laymen and academics.

BOLLENHUT Traditional Black Forest women's hat characterized by a flat brim with colored pom-poms on the crown.

BOMBARDE SLEEVES Wide sleeves on an outergarment. Also called ducal sleeves. Fashionable during the 14th and 15th centuries.

BONGRACE In the 16th century, a projecting brim, usually detached, of a bonnet, coif, or cap worn to protect the complexion.

BONNET À FLAMME Tasselled cap worn by French dragoons in the 17th century.

BOOT CUFFS Style of cuff on a man's coat in the 1720s, 1730s, and 1750s characterized by a large fold reaching back as far as, and even beyond, the elbow.

BOUBOU Long flowing men's overgarment worn in West Africa.

BOURRELET The padded brim of a man's hood, or a circular padded roll worn as a headdress, or as a component of one, during the 15th century.

BRACCAE Roman name for pants of various lengths worn by Celtic tribes, and which eventually found their way into the Roman wardrobe.

BRAGOU-BRAZ Traditional Breton men's breeches, generally full in the leg.

BRAIS Shorter pants, often woven from linen, worn throughout Europe in the late-Roman period into the Middle Ages. Often combined with chausses (hose) for fuller cover.

BRIGANDINE Sleeveless, fitted protective garment of cloth or leather interlined with overlapping metal plates riveted to a foundation.

BRUSTFLECK Traditional Tyrolean vest worn with a joppe.

BUCKET-TOP BOOT Man's boot with bucket-shaped fold at the top. Often decorated with spurs at the heel and stockings, sometimes lace-trimmed, inserted into the "bucket." Popular in the 17th century.

BUFF COAT Buff-leather coat, either sleeved or unsleeved, worn as protection against blades, sometimes in conjunction with light armor but frequently without. First appeared in the 16th century and continued to be used throughout the 17th.

BUFF JERKIN Protective jerkin made of buff leather. Used in the 16th and 17th centuries.

BUFF LEATHER Strong, heavy, but supple oil-tanned leather, often made of ox hide.

BUFU Surcoat, often highly decorated and made of silk, worn by male members of the Chinese imperial court.

BUNAD Traditional costume from Norway characterized by elaborate designs and decorated with embroidery, scarves, shawls, and jewelry.

BURGONET Close-fitting 16th-century helmet with cheek guards.

BUTTERFLY HEADDRESS Northern-European style of headdress from the 15th century involving fabric being draped over a wire frame creating a "butterfly" effect.

BUZI Square insignia badge worn by members of the imperial court in China to denote rank.

CALCEUS Roman ankle-high shoes for formal wear that covered the whole foot.

CAMISA Italian for "chemise."

CAMPAIGN WIG Style of men's 17th- and early 18th-century wig in which the hair is divided into three sections with one or more of these hanging sections knotted and tied back with a ribbon.

CAPADÜSHLI Small bonnet traditionally worn by women in the Lucerne region of Switzerland.

CAPOTAINE Curly brimmed, tall-crowned hat popular in the 16th century.

CAPUCCI Italian for "hoods."

CARACO An informal three-quarter length woman's jacket fashionable during the second half of the 18th-century. Loose, sack-back versions were popular in France while fitted versions were more popular in England.

CASAQUIN French name for a woman's fitted, hip-length jacket popular in the mid-18th century.

CASSOCK Close-fitting ankle-length garment worn now by the clergy but developed from everyday wear in the late Roman Empire.

CHAOPAO Women's silk robe worn by members of the Chinese imperial court.

CHAOQUN Women's silk skirt worn by members of the Chinese imperial court.

CHAOZU Necklace worn by members of the Chinese imperial court.

CHASING Method of ornamenting metal by indenting with a hammer and tools but no cutting edge.

CHASUBLE Sleeveless outergarment, the principal vestment worn by the officiating priest at Mass.

CHAUSSES Medieval term for hose; also a term for armored hose.

CHIGNON Knot of hair arranged at the back of the head.

CHITON A rectangular Greek tunic, generally made of one or two pieces of linen or wool sewn together along the sides and pinned across the top, worn knee-length by men, and by both sexes in a long version.

CHLAMYS Originally used by soldiers, this was a short cloak from ancient Greece, sometimes worn pinned at one shoulder leaving one arm free, sometimes pinned at the throat.

CHOGA Richly decorated loose, sleeved outergarment of Turkic origin made of soft wool, silk, or velvet.

CHOLI Midriff-bearing blouse worn by women in the Indian Subcontinent and Sri Lanka in conjunction with the sari.

CHONGKRABEN Traditional Thai skirt or hipwrapper worn by both sexes and all classes.

Glossary

CHOPINE Women's platform shoe of the 16th and 17th centuries with a very high sole designed both to increase height and protect the feet from dirt.

CHROMOLITHOGRAPHY Chemical color-printing process invented at the end of the 18th century that allowed printers to print in color rather than hand-coloring black-and-white reproductions.

CHUNRI Red bridal veil worn by Mughal women.

CHURIDAR Type of pyjama gathered at the ankles and worn by both sexes.

CIOPPA Tuscan name for houppelande.

CODPIECE Piece of cloth used to cover the crotch between the two legs of men's hose once doublets had shrunk well above the waist by the late 15th century. Initially plain, these became fashion items of some excess during the 16th century.

COIF Close-fitting plain cap, usually linen, that covered the top, back, and sides of the head, and tied beneath the chin. Worn by both sexes and all classes across Europe from the end of the 12th to the mid-15th century. In the 16th and 17th centuries, an undercap worn by women and often richly embroidered.

COMBOY Traditional Sri Lankan ankle-length hipwrapper worn by both sexes, similar to the Indian lungi.

COMPOSITE ARMOR Full-plate armor combined with mail.

COPE Semicircular cape used as a processional garment by the clergy.

CORNO Official headgear of the Venetian doge, distinguished by a large "horn" (corno in Italian) curving up the back of the crown.

CORSELET Body armor covering the torso.

COTTA Medieval and Renaissance Italian sleeved dress, often made of rich, lightweight material such as silk. It was worn over the chemise.

COTTE Medieval undertunic worn next to the skin by both sexes.

COUTÈRE Plate armor for the elbow, also called cowter.

COWTER Plate armor for the elbow, also called coutère.

CRACKOWES In the 14th and 15th centuries, shoes or hose with excessively long, pointed toes. Also called poulaines.

CROISURES À LA VICTIME In the 1790s, criss-crossed red ribbon trim on a woman's dress that signified the blood of victims of the guillotine in the French Revolution.

CUCULLUS In Roman times, a cowl and hood that covered the head and shoulders. Later, a hooded monastic garment.

CUIRASS Piece of armor covering the torso from neck to waist, of various materials, including leather or metal.

DAGGED EDGES Edges of sleeves and other edges decoratively cut away with pointed, rounded, or squared-off serrations. Particularly popular during the 14th and 15th centuries.

DALACHI A kind of Manchu women's headwear with a stiff board inserted in order to give it a flat, horizontal profile.

DALMATIC Wide-sleeved, often highly decorated overgarment worn in the Roman Empire that developed into priest's vestments in the 4th century AD.

DAMASCENING Method of ornamenting metal with wave-like patterns or with inlaid work of precious metals.

DHOTI Traditional Indian dress for men comprising a length of unstitched cloth wrapped around the waist, pulled up between the waist and tucked into the waist.

DOGALE SLEEVE Wide, flowing sleeve in the style popularized by the doge of Venice in the 15th century. Also known as a ducal or bombarde sleeve.

DOGE Elected head of the Venetian state from c. AD 700 until 1797.

DORIC CHITON A loose, tubular tunic made of wool.

DOUBLET Short, close-fitting, sometimes padded men's jacket worn over a shirt. Worn from the 14th century to about 1670.

DUCAL SLEEVES Wide sleeves on an outergarment. Also called bomarde sleeves.

ECHELLES Column of decorative elements, particularly a column of graduated bows on a stomacher in the 18th century.

EINSTECKTÜCHL Bavarian name for a fichu.

FAJA Sash traditionally worn around the waist by men in Spain.

FALBALAS Decorative flounces on a petticoat, often of the same material as the garment or sometimes of lace. Also called furbelows.

FANCIES Knots of ribbon used to decorate both men's and women's clothing in the 17th century.

FASCELETE Style of traditional women's headdress from Loreto, Italy, formed by folding a simple kerchief placed over the head and shoulders. Sometimes pinned with a brooch.

FEDLA Traditional Norwegian women's headdress.

FERDAH Women's cotton shoulder wrap from Senegal.

FICHU Large, square kerchief worn by women during the 18th and early 19th century to fill in the low neckline of a dress or bodice.

FILLEADH MÓR The "great kilt," traditionally made from many yards of striped and multicolored woven wool tweed, tightly pleated and belted around the waist, leaving a length of loose fabric thrown over the shoulder for use as a cloak or blanket.

FIRESTEEL A piece of high-carbon steel used together with a flint and tinder to light a fire. B-shaped firesteels and flints form the collar of the 15th-century Burgundian Order of the Golden Fleece.

FLAMMEUM Roman bridal veil.

FLICKHUCHKAL Traditional Scandinavian headdress.

FONTANGE Towering women's headdress made of wired tiers of linen and lace. First appearing at the French court in the 1680s, its preferred height varied over the years of its popularity. Called a commode in English.

FRENCH FARTHINGALE Wheel-shaped hooped petticoat that began to gain in popularity over the cone-shaped Spanish style in the late 16th century. Also called a wheel farthingale.

FROCK COAT 18th- and 19th-century men's coat. In the 18th century the frock coat, originally a sporting style, had a small turn-down collar and small or no cuffs. Around 1815 it reappeared in a new form with a turn-down collar and revers, a seam at the waist, and full skirts that lapped center front. It became the standard man's coat for formal daywear during the second half of the 19th century.

FROG-MOUTH HELM Full-face helmet with tiny viewing slits used by knights in jousting tournaments.

GABLE HOOD Also called a pediment or English hood, this was a distinctively English style of women's headdress consisting of a piece of cloth wired to form a pointed arch that framed the face. Worn over an undercap and fashionable *c.* 1500–45.

GALBINUS Latin name for greenish-yellow color used on expensive items of clothing in ancient Rome.

GAMURRA In the 15th century, the Tuscan term for the dress all women wore directly over the chemise. Usually made of wool, or occasionally silk, it fitted the body closely, and was worn by itself informally and beneath an overgown out-of-doors or for more formal occasions.

GARDECORPS 13th- and early 14th-century hooded overgarment with full sleeves that were slit to allow freedom of movement.

GESCHNÜR Chain lacing with decorative hooks from Bavaria.

GETA Raised, or platformed, wooden clogs worn by both sexes in Japan when streets were wet or muddy.

GHAGRA Indian women's full skirt that falls to mid-calf or to the ankle.

GIORNEA Overdress worn by Renaissance Italian women, open down the front and sides to show the garment beneath. Sometimes with detached sleeves. Also, a man's open-sided overgarment, sometimes decorated with embroidered devices.

GOFFERED Pleated or crimped, often in a honeycomb pattern.

GORGET Armor to protect the neck. Both mail and plate versions were known.

GREATCOAT A large man's overcoat, originally worn by coachmen, that crossed over into fashionable dress. Could be single- or double-breasted with a variety of collars, and in the late 18th century they often had shoulder capes.

GREAVES Armor for the shin.

HAKAMA Split skirt worn by Japanese men of the warrior class for formal and outdoor activities.

HALDIDI Form of ta'wiz made of a particular kind of jade and sometimes inlaid with gold or gemstones.

HAORI Short Japanese coat worn over the kosode or kimono.

HAUBERGEON A mail shirt; a shorter version of the hauberk.

HAUBERK Knee- or thigh-length, sleeved coat of mail that was the principal armored garment of knights from the 11th to the 13th century. Usually split at center front and back for ease in riding.

HAUSSE-COL A piece of plate armor protecting the neck.

HAUTE-PIÈCE Armor intended to protect the wearer's neck, specifically flanges that extend from the shoulder pieces (pauldrons) of a suit of plate armor.

HENNIN 15th-century women's conical headdress worn in Normandy and Brittany. A term, now believed to have been derogatory, also sometimes applied to the tall, steeple headdresses that was fashionable all across northern Europe in the 15th century.

HESSIANS Calf-high riding boots with a distinctive curve up toward the knee and tassel trim. Originally a military style, hessians became fashionable during the late 18th century.

HEUQUE Men's sleeveless overgarment, worn in northern Europe during the 15th-century.

HIMATION Long, rectangular draped cloak from ancient Greece often worn over one shoulder and around the body, leaving one arm free. Worn by men and women.

Glossary

HOPLITE Greek heavy infantryman who formed the backbone of all Greek armies for centuries.

HOSE Generic term for garments covering the legs and lower body.

HOUPPE Dutch women's headdress, also worn in the Rhône-Alpes region of France, characterized by its chimneylike shape and draped black silk. Also known as a huiken.

HOUPPELANDE A voluminous overgown fashionable in northern Europe c. 1380–1420. It was worn by both men and women; the men's version could be long or short, while the women's was invariably long.

HUL Traditional white cap worn by Dutch women, particularly in the south of the country.

IKAT Fabric in which the warp and/or weft yarns have been resist-dyed before weaving.

IONIC CHITON Easy-fitting chiton made from linen, usually pleated or crimped.

JAMA Cotton or silk long-sleeved, knee-length outergarment worn in the courts of central and northern India during the 16th and 17th centuries. The fitted upper portion was folded over and fastened under the armpit.

JAMDANI Expensive muslin sari from Dacca, Bangladesh.

JINGJU Beijing Opera, a form of classical Chinese opera derived from older schools, including Kunqu and Yiqiong, which became popular with the Chinese court during the early to mid-19th century.

JOPPE Traditional Tyrolean jacket.

JUDENHUT Cone-shaped, pointed white or yellow hat worn by European Jews in the Middle Ages as a distinguishing garment. Its wearing was enforced by the Fourth Lateran Council of 1215.

KALGI Decorative aigrette made from the feathers of the gray heron in the Mughal Empire in India.

KAMARBAND Broad sash that protected the lumbar region, worn with the angaraka. Developed into the European cummerbund.

KAO QI "Armor Flags" used to indicate that a character in a Beijing Opera has been kitted out for battle.

KATANA A type of Japanese sword.

KESA Japanese priest's vestment sewn from patches of used clothing that wrapped around the body and over the shoulder, and knotted at both ends through a ring.

KINKHAB Indian heavy and sumptuously decorated brocade of fine flattened precious metal wound around a core of strong silk fiber.

KIRTLE A laced garment, sometimes long-sleeved, worn over a chemise or smock. Originally worn by both sexes, it continued in one form or another to be worn, almost exclusively by women, from the later Middle Ages into the 17th century. After 1545 the term denoted a skirt only.

KLUT Traditional Swedish women's headdress of starched linen draped over a frame.

KOLPOS The bulge at the midriff caused by wearing a chiton bloused over a belt.

KORE Commemorative sculptures from ancient Greece.

KOROMO Japanese priest's formal robe.

KOSODE Older form of Japanese kimono, worn by both sexes, that developed into an overgarment from an undergarment worn during the Heian Period (794–1185).

KROSSE Cape, often decorated, worn by indigenous peoples of southern Africa and made of leather and skins.

KULLA Swedish traditional scarf headdress made of starched cotton folded into a triangle and tied around the head.

KURTA Long, loose-fitting shirt with either a rounded or a narrow collar worn in Mughal India and later.

KYAHAN Leggings worn by both men and women in Japan under outergarments.

LANDSKNECHT Late 15th- and 16th-century Swiss or German mercenary characterized by colorful, heavily slashed clothes.

LAPPET Hanging fold or flaps of cloth or other material.

LEDERHOSEN Southern German and Tyrolean men's leather breeches.

LEG O' MUTTON SLEEVE A woman's sleeve fashionable originally from c. 1828–35 and again from c. 1889–96. Characteristically has a large gathered puff at the upper arm and a tight or narrowing sleeve from elbow to wrist.

LIRIPIPE Long, pendant tail of a hood.

LODEN Feltlike woolen fabric used for making breeches in northern Tyrol.

LORICA SEGMENTATA Roman armor constructed of overlapping metal plates articulated with leather straps.

LUNGI Traditional Indian wrap of either cotton or silk worn around the waist and falling like a narrow skirt. Worn by men and women in some areas but by men only in the largest southern Indian state of Tamil Nadu.

MAMIAN QUN "Horse-face skirt," a style of women's skirt worn during the Qing Dynasty (1644–1911).

MANIPLE Ornamental, narrow-fringed strip worn over the left forearm by clergy.

MANTEO Traditional skirts worn by Castilian women, made of yellow or red baize.

MANTILLA Lightweight lace or silk scarf traditionally worn over the head and shoulders, sometimes over a high comb, by women in Spain and Latin America.

MANTLE A type of cloak or loose garment to be worn over other garments.

MANTUA A loose, one-piece woman's gown that developed in the 1670s–80s, characterized by a trained skirt that was swept up and draped behind. It was worn with a stomacher and a decorative petticoat.

MARSILLE Traditional Catalan men's short jacket.

MARY STUART BONNET A bonnet that was fashionable in the 1830s, whose wide sides and dipped brim recall the 16th-century French hood.

MATIXIU Horse-hoof-shaped cuffs popular with members of the Chinese imperial court in the late 19th century.

MINIVER The fur of the belly of the gray squirrel, characterized by its distinctive white shield shape surrounded by a gray border. Especially popular among the upper classes in the Middle Ages.

MI-PARTI Multi-colored.

MITER Ornamental gabled hat worn by Catholic bishops.

MO Japanese priest's skirt.

MONTERA Traditional pointed cap worn by men in Galicia in northwest Spain, characterized by the addition of pom-poms.

MORION A helmet used during the 16th and 17th centuries throughout Europe, characterized by a wide brim forming peaks front and back, and a high comb down the center of the crown. The morion was frequently highly decorated. Used principally by cavalry, light infantry, and archers.

MUREX Dye extracted from marine mollusks of the family Muricidae that was used to create imperial purple.

NAGAJUBAN Japanese underkimono worn for warmth.

NETHERSTOCKS A 16th-century term denoting the part of the hose covering the lower leg, the upper portion being known as upperstocks or trunk hose.

NIMA Transparent fine-cotton shirt worn by the male nobility in Mughal India.

OBI Wide sash used to secure the kimono. The style of tying this varied over time and according to the age of the wearer.

ODDIYANAM Indian decorative gold belt.

OORIJZER "Ear irons" used by Dutch women to secure in place and shape traditional headwear. Often crafted from silver or gold, the richness of these items announced the status and wealth of the wearer.

OSARIA Traditional Sri Lankan equivalent of the Indian sari.

PAENULA Roman hooded traveling cloak of leather, fur, or heavy wool.

PALETOT 19th-century short, loose overcoat for men cut without a waist seam. Also a women's short cloak or loose jacket.

PALLA Roman women's enveloping rectangular mantle.

PALLIUM Draped rectangular cloak without a fastening worn throughout Europe from Classical times onward.

PALLU Loose end of a sari, worn draped down the front.

PALUDAMENTUM Larger Roman version of the Greek cloak called a chlamys, which was fastened either at the throat or over one shoulder.

PANES Decorative strips of fabric produced either with strips of fabric joined at top and bottom or by slashing a length of material vertically, leaving top and bottom joined. Usually worn over a contrasting inner layer or lining.

PANETIÈRE A medieval waist-bag used to carry bread and other comestibles.

PARTLET Filling, sometimes of lace and often decorated, for the low or wide neckline of a woman's dress. Principally 16th century.

PATCH Small stiffened piece of black velvet or silk worn on the face by both sexes during the 17th and 18th centuries to highlight good features and hide blemishes.

PATKA Richly decorated unstitched band of cotton or silk wrapped around the waist and knotted at the front by men in the Mughal Empire in India and Central Asia.

PATTIYA Traditional Sri Lankan belt or sash worn by both sexes.

PAULDRON Upper-arm and shoulder armor.

PEASCOD BELLY Late-16th-century padded doublet that gave the wearer an exaggerated potbelly.

PÉDA All-purpose knife used by indigenous peoples in New Guinea.

PÈLERINE In the 18th century a woman's short, lightweight mantle tied at the neck with ribbons. In the 19th century a flat, wide, capelike collar, sometimes with long ends hanging down in front.

PELISSE In the 18th-century, a woman's loose lightweight cloak with wide collar and fur trimming. From the 1790s–1820s a woman's high-waisted, slender, long-sleeved coat available in many lengths.

PELLANDA Northern Italian name for houppelande.

Glossary

PEPLOS Greek item of clothing for women similar to a chiton but with the fabric of the top edge folded over and left hanging. The folded edges were pinned together along the upper arm.

PESHWAZ Women's open-fronted, full-skirted, high-waisted gown, often of high-quality muslin, worn in Mughal India.

PETASOS Felt hat from ancient Greece with round crown and flat brim.

PHASIN Traditional hipwrapper worn by Lao people.

PHENTA Parsi male headdress made of glazed, printed cotton on a wicker substructure.

PICKADIL In the 16th century, a border of stiffened tabs. At the end of the century the term also denoted a wired or stiffened support for a standing band.

PICKLEHUA Traditional Swedish men's felt cap constructed of four pieces.

PLASTRON A bodice front panel or section made of different material than the rest of the bodice.

POLEYN Plate armor for the knee.

POLONAISE A woman's dress fashionable during the 1770s and 1780s, characterized by a fitted bodice and a skirt, open down the center front, that was draped up into three puffs by means of internal ties or hooks. Worn with a decorative, often contrasting petticoat.

POULAINES In the 14th and 15th centuries, shoes or hose with excessively long, pointed toes. Also known as crackowes.

PYJAMA Generic term for various styles of cotton or silk pants gathered and fastened at the waist with a drawstring. Worn by both sexes in Mughal India.

QUATTROCENTO 15th century.

REBATO Wide, lace-edged, shaped collar of the late 16th and early 17th century, wired to stand up at the back of the head and worn with an underpropper.

REBOZILLA Traditional women's headwear in the Balearic Islands.

REDINGOTE A woman's coatdress modeled on the man's greatcoat, especially fashionable in the 1780s.

RETICELLA An early, characteristically spiky Italian lace based on cutwork filled in with needle-made motifs. Popular in the 16th century.

RÉTICULE Woman's small fabric handbag fashionable from the 1790s–1820s, derived from the knotting bag and often closed with a drawstring. Also known as "ridicule" and "indispensible."

REVERS Lapel.

ROBE À L'ANGLAISE A woman's dress with a fitted bodice, worn as an open robe over a decorative petticoat. Popular in the mid- and late-18th century.

ROBE À LA FRANÇAISE Also called a sack, this style of women's dress developed in the 1720s and continued to be worn for fifty years. Worn over hoops, it had a flowing back and distinctive triangular silhouette, and could be worn with its skirt open over a decorative petticoat or closed from the center front waist to the hem.

ROCHET White linen vestment resembling a surplice with close-fitting sleeves, worn by bishops.

SABATON Foot armor that was often extravagantly pointed, worn as part of a full protective suit.

SALLET Light helmet with or without a visor and with a projection over the back of the neck, used during the 15th and 16th centuries.

SANGHATI Shawl worn by Sri Lankan Buddhist monks in colder weather, often made of discarded cloth.

SARPECH Stemmed, featherlike gold plume embellished with pearls and gemstones, worn by Mughal royalty in their turbans.

SCAPULAR Long, wide band of cloth worn over the shoulders with an opening for the head as part of a monk's habit.

SCHEIBENBART Bunch of feathers used to decorate men's hats in northern Tyrol.

SCHLAPPE Traditional fan-shaped bonnet worn by married women in the Appenzell region of Switzerland.

SHALLA Expensive muslin sari from Chanderi, India.

SLASHING Slits of different lengths cut into a garment in a specific pattern, for decorative purposes. The style became popular in northern Europe by the end of the 15th century and later spread to Italy.

SLOPS A style of breeches popular in the first half of the 17th century characterized by their width.

SOLITAIRE A black ribbon from the bag of a bag wig that was brought around the neck and tied in front like a bow tie. In fashion from the 1730s to the 1770s.

SPANISH FARTHINGALE Cone-shaped, hooped petticoat that originated in Spain in the mid-15th century, spreading to the rest of Europe later in the century.

SPENCER Short jacket buttoned down the front worn by both sexes in the late 18th and early 19th centuries.

STEINKIRK A loosely tied cravat, the twisted ends of which were pushed through a buttonhole of the coat. Named for the way French soldiers supposedly wore their cravats at the Battle of Steenkerque (1692). Fashionable until about 1720.

STIKKEN Large metal button used to fasten the front flap of the breeches of men's traditional costume from the Zeeland region of the Netherlands.

STOLA Dress worn by Roman matrons. It was suspended from the shoulders by straps and was long enough to cover the feet.

STOLE Ecclesiastical vestment. A long band, usually silk, worn around the neck by bishops and priests, or over the left shoulder by deacons.

SUMPTUARY LAW Any law designed to limit or regulate the consumption of the population, especially to curtail perceived excesses. This could relate to food, luxury items, and clothing, among other things.

SUPPORTASSE Wire support for a ruff or standing band; also known as an underpropper.

SURCOAT Originally worn over armor, this developed into an outergarment, sometimes open sided, worn by both men and women in the Middle Ages.

SURPLICE Loose white outer ecclesiastical vestment, usually knee length and with open sleeves.

TABARD Tunic worn by a knight over his armor and emblazoned with his arms. Also had ceremonial and heraldic uses.

TABI Split-toed Japanese socks.

TABLION Japanese rectangular decoration on Roman clothing.

TAPA Coarse cloth made in the Pacific islands from pounded bark, especially of the paper mulberry, and often decorated with geometric patterns.

TASSETS Plate armor designed to protect the thighs that took the form either of separate, flexibly connected plates or a single plate that hung from the breastplate.

TAVANGER Breton women's apron.

TA'WIZ Mughal amulet made of a thin slab of gold, silver, or stone, and often inscribed with verses from the Qur'an.

TEBENNA Etruscan mantle with rounded edges that developed into the Roman toga.

THAVANI Half sari that covers the chest and wraps around the back.

TIPPET In the Middle Ages, long streamers hanging from the sleeves, later becoming scarflike strips of cloth draped over the arms and above the elbows. In the 18th century, a scarf wrapped around the neck and covering the chest or tucked into the bodice, or a small cape.

TIRAYA Traditional Sri Lankan veil cloth worn by both sexes.

TOGA A large, often elaborately draped rounded woolen mantle worn in ancient Rome. Originally worn by both sexes, by the 2nd century BC, it was usually reserved for male citizens. The color and style observed a strict hierarchy and changed over time. It continued to be worn into the 4th century AD.

TONSURE Shaved bald area on the crown of a monk's head.

TOP BOOT Man's knee-high riding boot with a black or dark-brown leg and a turn-down top of white or light-colored leather. Popular in the late 18th century and early 19th century.

TOQUE A 16th-century soft hat with a narrow brim.

TREWS Type of traditional close-fitting Scottish men's pants constructed from a single piece of tartan.

TRICORN HAT In the 17th and 18th century, a man's hat with the brim turned up in three places to form an equilateral triangle. Worn with a point at the front of the head.

TRUNK HOSE Short, often onion-shaped hose extending from the waist about halfway down the thigh, worn from the 16th into the 17th century.

TUNICA The dress worn next to the skin, under the stola, by Roman women.

TUNICA RECTA "Straight" tunic worn by Roman brides for their wedding.

UNDERPROPPER Wire support for a ruff or standing band; also known as a supportasse.

UNDRESS CAP Men's cap worn at home in the 17th and 18th century when not sporting a wig. Often highly decorated.

UTTARASANGA Long uppergarment worn by Sri Lankan Buddhist monks, often made of discarded cloth.

VAMBRACE Armor for the forearms made of either leather or metal.

VENETIANS Very full men's breeches that closed at the knee. Popular during the 16th century.

VESHTI Tamil word for dhoti.

VESTA Long, ample Venetian official robe with a high collar and ducal sleeves. Worn during the Renaissance.

VIRAGO SLEEVE A style of paned women's sleeve fashionable in the 1620s and 1630s. It was gathered into two puffs by a ribbon or fabric band above the elbow.

WAIST SEAM Seam cut into a coat or jacket at the waist to make it more fitted.

WARAJI Traditional Japanese straw sandals.

WELT STRIP Insert or seam for ornament or reinforcement.

WHEEL FARTHINGALE Wheel-shaped hooped petticoat that began to gain in popularity over the cone-shaped Spanish style in the late 16th century. Also called a French farthingale.

YING KAO Female "hard armor" in Beijing Opera.

YUNJIAN "Cloud collar," a style of cape attachment used by female characters in Beijing Opera.

ZORI Traditional Japanese thonglike footwear, made from a variety of materials.

Bibliography

ANDERSON, RUTH MATILDA, *Hispanic Costume 1480–1530*, The Hispanic Society of America, 1979

ARNOLDI, MARY JO, and MULLEN KREAMER, CHRISTINE, *Crowning Achievements: African Arts of Dressing the Head*, University of California, 1995

ASHELFORD, JANE, *The Art of Dress: Clothes and Society 1500–1914*, The National Trust, 1996

ASHELFORD, JANE, *A Visual History of Costume: The Sixteenth Century*, B.T. Batsford Ltd., 1983

BACLAWSKI, KAREN, *The Guide to Historic Costume*, B.T. Batsford Ltd., 1995

BARBER, ELIZABETH WAYLAND, *Women's Work: The First 20,000 Years—Women, Cloth and Society in Early Times*, W.W. Norton & Company, 1994

BISHOP, M.C., and COULSTON, J.C.N., *Roman Military Equipment*, B.T. Batsford Ltd., 1993

BONFANTE, LARISSA, *Etruscan Dress*, The John Hopkins University Press, 1975

BURNHAM, DOROTHY, *Cut My Cote*, Royal Ontario Museum, 1973

BYRDE, PENELOPE, *The Male Image*, B.T. Batsford Ltd., 1979

BYRNE, MURIEL ST. CLARE, Ed., *The Lisle Letters*, Chicago University Press, 1983

CAMDEN, WILLIAM, trans. PHILÉMON HOLLAND, *Britain, or a Chorographicall Description of the most flourishing Kingdomes, England, Scotland, Ireland*, G. Bishop and J. Norton, 1610

CARR, GILLIAN, "Woad, Tattooing and Identity in Later Iron Age and Early Roman Britain," *Oxford Journal of Archaeology* 24, 2005 (273–294)

CHENOUNE, FARID, trans. DEKE DUSENBERRE, *A History of Men's Fashion*, Flammarion, 1993

CROCKER ART MUSEUM, *Poseidon's Realm: Ancient Greek Art from the Lowie Museum of Anthropology*, Crocker Art Museum, 1982

CUMMING, VALERIE, *A Visual History of Costume: The Seventeenth Century*, B.T. Batsford Ltd., 1984

CUNNINGTON, C. WILLETT, and PHILLIS, *The History of Underclothes*, Dover Publications, 1992

DAVENPORT, MILLIA, *The Book of Costume*, Crown Publishers Inc., 1948

DE MARLY, DIANA, *Fashion for Men*, Holmes & Meier, 1985

DE MARLY, DIANA, *Working Dress: A History of Occupational Clothing*, B.T. Batsford Ltd., 1986

DUNBAR, J. TELFER, *The Costume of Scotland*, B.T. Batsford Ltd., 1981

EVANS, JOAN, *Dress in Medieval France*, The Clarendon Press, 1952

FERNANDEZ, DOMINIQUE, *et al*, *Moments de Mode à Travers les Collections du Musée des Arts de la Mode*, Herscher and Musée des Arts de la Mode, 1986

FOSTER, VANDA, *A Visual History of Costume: The Nineteenth Century*, B.T. Batsford Ltd., 1984

FOSTER, VANDA, *Bags and Purses*, B.T. Batsford Ltd., 1982

FOX-DAVIES, ARTHUR CHARLES, *A Complete Guide to Heraldry*, T.C. and E.C. Jack Ltd., 1929

GAIRDNER, JAMES, Ed., *The Paston Letters: AD 1422–1509*, Chatto & Windus, 1904

GRAPE, WOLFGANG, *The Bayeux Tapestry*, Prestel-Verlag, 1994

HERALD, JACQUELINE, *Renaissance Dress in Italy, 1400–1500*, Bell & Hyman, 1981

HETT, FRANCIS PAGET, Ed., *The Memoirs of Susan Sibbald*, John Lane The Bodley Head Ltd., 1926

HOLLAND, VYVYAN, *Hand-Coloured Fashion Plates 1770–1899*, B.T. Batsford Ltd., 1955

HOLLANDER, ANNE, *Fabric of Vision, Dress and Drapery in Painting*, National Gallery Co. Ltd., 2002

HOLLANDER, ANNE, *Sex and Suits*, Knopf, 1994

HOTTENROTH, FRIEDRICH, *Le costume, les armes, les bijoux…anciens et moderns, dessinés et descrits par Friedrich Hottenroth*, A. Guérinet, [188–]

HOUSTON, MARY G., *Ancient Greek, Roman and Byzantine Costume & Decoration*, Adam & Charles Black, 1947

KELLY, FRANCIS M., and SCHWABE, RANDOLPH, *A Short History of Costume and Armour, Chiefly in England, 1066–1800*, Charles Scribner's Sons, 1931

KÖHLER, CARL, and VON SICHART, EMMA, trans. ALEXANDER K. DALLAS, *A History of Costume*, Dover Publications, 1963

LATHAM, ROBERT, and MATTHEWS, WILLIAM, Eds., *The Diary of Samuel Pepys*, University of California Press, 1983

LE BOURHIS, KATELL, Ed., *The Age of Napoleon*, Metropolitan Museum of Art/Harry N. Abrams, 1989

LE GOFF, RAICHEL, "Venetian Portraiture 1475–1575: Mistresses and Courtesans," *ARTNewspaper.com*, 1994

LEVEY, SANTINA M., *Lace: A History*, W.S. Maney & Son, 1983

LLEWELLYN-JONES, LLOYD, Ed., *Women's Dress in the Ancient Greek World*, Duckworth & Co. Ltd., , 2002

MAEDER, EDWARD, *et al*, *An Elegant Art: Fashion and Fantasy in the Eighteenth Century*, Los Angeles County Museum of Art and Harry N. Abrams, 1983

MAYO, JANET, *A History of Ecclesiastical Dress*, B.T. Batsford Ltd., 1984

MEYRICK, SAMUEL RUSH, and HAMILTON SMITH, CHARLES, *The Costume of the Original Inhabitants of the British Islands, from the Earliest Periods to the Sixth Century …*, Dowding, 1821

MIDDLETON, JOHN HENRY, *Engraved Gems of Classical Times*, Cambridge University Press, 1891

MOLLO, JOHN, *Military Fashion*, G.P. Putnam's Sons, 1972

MOORE, DORIS LANGLEY, *Fashion Through Fashion Plates 1771–1970*, Clarkson N. Potter, Inc., , 1971

MORYSON, FYNES, *An Itinerary*, Theatrum Orbis Terrarum Ltd. and Da Capo Press, 1971

NEWTON, STELLA MARY, *The Dress of the Venetians 1495–1525*, Scolar Press, 1988

NEWTON, STELLA MARY, *Fashion in the Age of the Black Prince*, Boydell Press, 1980

OLIAN, JOANNE, "Sixteenth-Century Costume Books," *Dress* 3, 1977 (20–48)

PIPONNIER, FRANÇOISE, and MANE, PERRINE, trans. CAROLINE BEAMISH, *Dress in the Middle Ages*, Yale University Press, 1997

RACINET, ALBERT CHARLES AUGUSTE, *Le Costume Historique*, Firmin-Didot et cie, 1888

RACINET, ALBERT CHARLES AUGUSTE, *The Historical Encyclopedia of Costume*, Facts on File, 1988

RIBEIRO, AILEEN, *A Visual History of Costume: The Eighteenth Century*, B.T. Batsford Ltd., 1983

RIBEIRO, AILEEN, *Dress and Morality*, B.T. Batsford Ltd., 1986

RIBEIRO, AILEEN, *Dress in Eighteenth Century Europe 1715–1789*, B.T. Batsford Ltd., 1984

RIBEIRO, AILEEN, *Fashion and Fiction: Dress in Art and Literature in Stuart England*, Yale University Press, 2005

RIBEIRO, AILEEN, *Fashion in the French Revolution*, Holmes & Meier, 1988

RUNCIMAN, STEVEN, *Byzantine Civilization*, Longmans, Green & Co., 1933

SCHOESER, MARY, *Silk*, Yale University Press, 2007

SCHOESER, MARY, and DEJARDIN, KATHLEEN, *French Textiles from 1760 to the Present*, Laurence King Ltd., 1991

SCOTT, MARGARET, *Late Gothic Europe*, Mills & Boon Ltd., 1980

SEBESTA, JUDITH LYNN, and BONFANTE, LARISSA, Eds., *The World of Roman Costume*, University of Wisconsin Press, 1994

SNODGRASS, A.M., *Arms and Armor of the Greeks*, John Hopkins University Press, 1999

STEELE, VALERIE, *Paris Fashion: A Cultural History*, Oxford University Press Inc., 1988

SWANN, JUNE, *Shoes*, B.T. Batsford Ltd., 1982

TARASSUK, LEONID, and BLAIR, CLAUDE, Eds., *The Complete Encyclopedia of Arms & Weapons*, Simon and Schuster, 1982

The Taylor's Complete Guide; or a Comprehensive Analysis of Beauty and Elegance in Dress, Allen and West, 1796

VECELLIO, CESARE, *Vecellio's Renaissance Costume Book*, Dover Publications Inc., 1977

WALRY, LOUIS CONSTANT and GILBERT MARTIN, ELIZABETH, *Memoirs of Constant, first valet de chambre of the emperor, on the private life of Napoleon, his family, and his court*, Charles Scribner's Sons, 1895

WILSON, BRONWEN, *The World in Venice: Print, the City, and Early Modern Identity*, University of Toronto Press, 2005

WILSON, LILLIAN MAY, *The Clothing of the Ancient Romans*, Johns Hopkins Press, 1938

Index

A

aba (*abayeh*) 218
"acorn cup" hats 320
aegis 28
Africa 257, 258–67, 334–5,
    336–7
aigrettes 170, 200, 201, 253
aketon 48
Albania 254, 255
albs 92, 93
Algeria 258, 259, 260–1,
    334, 335
alparagatas 240
Amazons 18
Americas 257, 272–5, 336–7
Anatolia 18–19, 213, 214–17
angaraka 204, 205
angarki 204
angavastram 207
Anglo-Normans 50–1
Anglo-Saxons 42, 50–1
antaravasaka 211
apparels 93
aprons 125, 127, 155,
    285, 290–1
Arabs 20, 21, 258, 260
arisaid 233
armor
    ancient Greece 28–9
    ancient Rome 32–3
    Chinese opera 190, 191
    composite armor 137
    costume armor 120
    France 66–7, 136, 153
    Germany 120–1
    half armor 137
    headwear 322–33
    Italy 137
    mail 32, 48–9, 50, 67, 137
    Middle Ages 48–9
Assyria 16–17
Austria 234, 235

B

bag sleeves 54
bag wigs 163, 327
bags 310–11

baizhe qun 189
baju panjang 270
baldricks 165
Balearic Islands 242–3
Bangladesh 199
Banjara people 204, 209, 333
banyans 162
barbets 74
bardocucullus 45
bascinets 323
bashliks 329
Bavaria 234, 291
beads, glass 286
becho 118
bellen 230, 231
Berbers 258, 260, 261,
    334, 335
berettas 84, 321
bergères 230, 236
bezants 53, 77
Bhutan 199
bicorne hats 169, 326
bidang 271
birettas 111, 122
blackwork embroidery 289
bodices, pointed 154,
    283, 286
bollenhut 235
bombarde (*ducale*) sleeves
    54, 128
bonnet à flamme 168
bonnets
    men 324, 325
    women 181, 319
boot cuffs 163
Borneo 270–1, 337
Botswana 266, 337
bourrelets 65
Boyars 248
braies 43
brigandines 66, 136
Britons 38–9
Brittany 246
brustfleck 234
bucket-topped boots 140,
    146, 147, 313
Buddhist dress 193, 210, 211

buff coats 152, 153
buff jerkins 141, 153
buffoons 309
bufu 186, 187
Bulgaria 254, 255
Burgundy 47, 105
Buryats 222
bustles 287
butah motifs 219
butterfly headdress 56, 314
buttons
    Middle Ages 73, 74, 75,
        78, 79, 293
    Renaissance 145, 146
buzi 186
Byzantium 40–1

C

Cabinet des Modes
    (magazine) 170
Cadogan wigs 171
calzonchillas 273
camisia 107
campaign wigs 159
canezou 211
cannions 296
capadüshli 236
cape à capuchon 299
capotaine 317
cappucci 82
caps, women's 318
çarma 334
Carolingian costume 44
casaque 298, 299
casaquin 167, 285, 287
cashmere shawls 172–3, 202
cassocks 92, 147
cauls 319
Celts 38–9, 42
chador 220
chaopao 186
chaoqun 186
chaperon style headwear 324
chasubles 93
chausses 50, 89
chemise de la reine 285
Chile 272–3

China 185, 186–91,
    332, 333
chitons 19, 22, 23, 24, 25,
    26, 27
chlamys 24, 25, 29
choga 204
choli 203
chongkraben 196, 197
chopines 116
chundas 333
chunri 203
church vestments 92–3
churidar 209
cioppas see houppelandes
cloaks 146, 298–9
coats, men's 300–1
    see also frock coats;
    greatcoats
codpieces 87, 118, 119, 120,
    126, 130, 132, 296, 297
coifs 75, 321
comboy 210, 211
comeo sleeves 119
commodes (*fontanges*)
    160, 161
composite armor 137
copes 92
cornettes 315
corno 81, 321
Cossacks 250, 251
costume armor 120
costume books 97, 130,
    131, 142
cottas 85
cottes 59, 68, 69
cotton 13, 185, 264, 272
couters 50
crackowes 79
cravats 158, 179, 306,
    307, 308
crests 66, 67
crinolines 181
Croatia 252, 291
croisures à la victime 175
cucullus 31, 38
cuirasse 28, 33
    "muscle" cuirasses 29, 32

Index

kerchiefs 76, 142, 306, 308, 309
kesa 193
khalats 218, 222
Khanty people 249
khepresh 15
Khoikhoi people 267
kimonos *see kosodes*
kinkhab 207
Kirghiz people 222–3, 332
kirtles 57, 60, 61, 76
klut headdresses 227
kontusz 250, 251
kosodes 192, 194–5
krakouska 330
kulah 219
kulla 226
kurtas 201
kusak 216
kyahan 192, 193

L

lacing/laced closures 77, 86, 129
landsknechts 109, 120, 123, 133
Laos 185, 196, 197
lederhosen 234
leg-of-mutton sleeves 180
liangmao 186
libas 218
Liberia 265
linen 13, 14, 24, 154
liripipes 81, 83
loden 235
Longobards 73
Loreto 239
lungi 207
Lydians 18

M

mail (armor) 32, 48–9, 50, 67, 137
Malaysia 270–1
mamian qun 191
Manchu dress 185, 188–9
mang 190

maniples 92
manteos 241
mantillas 166, 308, 309
mantles 58, 78, 181
Mantua 106
mantuas 155, 160, 166, 286
marsille 240
"Mary Stuart" bonnets 181
Medes 20
Melanesia 268, 269
mememto mori 66
mente 253
merasim kaftani 214
Merovingian costume 44
Mexico 272, 273
mi-parti clothing 74, 86, 87, 296
Milanese dress 84, 104, 118, 119
  regional 239
military dress 15, 19, 20, 90, 108–9, 136, 145, 152–3, 168–9, 179, 259, 299, 301, 304
  see also armor
millstone ruffs 142, 144
miniver 57, 69
miters 92, 93
monastic dress 94–5
morions 153, 323
mourning 98, 111, 115, 155, 315
muffs 143, 148, 158, 164, 170
Mughal dress 200–1, 202, 203
mukta 207
"muscle" cuirasses 29, 32

N

naqsh 221
Native Americans 274–5, 336–7
Neoclassical style 174–5, 178–9, 250, 318, 319
Nepal 199
Netherlands 76, 128–31, 140, 141, 144–5, 230–1, 284, 291, 328

New Guinea 268
nightcaps 64, 327
nightgowns 158, 159
nima 201
Normandy 246, 247
Normans 50, 51
Norway 228–9, 290
Nubia 264

O

obi 192, 193, 194, 195
Oceania 257, 336, 337
oorijzer 231
orders of chivalry, men's dress and 79, 113, 164–5
Oromo (Galla) people 262, 336
Ottoman Empire 76, 213, 214, 216, 248, 254

P

Padua 239
paenula 31
Pakistan 199
palla 31, 36–7, 37
pallium 39, 41
paltok 292
paludamentum 35, 41
panetière 61
paning 91, 126, 134, 149, 297
panniers 286
  see also hooped petticoats
pantaloons 179, 183
Parsis 205
pas kontuszowy 250, 251
pashmina shawls 172
patches 160
pattiya 210
pauldrons 120
peascod belly 110, 134, 294, 295
pelerine 180
pelisses 180
pellandas see houppelandes
peploi 26, 27
Persians 20, 21, 213, 218–21
peshwaz 209

pet-en-l'air 285, 287
petasos 25
petticoat breeches 145, 156, 158
phasin 196, 197
phenta hats 205
Philippines 270
Phoenicia 16, 17
Phrygian caps 19, 38, 42
Phrygians 18–19
picklehua 227
pirahan 218
plaid 39, 42, 44, 194, 195, 232, 233
pointed bodices 154, 283, 286
Poland 225, 250–1, 328, 330
poleyns 50, 120
polonaise 166
Polynesia 268–9
ponchos 273
Portugal 90–1
poulaines 61, 79, 312
pschent 14, 15
Puritans 140
purple 33, 34, 35, 41
pyjama 201

Q

Qing dynasty 185, 186, 188
qumbaz 217

R

Racinet, Auguste 6, 7–9, 13, 33, 38, 43, 49, 64, 68, 69, 71, 81, 88, 100, 101, 126, 130, 131, 136, 137, 146, 148, 155, 170, 175, 196, 202, 206, 214, 216, 226, 257
Rajput dress 200, 202
ramie 192
rebato 138
rebozilla 242
redingotes 170
reticules 175, 247, 311
riding dress 151, 154, 171, 289, 299, 308, 312

Picture Credits

All illustrations have been reproduced from the following:

Hottenroth, Friedrich *Trachten, Haus-, Feld-und Kriegsgeräthschaften der Völker alter und neuer Zeit*, Stuttgart, Verlag von Gustav Weise, 1884

Racinet, Albert, *Le Costume historique*, Paris, Librairie de Firmin-Didot et cie, 1888

NOTES ON CONTRIBUTORS

MELISSA LEVENTON is a freelance consultant curator, and was Chief Curator of Textiles at Fine Arts Museums of San Francisco until 2002. She teaches Fashion History at the California College of Art, and has published numerous books, including *Art Wear: Fashion and Anti-Fashion*, also published by Thames & Hudson.
Contribution: The Ancient World, The Roman Empire, Europe in the Middle Ages, Renaissance Europe, Modern Europe, 1650–1840, Accessories Through the Ages.

MICHELLE WEBB FANDRICH is a fashion and textile historian and appraiser. She holds an MA in Visual Culture: Costume Studies from New York University and has served on the curatorial staff of museums such as the Metropolitan Museum of Art Costume Institute in New York and the Los Angeles County Museum of Art (LACMA).
Contribution: European Regional Dress, Clothing Through the Ages, Accessories Through the Ages.

ROCHELLE KESSLER has been active in the museum and academic fields for over twenty-five years, receiving graduate degrees from the University of Arizona and the Institute of Fine Arts, New York University. In addition to writing many publications, she has held curatorial positions at the Pacific Asia Museum, Pasadena, the Los Angeles County Museum of Art, and the Arthur M. Sackler Museum, Harvard University Museums. She has also served as collections manager and educator at The Metropolitan Museum of Art, New York, and was an international exhibition project liaison for the Smithsonian Institution's National Museum of Natural History and Cooper-Hewitt National Design Museum, New York.
Contribution: The Ancient World, South Asia, Antatolia, Persia and Central Asia

BOBBIE SUMBERG received an MA and a PhD from the University of Minnesota, Department of Design, Housing, and Apparel. She is co-author of *Sleeping Around: The Bed from Antiquity to Now*, and has published articles on dress and textiles in Nigeria and Côte d'Ivoire and on ethnic dress. She currently holds the position of Curator of Textiles and Costume at the Museum of International Folk Art in Santa Fe, New Mexico.
Contribution: Africa, Oceania and the Americas, Accessories Through the Ages.

DALE CAROLYN GLUCKMAN is a retired costume and textiles curator and department head at the Los Angeles County Museum of Art. She has lectured and published widely on the subject of Asian textiles and dress including the exhibition catalogues *When Art Became Fashion: Kosode in Edo-period Japan* (1992) and *Fabric of Enchantment: Batik from the North Coast of Java* (1996). She is currently an independent curator and consultant based in Los Angeles.
Contribution: East and Southeast Asia, European Regional Dress, Africa, Oceania and the Americas, Accessories Through the Ages. the Ages.

JUANJUAN WU is Assistant Professor in apparel and textiles at the State University of New York College at Oneonta. She has authored, co-authored and edited six books on fashion and apparel in China, and is currently writing *Chinese Fashion from Mao to Now*, which will be published by Berg in 2008. A former journalist and editor for a leading fashion magazine in Shanghai, Wu's research and professional interests include aesthetics, clothing design and fashion studies.
Contribution: East and Southeast Asia.

HOLLIS GOODALL is Curator of Japanese Art at the Los Angeles County Museum of Art. Since joining the curatorial staff there in 1988, she has overseen 250 installations in the museum's Pavilion for Japanese Art. In addition to planning installations and collection management, Goodall has worked at LACMA on a number of special exhibitions with publications including, "When Art became Fashion: Kosode in Edo-period Japan," 1992; "Shin-hanga: New Prints in Modern Japan," 1996; "Hirado Porcelain of Japan from the Kurtzman Family Collection," 1997; and "Munakata Shiko: Japanese Master of the Modern Print," 2002. She also contributed to the catalogue for the National Museum of Art's, "Edo: Art in Japan, 1615–1868" in 1998, and was primary author on the book, *The Raymond and Frances Bushell Collection of Netsuke: A Legacy at the Los Angeles County Museum of Art*, in 2003.
Contribution: East and Southeast Asia.